Not long after, she ___
sidewalk in front of t___
about a confrontatio___
with a man outside the Rice Lofts. "I'm worried
about you," Carroll told her. "You should buy some
pepper spray or something, if you're going to be
walking around downtown alone at night."

"No one is going to fuck with me," Ana said,
frowning. Then she bent down and pulled off one
of her shoes, a black stiletto with a thick platform
and a long slender heel. In a statement that would
later seem prophetic, she said, "If they do, I'll get
them in the eye with this."

Praise for KATHRYN CASEY

"Casey is a true crime great: fascinating cases,
extensively researched, beautifully told."

Gregg Olsen, #1 *New York Times* bestselling
author of *Abandoned Prayers*

"She explores incredible crimes . . .
with a deft and experienced hand."

Ann Rule

"Casey stakes her claim as one of
the best in the business."

M. William Phelps, author of *Perfect Poison*

"Kathryn Casey ranks among
the elite of true crime writers."

Carlton Stowers, Edgar® Award-winning
author of *Careless Whispers*

By Kathryn Casey

Non-Fiction
POSSESSED
DELIVER US
MURDER, I WRITE
DEADLY LITTLE SECRETS
SHATTERED
EVIL BESIDE HER
A DESCENT INTO HELL
DIE, MY LOVE
SHE WANTED IT ALL
A WARRANT TO KILL

Fiction
SINGULARITY
BLOOD LINES
THE KILLING STORM

KATHRYN CASEY

P⬟SSESSED

THE INFAMOUS TEXAS STILETTO MURDER

wm

WILLIAM MORROW

An Imprint of HarperCollins*Publishers*

POSSESSED is a journalistic account of the investigation and conviction of Ana Trujillo for the 2013 murder of Stefan Andersson in Houston, Texas. The events recounted in this book are true, although some names have been changed to safeguard the privacy of certain individuals. The personalities, events, actions, and conversations portrayed in the book have been constructed using court documents, including trial transcripts, extensive interviews, letters, personal papers, research, and press accounts. Quoted testimony has been taken from trial and pre-trial transcripts and other sworn statements.

POSSESSED. Copyright © 2016 by Kathryn Casey. All rights reserved. Printed in the United States of America. No part of this book may be used or reproduced in any manner whatsoever without written permission except in the case of brief quotations embodied in critical articles and reviews. For information, address HarperCollins Publishers, 195 Broadway, New York, NY 10007.

First William Morrow mass market printing: October 2016

ISBN 978–0–06–230051–5

William Morrow® and HarperCollins® are registered trademarks of HarperCollins Publishers.

16 17 18 19 20   QGM   10 9 8 7 6 5 4 3 2 1

In memory of my friend and mentor Ann Rule,
who is missed and will never be forgotten.

Some names have been changed in this book: Stan Rich, Teresa Montoya, and Christi Suarez.

POSSESSED

Prologue

In his starched, blue-shirted uniform, Houston P.D. officer Ashton Bowie circulated through the eighteenth floor hallway of The Parklane, one of Houston's most stylish high-rise addresses, a smoky glass and off-white paneled structure that soared over the sixteenth hole of a lush green golf course. In daylight, floor-to-ceiling windows from the thirty-five floors offered breathtaking views of the city's impressive skyline.

At 3:41 A.M. when the 9-1-1 call hit, however, darkness cloaked the nation's fourth largest city. On the phone, a desperate-sounding woman pleaded for help. Yet the apartment number on the transmission posed a problem. Dispatched to an assault in progress in apartment 1801, once he stepped off the elevator, Bowie saw that the apartments were designated by the floor number and a letter. Where was the crisis? In apartment 18A? 18D? Behind which closed door?

A fit man, Bowie worked the graveyard shift in this section of Houston, dominated by the elegant museum district, the hallowed halls of Rice University, and the expansive facilities that made up the Texas Medical Center, the largest hospital and medical research complex in the world. Among H-town's most expensive neighborhoods, the area suffered its share of common crimes: burglaries, robberies, shoplifting and car heists. This type of call, one potentially involving violence, was rare.

In The Parklane, Officer Bowie worked his way from
door to door, lingering at times, listening intently, assuming the assignment could involve a domestic-violence situation, among the most dangerous for any officer. Entering
a private residence where two people fought in the middle
of the night, perhaps one armed, was unpredictable. When
tempers and emotions flared, anything was possible.

Suddenly, from deep inside apartment 18B, Bowie heard
a woman's moans, muffled by a thick door. He walked up
and listened. Confident that the sobbing came from inside,
his hand on the gun in his holster, he knocked.

"Police! Open up!"

A slight hesitation, then the door cracked open far enough
to reveal a slice of a woman's face, mostly concealed behind
the door. "Did you call 9-1-1, ma'am?"

"Yes," the woman said, her words slurred.

At five-foot-five, the woman appeared to be of Latin descent, thick, long, dark hair held in a clip at the top, falling
about her face and gathering around her shoulders. Something muddy looking marked her forehead and cheeks.

"What's wrong?" he asked. The woman looked unsteady,
weaving slightly.

Not answering, she eased the door open a bit wider. Exposed to the light from the hallway, Bowie judged that the
smudges on the woman's forehead, cheeks, and chin resem-
bled blood. Her hands and her hair were streaked. Her lacy
black tank top revealed little, but blood covered and saturated the legs of her jeans, especially around the knees. So
much blood. The scene recalled a horror movie, one where
the art director had been ordered to ramp up the gore. In real
life, so much blood meant only one thing—someone was
dead or dying.

"Are you hurt?" the officer asked. The woman didn't
appear to be, but he wondered if it was possible that the
blood was hers. The woman shook her head no, and Bowie
caught a strong whiff of alcohol.

"He was holding me, and he wouldn't let go," she said,

an eerie hollow whine to her voice. Now that he'd heard her speak, Bowie realized the woman had a Spanish accent, garbled by what appeared to be an overconsumption of liquor. "I said, 'Stefan! Let me go!'"

"Who is Stefan?" he asked.

"My fiancé," she said. "Come in."

The woman stepped back and opened the door into the foyer. She then pointed into the apartment, down a short hallway, one that T'ed off at a wall that separated the entry from the apartment's interior. Officer Bowie edged inside, his hand still hovering over the service weapon in his holster, his eyes surveying the scene.

"Are there any weapons?"

"No," she said, choking out the word.

Once inside, Bowie's eyes trailed the brief hallway's off-white walls. Low to the floor, dark reddish-brown smudges and spots spattered in a chaotic pattern. More blood. Beside him, the woman sobbed. "He was holding me. He wouldn't let me go," she wailed. "I told him, 'Stefan, please! Please! Let me go!'"

Then Bowie saw the man sprawled on the floor, on his back, at the end of the hallway, his hands flung above his head. Beside him, near his face, more crimson pooled on the off-white carpet. At first, the officer, who walked forward for a closer look, assumed the cause of so much bleeding must have been a bullet. That, however, didn't seem to be the case. Careful not to contaminate the scene, Bowie bent down for a closer look and judged this was something else. He wasn't sure what. It looked like the white-haired man on the floor had been attacked with something, beaten about his head. Dozens of cuts, dents, and bruises pocked the face and scalp of the man on the floor, garish, seeping wounds.

"Sir, sir!" the officer said, but there was no answer. From the look of the man, Bowie hadn't expected one.

"I tried to give him CPR," the woman said. "Can you try?"

Yet the officer never started CPR. The blood on the carpet was already drying. In Officer Bowie's estimation, any opportunity to save the man had long since passed. Judging from the coagulating blood on the carpet and the cold, pale look of the body, the officer judged that the man on the floor had been dead for some period of time.

"What happened?" Bowie asked, turning his attention fully on the woman.

"We were arguing," she said. As she talked, she grew calmer, but her voice was urgent, and her words rushed out in a torrent, jumbled, perhaps a result of the alcohol the officer smelled even more clearly now that she stood beside him. "He wouldn't let me leave. He was holding me, and he wouldn't let me go. I said, 'Stefan, let me go!'" This time when she recounted what she'd told the dead man, the woman held on to the vowels, turning her entreaty into a plea: "Pleeeeease, Stefan! Pleeeeease, let me go!"

Officer Bowie looked down and again considered the man's corpse, his face covered in a bizarre patchwork of wounds. The woman said there wasn't a weapon, but it was obvious that she hadn't done so much damage with her hands. "What did you hit him with?"

The woman's face twisted into a pained grimace, and she pointed a bloody finger toward something on the floor near the dead man's head, a size-nine, cobalt-blue suede stiletto, its five-and-a-half-inch heel stained with blood that held tufts of what appeared to be strands of the dead man's white hair.

"My shoe," she said. "I hit him with my shoe."

In the year that followed, the shock waves of the killing inside Parklane 18B echoed past the streets of Houston, mesmerizing the nation and the world. A sexy woman's shoe might have been a recurring weapon in movie plots, but on that awful June morning, in a posh Houston high-rise, it became reality.

Compounding the mystery surrounding the case was the identity of the dead man: Dr. Stefan Andersson, a brilliant scientist and researcher who investigated the interactions of hormones and steroids, and the way both impacted women's bodies during pregnancy. At the University of Houston, Andersson, an esteemed professor, lectured medical students.

Yet questions emerged from that night when the call went out and homicide detectives flooded Andersson's apartment. Was the professor living a double life?

Those who knew him described the scientist as a quiet, kind, and generous man. But Ana Trujillo, the woman who'd beaten Andersson almost beyond recognition, characterized the dead man in vastly different terms. She called him controlling and abusive, to the point where she had no option other than to defend herself with the only weapon available.

"He wouldn't let me go," she insisted, when she recounted to investigators the events of that night. "He pushed me . . . he grabbed me . . . he . . ."

But who was Ana Trujillo? And was she to be believed? Why, if not fearing for her life, would she kill the man? Perhaps a clue waited at the scene of the killing.

After Trujillo was transported to Houston Police Department's homicide bureau for questioning, the forensic unit took over Andersson's apartment. One officer inspected Trujillo's purse. Out of the black-leather sack with a drawstring, he pulled a pair of white tennis shoes, a black-and-white, snake-patterned wallet, and one more item: a thin, stained, and worn book with a white-wire spiral binding. Its gold-and-purple cover bore the title: *Tarot.*

The paperback was open to page twenty-one, on which the author explored the meaning of card number thirteen, accompanied by a chilling illustration of a skeleton on horseback, holding a sickle and wearing a hooded cape.

On the night she killed Stefan Andersson, Ana Trujillo had the *Tarot* book in her purse open to the death card.

Chapter I

Decades pass, yet childhood memories remain. Early experiences imprint and shape, the good and the bad, the hopeful and the disappointing, the joyous and the tragic. Adults may try to overlook their pasts, but can they ever truly be forgotten? For the child within calls out, reminding the adult where he came from, branding who he will be, how he will react, and forever influencing his self-image, his relationships, and his life.

In Stefan Andersson's case, his beginnings would not only impact how he lived his life but eventually how he died.

Green forests, blue skies, lakes, and snowcapped mountains, a Scandinavian country that neighbors with Norway and Finland, Sweden has a long, rugged coastline and less than 10 million citizens. In area, Sweden is the third largest country in Europe, but its population is scattered, giving much of it a rural feel, farms and cities, quaint towns and villages, forests and open land. The outer reaches lie in the Arctic Circle, and Sweden boasts spectacular displays of the northern lights. Winters are cold and snow-covered, with as little as three hours of sunshine a day. Summers are cool, green, with only a few hours of darkness.

Stefan was born in Västerås, in central Sweden. On the shores of Lake Mälaren, a city of 110,000, it's on land inhabited for more than three thousand years, since before the Viking era. On the outskirts lies a primitive burial mound, Anundshög, two hundred feet long and thirty feet high, dating to between A.D. 250 and 500. An industrial city, Västerås is surrounded by farmland, and, because of the prevalence of the green gourds, it's known as the cucumber city.

At his birth, Stefan was named Alf Stefan Andersson. Throughout life, he would forgo use of his first name in favor of Stefan, perhaps to differentiate himself from his older brother, Alf, a toddler who tragically died while their mother carried Stefan in her womb. His parents named him in honor of their dead firstborn. But Stefan found it gloomy and told friends that he wondered if his growing up would have been happier if his parents had not grieved so for their lost child that they'd given him Alf's name.

From the outside, the Andersson home appeared unremarkable, an older, quaint house on a typical, quiet street, with two parents, Irene and Harry. A sweet but passive woman, Irene cared for the children, Stefan, followed by daughters Marie and Anneli. Harry had a secure position working for the railway system. But behind closed doors, Stefan described his childhood as fearful and turbulent.

Throughout his life, Stefan confided in friends about his parents' volatile relationship, often describing his father as a bully, abusive to his mother, leaving their only living son regretting not being able to save his mother from his father's temper. While not detailing specific incidents, Stefan implied that the abuse was physical, and admitted that he, too, felt the sting of his father's wrath. Many of his friends viewed this heartache as one of the defining experiences of Stefan's life. "He came to identify with his mother," said a good friend. "They were both similar in temperament, easygoing, kind, and both his father's victims."

Other characteristics emerged that would portend the path his life would take.

Even as a child, Stefan had an exceptional mind, the kind that continually asks questions and seeks answers, searching for insight by pulling together the pieces of the puzzles.

At a young age, his keen intellect garnered attention. When he was ten or eleven, Stefan, like many young boys, built toy airplanes, but his curiosity took over, and he considered military aircraft, and the methods used to hide it from enemy forces. Intrigued, he began drawing his own camouflage designs on paper at the kitchen table, while his sisters watched. When finished, he chose his favorites and sent them to the FOA, Sweden's military research department. A general responded, highly complimentary of Stefan's work, saying he'd passed it on to those in the field, and they were impressed.

When Stefan later recounted the story, however, he'd contend that his father was less than happy. When the general's letter arrived, rather than express pride at his son's talents, Harry Andersson fumed, livid that Stefan had drawn attention to the family. "Better to blend in," Harry told him. "It's never good to stand out."

Decades later, Stefan would receive a letter from the general's wife, after her husband's death, recalling how he often mentioned Stefan and wished that he'd had a son like him. Cherishing the letter that brought the validation his relationship with his own father never would, Stefan kept it with him always.

Over the decades, his father's disapproval and violent nature shadowed Stefan, resulting in a constant state of self-doubt. "I was supposed to be of a Lutheran mind-set," Stefan told a friend. "Work hard, not question authority, and live a simple life, like my father. That I didn't do that met with disappointment."

Yet in many ways, Stefan's early life was good. He loved his mother and his sisters, and his father, despite the pain. And Stefan did well in school. There was much to enjoy in his native land. Sports were popular in Sweden. Despite the lack of sunshine, tennis, hockey, soccer, and bandy (a game similar to ice hockey) flourished. In the summers, residents congregated outdoors, on the shores of the lake, surrounded by rolling hills and shade trees, for picnics. In the winters, when the lake froze over, they enjoyed ice-skating and skiing on nearby mountainsides.

In 1972, at the age of eighteen, Stefan, five-foot-nine with shaggy, blond hair the color of ripened wheat, and inquisitive, deep-set blue eyes, left home and moved one hundred miles north to Gävle, where he served what was then a period of compulsory military service for Swedish men. Separated from his domineering father, Stefan began to find himself. Soon, he made friends, athletes, many of whom would later become professional hockey players. On the summer solstice, they took a nine-kilometer bike trip from the small town of Norrlandet. The pilgrimage became an annual event for the friends, about three dozen of them. In the coming years, no matter where Stefan's work took him, each June he returned to Sweden, to visit family, and to bike through the stunning Swedish countryside.

After his conscription ended, doing what middle-class Swedish sons were expected to do, Stefan signed up for a program to learn a trade. He chose welding, enrolling in a trade school in Gävle. At the same time, he developed an interest in weight lifting, and before long, he was muscular and bench-pressed more than three hundred pounds. Enthusiastic about the sport, Stefan entered competitions, winning trophies and medals, then turned to teaching and training other athletes.

Something about athletes especially appealed to Stefan, who often remarked that he admired not only their incredible power but their passion for their sports. At strength competitions, he met and befriended a group of Russian weight lifters, some bound for the Olympics. As his welding training drew to a close, Stefan traveled with the Russians, acting as a trainer and seeing the world. On a grand adventure in St. Petersburg, he drank vodka and dated dancers from the Bolshoi Ballet. Later, he'd laugh boisterously and tell the story of how on a trip to Moscow, he peed on a Kremlin wall.

Stefan in an early photo
(Courtesy of Annika Lindqvist)

Although it was a brief interlude in his life, his weight-lifting experiences had a profound influence. At the time, many of Stefan's friends relied on steroids and other drugs to build strength. Watching them take the pills, seeing the sometimes remarkable results as their physiques developed, he became captivated by the profound effect of a small pill. "Stefan said it transformed the athletes," said an old friend. "From that point on, he was fascinated with the power of chemistry on the human body. That was the spark that ignited a lifelong interest."

At the welding school, impressed with their student's extraordinary mind, his teachers had suggested that Stefan continue his education by attending a university. Yet that wasn't something he initially felt comfortable pursuing. He knew what his father expected of him and didn't consider that a possibility. No one in his family had ever attended college, and it appeared out of his reach. But before long, Stefan began to consider the potential, and when he did, he recalled his experiences with the Russian weight lifters. His intellectual curiosity stirred, Stefan felt drawn to study chemistry and its effects on the human anatomy, wanting to decipher its mysteries.

In 1979, Stefan registered at Uppsala University, enrolling in the pharmacy school. Dating back to 1477, Uppsala was Sweden's first university and specialized in science and research. Stefan's years there would be memorable ones. He loved the school and its traditions, the annual spring Walpurgis, called the donning of the caps, where students wore white sea-captain hats, marking the completion of their time in the upper secondary school. The day began with a champagne breakfast and float races on the nearby river rapids, followed by herring lunches. Enthusiastic about the future, he worked with his professors in their laboratories, assisting with research, made close friends, and envisioned ever larger horizons.

Uppsala University
(Courtesy of Aftonbladet)

After earning a master's degree in pharmacy, Stefan stayed on at Uppsala, working on a doctorate in pharmaceutical biochemistry. During those years, Stefan assisted his professors on research, later published in several scientific journals, on the isolation and identification of a protein that helps produce bile acids from cholesterol and modifies vitamin D to a more active form. His doctoral thesis, entitled *Cytochromes P450 in Biosynthesis of Bile Acids and Metabolism of Vitamin D3*, was also published that year. Through his work, Stefan achieved recognition within his discipline and was granted patents on his discoveries.

At Uppsala, Stefan's graduation ceremony unfolded in the school's grand auditorium, through the main entrance engraved with "To think free is great, but to think right is greater," the words of Thomas Thorild, an alum and a famous jurist. Along with his diploma, Stefan received a gold ring commemorating his achievement and symbolizing his dedication to his science. That evening, there was a banquet at Uppsala Castle, built in 1549 by King Gustav I, in modern times housing three museums and serving as the residence of the county's governor.

Yet as far as Stefan had come, one thing remained static. His great sadness, Stefan would later say, was that despite his academic success, Harry Andersson still didn't appear proud of his son's accomplishments. "It drove even more of a wedge between them that Stefan wanted to better himself," said a friend. "His father didn't understand a son who wanted more."

As much as he loved Sweden, Stefan needed space to grow and felt drawn to see the world. His doctoral thesis had received attention and offers arrived from research facilities around the world. As he reviewed his options, there were some possibilities that appealed more to him than others. Many Swedes speak English, and Stefan did as well, so there was the lure of transplanting to a country where he wouldn't have to learn a new language. The other overriding temptation was climate. Stefan had lived his life in a country with little sunshine much of the year and cool summers. He was a man who worshipped blue skies and hot weather. Growing up in Sweden, he'd suffered through too many long, dark winters. One offer that intrigued him came from the University of Texas Southwestern Medical Center in Dallas. That was the one he accepted.

In 1986, diploma in hand, Stefan Andersson accepted a postdoctoral position at UTSW. He packed his bags and moved to Texas for further training and mentoring in one of the center's many research labs, and for the sunshine.

Chapter 2

At the University of Texas Southwestern Medical Center, Stefan became a postdoc under the auspices of Dr. David W. Russell in the department of molecular genetics. In 1986, when Stefan moved in, Dallas was in its heyday, made internationally famous by the then-wildly-popular prime-time soap opera bearing its name, starring Larry Hagman and Linda Gray.

Unlike its fellow Texas metropolis, Houston, Dallas wasn't as impacted by the eighties oil crunch. The city was more diversified, with high tech prospering, Southwestern expanding and gaining a reputation in the medical world, as was Dr. Russell for his research into cholesterol and its impact on the body.

Soon Stefan, who his colleagues rarely called Dr. Andersson, immersed himself in Russell's endeavors. In the lab, Stefan cut a dashing figure, his soft Swedish accent, his shaggy dark blond hair and intense blue eyes, wearing a white coat over a shirt and jeans. His mind on his research, not his dress, he sometimes arrived a bit wrinkled in the mornings but never appeared self-conscious about it. Instead, he channeled his energy into his inquiry, attempting to decipher the secrets of the human body.

Away from the campus, Stefan settled into Dallas, renting an apartment in The Village. A popular residential area for professionals, it was a patchwork of more than a dozen apartment and town-house developments, built on 307 roll-

University of Texas Southwestern Medical Center

ing green acres of a former golf course. Close to Central Expressway and just minutes from downtown Dallas, tucked into lush trees, the complexes offered tennis courts and swimming pools, and overall there were community biking and jogging paths, a gym, green esplanades, and towering gnarled live oaks. Most of the nearly ten thousand residents were couples without children or singles.

"Everyone I knew in Dallas lived in The Village at one time or another," said a friend of Stefan's. "It was a good place to start out, to meet people." Crowds gathered at weekday happy hours, but The Village was particularly lively on weekends, when impromptu pool parties sprung up; music played on boom boxes, while residents mingled, talked, and drank, taking the occasional cool-off dip in the pool. Entertainment choices abounded, with the vast development's western boundary, Greenville Avenue, a restaurant row with bars, nightclubs, and eateries.

Renting a first-floor apartment, Stefan became a regular

at the pool. On weekends and summer afternoons, wearing his swimsuit, he rarely entered the water but rather lounged bare-chested on a chair, soaking up the hot Texas sun, often reading a scientific journal or perusing reports he brought from the lab. Although he knew how to cook, he did little of it, with the exception of an occasional omelet for dinner, preferring to eat his meals out.

Larger than any city in Sweden, perhaps Stefan felt the need to cut Dallas down to size, to make it more manageable. With his chaotic childhood, it wasn't surprising that he reined in his life, making Dallas seem smaller by carving out a comfort zone that included his apartment, The Village, the medical center where he worked, and the nearby Greenville Avenue restaurants and clubs.

At work, Stefan flourished, his postdoc progressing, as he became a member of the American Society for Biochemistry and Molecular Biology and of the Endocrine Society. His successes in the lab mounted, and in the late eighties he helped identify and clone two genes, while exploring how testosterone was converted to an androgen in the prostate. In 1989, he was the lead author of a paper in the *Journal of Biological Chemistry* exploring the role of 5a-Reductase, a steroid essential in the process of differentiating sex in a fetus. Through his research, he worked with scientists around the world, including a visiting professor from Russia. In many ways, on a microscopic level, Stefan Andersson was on a grand quest, investigating life's essential elements by studying the interactions of enzymes, steroids, and hormones in the womb and the fetus.

It was a heady time for Stefan, seeing his name in scientific publications, exploring exciting possibilities.

Although he'd dated off and on, no serious relationship opened up until 1989, when he met Jackie Swift, an attractive, dark-haired woman whose mother was Comanche and Fort Sill Apache. By then, Stefan was in his mid-thirties, and Jackie was more than a decade younger. She'd left home for Dallas, eager for challenge and excitement.

In The Village, Jackie moved with a roommate into a ground-floor apartment, and in 1989 she encountered Stefan one afternoon at the pool.

On their first date, Jackie, who had a two-year associate's degree, had to coax Stefan to tell her what he did. "I really don't like to talk about that because it can be a little overwhelming," he said, but finally explained that he had a PhD and conducted research at the medical center. Trying to put her at ease, he described his doctorate as "like a driver's license to do something, a kind of work."

Yet as they talked, his expression lit with excitement about his work, and she was even more impressed with his humbleness. "He was sweet, gracious," she said. "And at the same time, clever and engaging. He never made me feel like he thought he was smarter or better than I was."

Over time, she would learn that Stefan saw very little difference in people based on their educations or their stations in life. When he and Jackie went out walking and encountered a homeless person on the street, Stefan often asked her to wait while he went into a store, coming out with food and drink to give to the man. But it was what Stefan did afterward that seemed remarkable to Jackie. Rather than just hand the man the food and leave, he paused to talk, asking about the homeless man's life and interests. Before long, Stefan and the stranger nearly always found something they both felt passionate about, and they'd laugh like old friends. "Stefan really transcended boundaries," Jackie said. "He didn't pigeonhole people because of social position or education."

Not long after they began dating, when Jackie brought him home to Yukon, Oklahoma, to meet her parents, her dad, Dick Swift, at first worried. At twenty-three, Jackie seemed too young to settle down, especially with a man of thirty-five, but soon Dick, a home remodeler, set aside any misgivings. "Stefan and I became really good friends," said Swift. "We just hit it off."

On that trip, Dick Swift took Stefan to see a friend's collection of Native American art. Afterward, Jackie's father was impressed with how much Stefan absorbed at the meeting, information about types of works and the artists. "He seemed to grasp a deeper meaning in things," said Swift. "He took the time to understand."

"Stefan was this blond, good-looking guy. He wore his hair long, glasses, a leather jacket, and biker boots. He was kind of rugged attractive. He looked a little like a rocker. But the conversations made me fall in love," said Jackie, who found Stefan worldly and captivating. They talked of his life in Sweden, his work, and her life, what she wanted for the future. Her parents had urged her to pursue college, but she'd balked at the idea. Stefan never pushed. Instead, he simply offered to be there for her, to help if she wanted to go.

Something else attracted her to Stefan, however. "He was one of the first people to have confidence in me, to say I was smart enough, good enough to succeed," she said. Yet as he championed her, she sensed that he battled his own self-doubts. He talked often of his painful childhood, his kind mother, and his cold, judgmental father.

As it had in Sweden, at Uppsala, Stefan's work wasn't going unnoticed. In 1991, he received an offer from Merck, one of the largest and most successful pharmaceutical companies in the world. The position required that Stefan move to the East Coast. They'd offered him substantially more money and the opportunity for advancement, for while his academic research was intellectually stimulating, it was not something that would ever make him rich.

That August, Jackie and Stefan married in a ceremony in Stefan's apartment, officiated by a judge and witnessed by only her family. Everyone laughed when, during their vows, a Federal Express driver interrupted, banging on the door with a delivery. That evening, they held a reception for friends at the pool where they'd first met.

Two weeks later, the newlyweds began their move. While his office was in New Jersey, Stefan wanted the experience of living in New York City, and they rented an apartment on the nineteenth floor in a high-rise on West Sixtieth, a block and a half from Columbus Circle and Central Park, with windows overlooking the skyline. Jackie bought furniture and decorated, something in which Stefan showed little interest. "He liked nice things," she said. "But he wouldn't have done that for himself. He just didn't care that much. He wasn't into possessions."

In New York, Jackie and Stefan embraced the city by exploring the museums, clubs, and restaurants. Each workday, Stefan rose early and left for the train station, to begin his commute. In the evenings, he returned home late and often tired. Yet they found life exciting, including trips, one to Venice, where they had their picture taken on a gondola.

Jackie and Stefan in Venice

In just five years, Stefan's life had drastically changed, growing up in Sweden and now married and living in the biggest city in the United States, collaborating with respected scientists and traveling the world. In New York, the couple frequented small, ethnic restaurants in the evenings. One afternoon, they walked down the street and noticed someone with a well-built figure in a revealing dress. Jackie looked at Stefan as they passed by, and both realized it was a man. "I can't wait to tell everyone we were ogling him," Stefan said with a hearty laugh.

Yet in so many ways, Stefan remained the same man with whom Jackie had fallen in love. In New York, as he had in Dallas, Stefan stopped whenever he saw a homeless person on the street, handing over a few dollars or buying food. There was a kindness about her husband that Jackie found endearing. No matter all Stefan had achieved, he still saw himself as no different from the man living on the street, whom he judged as simply down on his luck.

Yet for Jackie, the transition wasn't as easy. While excited to live in the city with Stefan beside her, she often felt lonely and homesick. Much of the time she spent alone since she had few friends, and Stefan routinely worked late into the evenings and on weekends. "I wanted more of his time and attention," she remembered. When she complained, he gave her money to go shopping, but not what she truly wanted, time with him. It wasn't that the marriage was visibly troubled since they rarely fought, and when they did, he remained steadfastly calm, never raising his voice.

"You need to get a hobby," Stefan told her when she complained about his frequent absences.

"You're my hobby," she said, and he just smiled.

It didn't help that in the evenings, he often stopped at a neighborhood bar on his way home from work, delaying his arrival even further. Stefan had been drinking since college, not usually to excess but nightly. Dick Swift would remember his daughter talking about Stefan's proclivity for a nightcap out and how it left her home alone. When he listened to

Jackie and heard the sadness in her voice, Swift worried that Stefan's drinking would hurt the marriage.

Working at a local clothing manufacturer but still some-what adrift in New York, Jackie slowly began to redefine her life. She'd left Oklahoma for Dallas years earlier, lured by a fast-paced urban lifestyle, entranced by the possibilities and excitement it offered. Yet as a consequence of leaving home, she'd inadvertently distanced herself from her Native American heritage. In New York, Jackie felt the strong pull of her ancestry, and she and Stefan attended events, in-cluding the opening of the movie *Geronimo: An American Legend* in 1993. At the American Indian Inaugural Ball, she wore a flowing black pantsuit and long, dangling earrings and Stefan a tux, and that same year she started a small nonprofit, the Manahatta Indian Arts Council, named after the tribe pushed off Manhattan by white settlers during the French and Indian War.

Buoyed by Stefan's support, Jackie became increasingly active in Native American events and organizations, includ-ing raising funds to finance a powwow featuring the Apache Fire Dancers in Gateway National Recreation Center. While her start in the city had been a lonely one, eventually Jackie settled into New York, putting down roots in the Native American community. When that happened, she began to think of the city as home, growing to love its bustle and end-less opportunities.

Meanwhile at work, Stefan published his Merck re-search, this time on enzymes involved in the formation of testosterone and estradiol. In the evenings, he continued to drop in at the local bars, to socialize and have a few drinks on the way home. There he met Wall Street analysts and brokers, who educated him on finances and investing, one day making friends with the manager of a large hedge fund. With his scientific background, Stefan understood statistics and calculations, and he began reading and study-ing the markets.

Although it might have seemed that they were both prospering in New York, four years after they arrived, in 1995, Jackie sensed that Stefan was unhappy. The long train commute wore on him, and he looked tired. Separated so much of the time, she didn't feel that they communicated as they once had, and before long, she realized that they'd drifted apart. They seemed to be living parallel yet separate lives.

"I've been offered a position in Dallas, at UT Southwestern," he said to her one evening. He explained that the invitation came from a prominent chair at the school and that he saw the offer as a great opportunity. Merck hadn't turned out the way he'd once hoped, he confided, and he'd decided that perhaps he wasn't a good fit for the corporate world. In academia, his research was more esoteric, its goal to answer questions, and if it took time to evolve, that was understood. But at Merck, a company with investors to satisfy, he felt pressured to move quickly and pursue profits.

"What are you saying?" Jackie asked.

"I think it would be a good idea to move back to Dallas," Stefan answered.

"After it took me so long to get where I am here?" Jackie said, astonished at the idea that the inroads she'd made could all be for naught. She thought about their lives, and the sense she had that they'd become more roommates than lovers. "You go to Dallas, and I'll commute," she said, in her heart seeing the parting as a separation.

The marriage ended without fighting or angry words. "Stefan wasn't like that. He never yelled. He never fought," she said. But to her mind, it seemed a natural progression since she believed Stefan was more preoccupied with his work and his career than their marriage. "I felt like I was a checklist item. I was unhappy."

That same year, Stefan moved back to Dallas while Jackie stayed in New York. The following year, Jackie traveled to Dallas and asked Stefan for a divorce. She'd grown, her life had changed, and it wasn't in Dallas any longer. She'd made plans to continue her education. As much as she cared for

Stefan, their marriage no longer fit. "It was very sad," she said. "It was hard."

For both of them, it seemed, for Stefan's friends would say that the divorce devastated him, perhaps because he never understood why it had happened. "He couldn't make sense of it," said one friend. "So he couldn't ever put it behind him."

Through the years, Stefan kept one of his wedding reception invitations as a remembrance, and he talked of Jackie fondly and often, sometimes musing about what could have gone wrong. Always he carried her picture in his wallet. "I think the divorce totally messed him up," said a close friend. "He was damaged by it. Stefan wanted a family. He wanted children and a home. But he never really believed he deserved it."

Chapter 3

To return to UTSW, Stefan accepted less money than he'd made at Merck, an $85,000 salary. As an associate professor, he had two responsibilities, the first running a lab funded by the National Institutes of Health (NIH) in the department of obstetrics and gynecology, where he'd investigate the roles hormones and steroids play in pregnancy and premature births. His second task required him to lecture to the school's medical students and PhD candidates on his areas of expertise and his research.

Making his return to his pre–New York life a complete circle, Stefan leased an apartment, this time a corner unit near the pool, at The Village, which he began referring to with a smile and a laugh as "The Ghetto." Whenever the weather permitted and he had spare time, he again became a familiar sight lounging around the pool, sunbathing and reading. It was there one afternoon that he met Mark Bouril, an engineer who lived in an adjacent apartment. Bouril had seen Stefan in the past, usually getting his mail, and thought that he seemed a bit gruff, but on that day, Stefan was reading a financial magazine, and the two men talked about the stock market and investments. Before long, Bouril, a runner, had Stefan jogging beside him on The Village paths.

In the evenings, Bouril and Stefan, both single, hung out together, going to dinner or sometimes watching Ingmar Bergman, Federico Fellini, and Mel Brooks movies. Bouril appreciated the way Stefan dropped lines from *Blazing Sad-*

dles or Monty Python into conversations. Particularly taken with German director Werner Herzog's movies, Stefan seemed drawn to his recurring theme of heroes who fought tremendous obstacles. Many of his favorite movies starred leading man Klaus Kinski. Stefan particularly admired the German actor's dead-eyed grimace, a look he copied, practicing before a mirror, then employing when forced to have his picture taken.

On another afternoon, Stefan bumped into Ran Holcomb, a CPA who lived in his complex. Soon Holcomb was giving Stefan financial advice and doing his taxes, and Bouril, Stefan, Holcomb, and other friends from The Village sometimes dropped in at happy hours at half a dozen of the nearby restaurants and bars, from the microbrewery Humperdinck's, where Stefan ate the barbecue and burgers, to a place called Two Rows, where he always ordered fish. After he was pulled over in his car one night when he'd been drinking, Stefan narrowed his restaurants down to those in walking distance of his apartment, so he didn't have to worry about imbibing and driving. "He was practical," said a friend. "He liked to drink, and this way it wasn't a problem."

Making something of a game of it, one night on their way home, Stefan with a group of hungry friends walked through the drive-thru at a Wendy's restaurant, with cars in front of and behind them, laughing as they put in their orders and carried their sacks of burgers home.

As much fun as Stefan had in Dallas, there were those times around the pool or on their nights out, when the conversations became serious. Many of his friends simply called Stefan "the scientist." And as Jackie had before them, they felt drawn to him for the conversations, his thoughts on the world. Always reading, he enjoyed discussing theories on life

While the others gave him a moniker reflecting his profession, Stefan sometimes called himself a nickname based on his beliefs. Like many scientists who are trained to accept as true only what they can see, touch, and calculate, Stefan was a secular man, an atheist, in his words, "the heathen from Sweden." While his atheism put him at odds with religious friends he made in Texas, it never became an obstacle. "He always treated our beliefs with respect," said one such friend. "It wasn't like he ever told us we were wrong, but rather that he held a different view."

One day, the conversation with Bouril turned serious, and Stefan talked about his opinions on life and death. "We're here for a brief time. So much happens that are accidents. When we can help each other, we should," he said. Then he went on to voice his concept of death, that when a person dies, they simply stop existing, "as if they'd never been born."

While some may have found his viewpoint sad, Stefan saw it simply as the reality of a living organism never intended to live forever.

At the restaurants, in the bars, Stefan struck up conversations with those seated around him, asking about their jobs and their histories. In the end, the people he invited into his life were those he said were "shooting from the hip," said a friend. "There were only two things Stefan couldn't abide, dishonesty and people who judged others more harshly than they judged themselves."

While he'd cobbled together a family of sorts out of his Dallas friends, Stefan still ached for a wife and children. Two years after his divorce from Jackie, he hadn't given up on the prospect of love. As in his career, he used his analytic skills to assess the possibilities and decided that the best way to meet and court a woman was on the dance floor. At a Dallas dance school, he signed up for lessons. As with everything else, he studied and practiced. On the floor, Stefan was graceful and intense, and he entered competitions. In love, however, it was a disappointment. Around that time, he did start a new relationship, but it was with a married woman, one who appeared to want him for what he could buy her. She borrowed $70,000 from Stefan to invest in a business and never repaid him.

Although not earning enough at UTSW to afford such things, Stefan had found some success in the financial markets. Each day, he rose early, checking the stats on the foreign exchanges before New York opened. He then put in his buy and sell orders, and left for work, checking off and on to see how his stocks performed.

Settled into his life in the U.S., Stefan returned to Sweden once a year, to ride in the annual summer-solstice bike trip he'd helped found while in college. While there, he visited family and friends. Yet Dallas had become his home, and he loved his life in the United States, leading him to, in the mid-nineties, become a U.S. citizen. He saw his future in America, one he hoped would someday include a wife and a family. "Stefan always said he was looking for the right woman," said a friend.

The Stefan Andersson his friends knew was a social person, who needed other people. At night, in the clubs, if seated at the bar alone, he talked to the bartender or other patrons. At his apartment, he left his television on, to hear the voices. "Stefan just loved people, being around people. He craved contact. And he loved women."

Not far from The Village, Stefan became a regular at Henk's European Deli and Black Forest Bakery. A little piece of his homeland, it offered herring, Wiener schnitzel, bratwurst, liverwurst, and sauerbraten. On Thursday and Saturday evenings, he claimed a table, and before long became friends with the staff, asking about their families, talking about their lives, giving the younger ones advice, including "always have a Plan B, because Plan A doesn't always work out."

Everyone at Henk's knew that Stefan had a crush on one of the waitresses, a tall blonde. Although she was married, he indulged in an innocent flirtation, one neither let go further. At the restaurant, he stayed late, talking to the waiters while they cleaned up and set the tables for the next day. Over the years, they all became close. "It was kind of like he was one of us," said one of the waitresses.

One evening, he gave the woman he clearly coveted
a ride home. As she got into the car, she wondered if he
would make a pass or do anything she'd have to reject. But
he didn't. He simply drove her home, then waited for her to
open her front door and disappear inside. "Very much the
gentleman," she said.

Meanwhile, in 1997 in Lund, Sweden, a young woman
named Annika Lindqvist was working on her PhD in cel-
lular molecular biology when her faculty advisor asked her,
"Where do you see your future?"

"I'd like to move to the U.S.," Lindqvist said, basing her
decision on reports she'd heard of good salaries and important research.

Musing over the possibilities, her advisor mentioned
a friend, a former colleague, Stefan Andersson. "He's in
Dallas."

"Is it warm there?" Lindqvist asked. As Stefan once had,
Annika, with dark blond hair, glasses, and a wide smile,
dreamed of an escape from Sweden's long, dreary winters.

"I think so. I'll contact him for you," the woman offered.

A short time later on her way to a camping vacation in
the Grand Canyon, Annika stopped in Dallas. Getting off
the plane, she encountered a clear, blue Texas sky and felt
the warmth of sunlight caressing her skin. Outside the ter-
minal, Stefan waited in the white Toyota Camry he'd had
for years. "You see this dent?" he asked, rather gruffly.
When she said she did, he asked, "Do you think women
won't date me because of the dent?"

"Well, if they don't date you because of the dent, you
don't want to date them," she answered, and Stefan looked at
her, considered her response, and laughed. That afternoon,
he gave her a tour of the lab, then out to dinner with his tight
group of friends. First impressions can shape relationships,
but Annika's of Stefan would be a passing one, as she sized
him up as rather a crusty older man. At forty-three, his hair
was prematurely greying, and he'd developed a slight stoop,

perhaps from leaning over computers and microscopes, which made him look somewhat older than his years.

Stefan
(Courtesy of Annika Lindqvist)

When she returned to Dallas two years later, after her graduation, Annika joined Stefan, working for him in his lab, renting an apartment near his in The Village. As a housewarming gift, one afternoon he gave her all of his pots, pans, and kitchen utensils. "I never cook," he announced, and before long she realized it was true. When she visited his apartment with friends, she found his cupboards and refrigerator bare, except for a carton of eggs and one small pot to boil them in.

As she looked around, she noticed a cabinet filled with prescription medicines, ones Stefan had stockpiled for years. As she grew to know him she'd realize that Stefan was something of a hypochondriac, continually asking his doctors for medicines but rarely taking them. Still, with a master's degree in pharmacy, he had a respect for pills and rarely if ever threw any out.

Seamlessly, Annika entered Stefan's life, working at the lab, joining his friends on their evening forays into Dallas nightlife. There were Sunday afternoons spent leisurely brunching at the Intercontinental Hotel, drinking mimosas and listening to jazz, and Friday evening happy hours at a local Mexican restaurant with a large outdoor deck and goblet-size margaritas.

Working with Stefan, Annika judged him to be rational

and highly analytical. Discussing possibilities, at work or over drinks, his mind filled with ideas not only for their research but for that of others at UTSW. Yet less than organized, at times he found focusing difficult, something Annika did exceptionally well. Quickly, they became a team, she implementing and organizing his ideas, while he moved forward on the research's bigger picture, investigating the effects of high blood pressure during pregnancy and the molecular mechanisms involved in premature births.

Over the years, Stefan grew to rely on Annika at work, and she realized that, but still her feelings were hurt the day she called in sick and he pushed to know when she'd be back, saying not that she needed to take care of herself but that he had work waiting for her. When she returned, however, coworkers surrounded her, asking about her health. "Stefan was so worried," more than one told her. "He was talking about getting a doctor for you."

Along with the others, Stan Rich lived in The Village and became a member of Stefan's circle of friends, going out many evenings. Rich was raised in Northern Europe, and he and Stefan had much in common. Like Mark Bouril, when Rich had first noticed Stefan at the complex, he had a scowl on his face, one Rich later recognized meant his new friend was deep in thought.

In the bars and restaurants, they laughed and joked, happy to be together. At times, Stefan suggested an evening at a north Dallas club, where he sashayed on the floor, deep into the tango or the flamenco. There one night, he spoke Russian to a woman while they danced. When she asked him what he did, Stefan stared at her, his face blank, and said, "I'm working for the KGB."

Shocked, the woman dropped her hands and walked away, stalking out of the club, leading Rich and the others to share a boisterous laugh.

After Annika joined, the group became even more of

a family, celebrating holidays at her apartment, including traditional Swedish Christmas Eves with pickled herring, salmon, and ham. At such occasions, colleagues with children attended, and Annika grew used to seeing Stefan, who so wanted a child of his own, ignoring the adults, instead sitting on the floor, playing with the youngsters. The same thing happened at a home with a dog. Drawn to the animal, Stefan stroked and talked to it. Before long, off and on he mused about adopting a black German shepherd, a breed he'd researched extensively on the Internet, impressed with the reports of their intelligence.

As gifted as Stefan was, Annika soon came to realize what others had about him, that he lacked a street-smartness, or perhaps common sense. The stories about him were legendary, like the time he complained his television was broken. Annika looked it over for him and realized that it was simply unplugged.

Another favorite story was the day Stefan knocked on Mark Bouril's apartment door with a quandary. One of the things Stefan loved so much about Texas was the cachet of the Wild West, and he began collecting antique guns, including old Winchesters and a stunning Smith & Wesson. That day, he'd been cleaning one on the kitchen counter, when he dropped a bullet that clattered into the sink and landed in the garbage disposal. His hand too large to reach inside to pull it out, Stefan knocked on Bouril's door for help. "So many Americans have guns, this must be a common problem," he said. "You must have a tool for this?"

Laughing, Bouril said he knew of no such tool, and the two men ended up rigging a tweezer-type apparatus out of chopsticks.

As they became closer friends, Annika saw things in Stefan that made sense after he confided in her about his upbringing, describing his father as abusive to him and to his mother. At times, Stefan seemed overeager to please, and he assiduously avoided conflict. "He'd sided with his mother.

They were very close, and he took on the pain of her abuse," she said. As a result, he was easily hurt.

One afternoon, he came to her with a thought he wanted to share, but Annika had no time to listen with a deadline looming. When he continued to talk, she snapped at him, "Not now!"

She looked up, saw the devastated look on his face, and quickly regretted her words.

As sympathetic as she was, however, Stefan's inability to stand up for himself frustrated Annika. Routinely, she counseled him to be more forceful, to fight for what he wanted, telling him that he needed to have confidence. Always, he agreed, but when a difficult situation presented itself, he crumbled rather than engage in any conflict. As the years passed, she grew to understand that it was too much to expect of him. "Any confrontation terrified him," she said. "It wasn't something he could control."

Outside the lab, too, Annika watched Stefan habitually back away from unpleasant situations. In a bar one night, an intoxicated woman for some unknown reason took offense to something Stefan said and moved toward him, poised to scratch his face. Not raising a hand, Stefan simply turned away. The woman's boyfriend moved in, grabbed her, and dragged her off.

"I could never hit a woman," he said to a friend. "My deepest fear is becoming my father."

Those who knew him would realize that the memory of his father's rage never left Stefan. In 2005, when his father died, at work Stefan seemed uncharacteristically remote and depressed, talking about how his father had never told him that he loved him or that he was proud of him, never acknowledged all Stefan had done with his life. "It saddened him that his father never approved of all he'd accomplished," Annika said. "He loved his father. He didn't dislike him. And he was disappointed that he'd never been able to please him."

As the years passed in Dallas, Stefan relied on his make-shift family of friends, looking out for each of them when he could. In his way, Stefan was something of a fixer, networking people. When his CPA friend, Ran Holcomb, was diagnosed with cancer, Stefan researched the type and connected him to physicians at MD Anderson in Houston to treat him. When Annika had a problem with her car, Stefan went through his list of contacts and found a repairman, handed it to her, and said, "Call this fellow. He's an expert on that part of the car."

At times, Annika mentioned something to him in passing, and later he'd approach her with the solution to her problem, an answer for her question, something he'd taken the time to investigate to help her. One of the most remarkable events was the time she mentioned to him that Hawaii was on her bucket list. Stefan said nothing, and she hadn't even realized that he listened. But a year and a half later, he gave her an American Airlines ticket to Hawaii as a Christmas gift.

Annika and Stefan
(Courtesy of Annika Lindqvist)

The friendship and respect grew between them, and Stefan trusted Annika. Over the years, she learned the disdain he had for those scientists he judged weren't dedicated to the truth, some he suspected misrepresented data to bolster their results and increase their prestige and grant money. At one point, he refused to work with a scientist after he questioned a study's results. For some scientists, their work was tied to their egos, but Stefan was simply intrigued by the quest to discover, to expand boundaries, so for him manipulating scientific data was unthinkable and inexcusable, because, said Annika, "it was truly all about the science."

In April of 2002, Annika and Stefan authored an article that ran in the *Journal of Biological Chemistry* entitled: "Enzyme catalysis and regulation; biochemical properties of purified recombinant human carotene 15."

By then, Annika and Stefan spent so much time together, meshed so well, that friends and colleagues assumed they were a couple. Instead, they were the closest of friends. Then, in the spring of 2004, their platonic relationship transformed into a romance. For months, their connection took what seemed a natural step, and they dated. In many ways, nothing had changed. They still went out with their group, frequenting the local restaurants and bars, laughing and having fun. While not overtly passionate, not prone to buying candy, sending poems or flowers, Stefan was loving, highly attentive, and gentle. "I'd sit down on a couch, and suddenly there would be a pillow next to me," she said. "It was a little like hovering over me."

There were things Stefan admired, and near the top of his list was a beautiful woman in high heels. For his fiftieth birthday that May, Annika made Stefan a framed collage of photos of him with his friends, along with handwritten notes, little greetings most of which read "Happy Birthday!" with short sentiments including "Official Old Fart," and "Looks like it's time to get that red convertible!" Tucked in between were suggestive photos of women in stiletto heels. In the center, Annika posted a note that read: "Shoe Fetish" in blue, with an arrow pointing at a picture of Stefan. At the time, all Stefan's friends laughed. Years later, it would seem both tragic and ironic.

While their friendship continued, Annika and Stefan's romance lasted only a matter of months. Later, she would decide that while similar in many ways, they were simply too different. Annika loved nature and the wilderness, while Stefan craved city life. She wanted to explore the world, and Stefan had grown set in his ways, wary of change, only wanting to visit places he'd already been, Sweden, New York, and to see a friend in Rio. Rarely happier than in a field bird-watching, Annika knew Stefan had no such desires. When she asked him to go hiking or camping, he'd suggest, "Why don't you just stay here, and we'll go out to lunch?"

Afterward, Annika realized that part of the problem was that Stefan didn't know what to do with her since she was independent and not looking for him to support her. Many of the other women he'd dated over the years had wanted something from him, including the married woman he dated when he first returned to Dallas, who still occasionally asked him for money or presents. Habitually, although they hadn't had a relationship in years, he bought the woman what she wanted, which grated on Annika. "I wondered why he couldn't just say no," she said. "But that wasn't Stefan. He had a hard time saying no to anyone. And if he once cared about a person, he always cared."

No bitter breakup, as quietly as their romance began, Annika and Stefan simply went back to being friends, perhaps closer after their brief affair. Although he was two years older than she, Annika thought of him as a younger brother, someone so accepting that he was easy to take advantage of and needed protection. "I loved Stefan dearly as a friend," she said. "But as a relationship, it didn't work. We just weren't a good match."

In 2007, Stefan traveled to Washington, D.C., for a conference, and called his ex-wife, Jackie, asking her to meet him for lunch. By then, she worked in the Indian repatriation branch of the Smithsonian Institute, assisting American Indian tribes reclaiming religious artifacts and human remains. Jackie had gone on with her life, completed her college education, married, and had children. In contrast, Stefan's life had changed little from when she first met him although he talked regularly about looking for the right woman to start a family. Perhaps he was still attempting to put that first marriage behind him. At lunch that day, Jackie and Stefan ate crab sandwiches and talked, but she would remember it as being uneventful. When he returned to Dallas, Stefan seemed no more settled for having seen her again.

That same year, Annika bought a one-story, four-bedroom house in a quiet neighborhood about ten minutes from The Village. Amplifying the differences between them, Stefan seemed unable to understand why she'd want to be tied down with a house. Yet before long, he dropped in off and on, happily sunning in her backyard, sipping wine, and talking. At times, he showed up on the weekend for a morning coffee, and stayed to have a beer or wine in the afternoon.

For the most part, Stefan seemed content at The Village, surrounded by his friends. He continued his research, and that year he published a paper on how estrogen and progesterone metabolize in the cervix during pregnancy. His personal desires progressed as well. For years, Stefan had talked about replacing his white Camry and exhaustively studied cars on the Internet. After so much thought, he chose a Mercedes and bought a four-year-old, silver CLK-320 coupe. Once he had it, he rarely drove it except to and from work, still staying close to his apartment or Annika's house, walking or taking a cab out in the evenings. "If he left the city limits, it must have been a mistake," Annika said with a laugh.

Stefan showing off his new car
(Courtesy of Annika Lindqvist)

At Henk's, the Bavarian deli and bakery, he met a German artist, Arie Van Selm. Later, Stefan purchased one of Van Selm's paintings, a large black crow called *Not an Everyday Bird*. Stefan and the artist became friends, occasionally talking on the phone, meeting for lunch, getting together for dinners. Explaining why he liked the painting, Stefan said he appreciated crows because they weren't the most loved of birds and were rather outsiders in the bird world. "I think Stefan saw himself in the painting," said Van Selm. In the following months, Stefan purchased two more of the artist's crow paintings, and Van Selm would say that he found Stefan to have a good sense of form and color. "We drank good wine together and talked art."

In the bars and restaurants, Stefan and his friends continued to gather in the evenings and on weekends. Stefan bought rounds of drinks, picked up more than his share of the tabs, and tipped heavily. His friends cautioned him that there was no need to, but he insisted. Some thought that he was overcompensating, that it was so important to him to be liked. Others thought that he did it to hide what they saw as his inner shyness.

Despite his many successes, in 2009 everyone in Stefan's life knew he was on edge. The economic downturn that began a year earlier was impacting NIH grants, and federal research money dried up across the country. As an associate professor, Stefan's position at UTSW wasn't tenured, and without the grant money to fund his investigation into molecular changes inside the cervix during pregnancy, he faced losing his position and his lab.

Furiously, he wrote grant proposals, worked on finding funding, but with the banks in turmoil and money tight, nothing emerged. Off and on over the years, Stefan had battled with depression, and he'd taken prescription meds to treat it, but the impending loss of his position loomed large, troubling him. Not as outgoing as usual, Stefan appeared anxious about his situation and his future.

That August, Stefan lost his position at UTSW.

Weeks later, an offer came in from a fellow Swede, Dr. Jan-Åke Gustafsson, the director of the University of Houston's new Center for Nuclear Receptors and Cell Signaling in the department of biology and biochemistry. Stefan felt flattered when Gustafsson, whose work focused on prostate-cancer research, invited him to Houston for a look at the new center, recently funded by then–Texas Governor Rick Perry. On the campus, Stefan's office would be in the ultramodern Science and Engineering Center building. Gustafsson made an offer, and Stefan accepted. At UH, Stefan agreed to a salary of $80,000, less money than he was making in Dallas, in exchange for a better title, that of a full professor. By then, the delayed NIH funding for his study had been renewed for an additional three years. While Annika remained in Dallas, going to work in another lab, the money enabled her and Stefan to continue working together, albeit long-distance.

Despite his excitement about the new opportunity, the pending move weighed heavily on Stefan. "He was upset," Annika remembered. "Moving to Houston was hard on him. He had his life in Dallas, his friends. He was comfortable there. He wasn't a man who liked change, and everything was changing."

Yet the world marches on, and all wasn't staying the same in Dallas either. About that time, Stan Rich married. At the wedding Stefan, while happy for his good friend, expressed regret at his own lack of a family. "I want to meet my match, my partner," he said.

When describing what he wanted in a woman, Stefan's blue eyes sparkled behind his glasses, and he chuckled. "I'd like a hot-blooded Latina," he said. "Someone who will tango and dance the salsa with me, and teach me to speak Spanish."

Such a woman waited in Stefan's future, but she would be far from a blessing.

Chapter 4

The move to Houston that December 2009, would prove difficult for Stefan Andersson. After nineteen years at UTSW, his move to UH meant that he worked in a strange setting with all new people, which left him feeling uncomfortable and alone. He rented a small apartment near the Texas Medical Center, a sprawling web of high-rises and skyscrapers made up of some of the largest hospitals, medical offices, and research facilities in the world, just west of downtown Houston. But the apartment was dim and lonely, without the camaraderie of The Village.

Soon after Stefan arrived, Stan Rich contacted Stefan to say that he'd entered Alcoholics Anonymous, after becoming aware that his drinking was out of control. Over the years, he and Stefan had been great drinking buddies. There were times when they drank heavily, and Stefan appeared worried about his own habits. "Do you think I'm an alcoholic?" Stefan asked Rich one night over one of many glasses of wine.

"I don't know. Maybe you are," Rich said. "Maybe we both are. But no. I don't think so."

They brushed it off. "It wasn't something I was ready to face at the time," Rich said later.

When Rich called and announced that he'd quit drinking, Stefan became quiet for just a moment, perhaps stunned, then said, "That's admirable."

There were facts that perhaps reassured Stefan that his

drinking hadn't reached an addiction level, that while his friend might be an alcoholic, he wasn't one. The first was that every year Stefan gave it up for a month or more, during the spring when he worked out to get ready for his annual bike race in Sweden. Moreover, his drinking had never affected his work, and he kept no alcohol in the house, never drinking alone. Still, on his forays out in the evenings or afternoons when he wasn't working, Stefan nearly always had a glass of wine or a drink in his hand.

If Stefan had been inclined to honestly assess the situation, perhaps so soon after his move to Houston didn't seem to be the most appropriate time. Struggling to find a comfort zone in the city, to map out new restaurants to frequent, places to go, without his support group around him, trying to meet new people, he felt ill at ease. As he'd done in the past, Stefan relied on his trust in the field of pharmacy and went to a doctor asking for help. One prescribed Xanax to mollify Stefan's anxiety.

Attempting to settle in that spring, Stefan bought furniture, a large black-leather couch and a chair and ottoman. Arranging it in his apartment living room, he fell and hurt his back, and a doctor prescribed painkillers. At the lab, Stefan had to stand while he worked, his tailbone too sore to tolerate sitting. Neither the Xanax nor the painkillers were supposed to be taken while consuming alcohol, but Stefan continued to drink. "His life was really going through a rough patch, and he was overmedicating," said Annika. "He seemed at a loss, out of his zone."

In his apartment one afternoon, Stefan passed out and fell down. When he came to, shaken, he called a colleague at UH, who summoned an ambulance. At the hospital, Stefan was diagnosed with an electrolyte imbalance, one that they pegged as related to the pills and his alcohol consumption. At the urging of colleagues, Stefan signed himself into the PaRC Rehab Center at one of Houston's largest hospitals, Memorial Hermann.

For the next ninety days, Stefan participated in a twelve-step program similar to Alcoholics Anonymous, which admits powerlessness over an addiction and seeks help from a higher power. As an atheist, Stefan couldn't ask a god he didn't believe in for help, couldn't turn his problems and his addiction over to an entity that he judged didn't exist. Instead, Stefan replaced the concept of a god in the program with something tangible, something he'd loved throughout his life: the sun.

After months of counseling and group sessions, lessons in redirecting his life, Stefan checked out of rehab with a PaRC baseball cap, one he said he'd worked hard to get. He returned to his research and his apartment. On and off, he called Stan Rich, saying that he wasn't drinking, and Stan knew that his old friend was trying. Stefan went to AA meetings, and he stayed home more at night, and told a friend that when he thought of drinking, he took out his admit report from the rehab center. "It's a sobering thing to read," he said.

Yet after so many years of going out nightly, finding companionship in restaurants and bars, Stefan must have found it difficult. In a new city, Stefan was alone, not going to the places where he felt the most comfortable, the restaurants and bars where he could be around people and enjoy their company. Before long, Stefan told Rich that he was drinking again, but he claimed to be monitoring how much, limiting himself to two or three beers or glasses of wine an evening.

Then something happened.

That fall, as his first year in Houston drew to a close, Stefan took one of his daily constitutionals and walked the path around Hermann Park, as close to New York's Central Park as Houston has to offer, a 407-acre expanse of green situated between the Texas Medical Center and Houston's stylish Museum District, close to the stately Rice University campus. A statue of Sam Houston on horseback marked the park's entrance, pointing visitors to the Houston Zoo, an outdoor theater where the symphony performed each summer, a jogging track, playgrounds, gardens, a small lake with paddleboats, and the Museum of Natural Science. That day, Stefan noticed a tall building, The Parklane. Next to a driveway leading to the porte cochere, a sign advertised apartments for rent.

A sleek thirty-five-story luxury high-rise, The Parklane rose above Hermann Park Golf Course's six-teenth hole. Inside the double glass doors at the entry, manned by round-the-clock valets, stood a glass-topped table with a large potted white orchid, atop a black-and-white-marble floor. To the right, at a large desk that matched the wood-paneled walls, sat a concierge, responsible for moni-toring a high-tech security system that included pass keys to access the building and resident floors, as well as recording the comings and goings of guests and deliveries.

The Parklane

An impressive address in one of Houston's priciest neighborhoods, The Parklane, like The Village, was geared toward professionals, mainly childless couples and singles, offering happy hours, parlors for greeting guests or waiting for limos or taxis, a fitness center, tennis courts, a pool, a parking garage, and surveillance cameras throughout the building and the grounds.

That day, Stefan toured 18B, a one-bedroom, one-bath corner unit. On the eighteenth floor near the elevator, it was T-shaped, with the wood-floored entranceway and kitchen making a wide stem that continued onto the beige-carpeted living room, the master bedroom to the left with a full bath, and a study open to the living room on the right. The kitchen was small, but Stefan still rarely cooked, not even owning dishes or pots and pans since he'd gifted them to Annika. Instead, the place had amenities that meant more to him: nine-foot ceilings with seven-foot panoramic windows that overlooked the golf course and the city, and two balconies with nothing impeding the rays of his beloved sun.

Stefan Andersson's move into The Parklane would mark his turning point in Houston. Overnight, his attitude toward the city changed. Never into possessions, for a man of fifty-six, Stefan had little. He brought his recently purchased black-leather furniture and placed a desk with a black-mesh chair in front of a curved corner window, then hung his three crow paintings on the living-room walls, including two above a flat-screen TV. The kitchen cabinets were bare, except for one he filled with his unused prescriptions in their original bottles, carefully organized. He had no dining-room or kitchen table, and only a single barstool near the kitchen counter. With its expansive views, the 1,211-square-foot apartment felt free, open, and bright.

Abhorring clutter, Stefan decorated the bedroom with only a bed and shelves crowded with books, nearly all non-fiction, exploring history, finances, business, or science.

Stefan smiling and happy in his apartment
(Courtesy of Annika Lindqvist)

"I'm a minimalist," he told friends. "I feel better with space around me."

In the months that followed, Stefan settled happily into his new home. In the mornings, he rose early to see the sun rise over the city. Then he sat at his desk on his laptop surrounded by windows and checked how the overseas financial markets had fared overnight. Sometimes he put in a buy or a sell order, or simply held to his current positions. Afterward, he drove to the University of Houston campus for a day's work in the lab. At times, there were lectures to give to medical students and PhD candidates on his research.

In the evenings and on the weekends, Stefan made Houston his own, as he'd once done with Dallas and New York. One of his first forays was to the Museum of Fine Arts—Houston, a nine-minute walk from his new apartment. There he became a member, which spurred invitations to attend parties surrounded by Picassos,

Stefan in a UH photo in the lab
(Courtesy of Staffan Larsson)

Rembrandts, and Monets, and to view special collections
at cocktail gatherings that marked the openings of new
exhibits. Always personable, he quickly made friends.
Sometimes he talked of his sister Anneli, who'd become
an art teacher and a sculptor in Sweden. In Houston, one
of the most diverse cities in the nation, with consulate
offices of ninety-four countries, ranging from Albania
to Venezuela, Stefan hobnobbed with native Texans and
transplants from across the United States. Nearly a quar-
ter of Harris County's residents were immigrants from
other countries, and at the museum, Stefan met many,
the majority working in the energy business in the city
known across the world as Big Oil's megacenter.

The fourth largest city in the U.S., anchoring a metropoli-
tan area of more than 6.6 million, Houston sprawls, splitting
off into neighborhoods and suburbs. For Stefan, it became
more manageable after he explored the Museum District,
surrounding The Parklane, and discovered restaurants and
bars within walking distance. Before long, Stefan was a
regular at Bodegas, a brightly decorated, Tex-Mex eatery on
the first floor of an office building, just half a block from the
art museum. There, Stefan claimed a barstool and ate tacos,
while drinking a beer or downing a shot of tequila. On Sundays, he indulged in festive brunches in the Hotel Zsa Zsa's
circular dining room, lined with plants and trellises. There
he feasted on omelets or pasta, enjoying the views through
windows overlooking a garden and the iconic Mecom foun-
tain, gifted to the city by a prominent oil magnate in the
sixties.

Two of Stefan's closest Houston friends were tied to his
homeland, Pernilla and Anders Berkenstam. Sandy-haired
with glasses, Anders had not only Sweden in common with
Stefan but professions. An associate professor at the University of Houston, he had a PhD and conducted medical research at the Methodist Hospital Research Institute. With soft
blond hair often pulled back, Pernilla had eyes that squinted
when she smiled, rosy cheeks, and an inclination to wear a

string of pearls. The Berkenstams lived in a nearby high-rise also overlooking the park, and friends described the couple as good companions, warm sorts who enjoyed a laugh.

On his evening forays, Stefan encountered others out dining, including Todd Griggs, a chief technology officer at a consulting firm, and his girlfriend, Bessie Garland, a petite nurse with chin-length dark hair. Before long, Stefan, Griggs, tall and good-looking, with dark hair and an Ivy-League manner, Garland and others formed a network not dissimilar to the one Stefan had enjoyed in Dallas, an eclectic group that included an engineer and a stockbroker, financial consultants and sales reps. In the evenings, they congregated at their favorite haunts, texting or calling to determine where dinner and drinks would be. They talked of their days, compared views on politics and current affairs, and enjoyed the company. For Stefan, a social creature who lived alone, the companionship raised his spirits.

As always, Stefan walked to the meeting places. His route

Stefan with Bessie Garland on St. Patrick's Day
(Courtesy of Todd Griggs)

usually took him past Hermann Park, where, in the early mornings, when the golfers hadn't yet taken over the course, the homeless gathered. Before long, he routinely stopped at a nearby convenience store, buying the group donuts for breakfast and sometimes a six-pack of beer and sandwiches to distribute for lunch. Although he'd always acted disinterested in nature to Annika, she judged Stefan had settled in the day he started talking about a squirrel he'd befriended while sitting on a bench behind the apartments. "I don't know what to do. There's a squirrel that keeps coming up to me," he said one day. "What do I give it?"

"Peanuts," she advised him.

Before long, he confided about how he spent mornings sitting on the bench, reading his newspapers and feeding the squirrel. "People will think I'm some strange old man who talks to squirrels!" he said with a chuckle.

On one particular morning, Stefan, his voice filled with excitement, called Annika to tell her that a bald eagle flew past his window. "It was probably a turkey vulture," she said, dubious. Later, she'd learn there were nesting eagles in the park, and it was likely that Stefan had been right.

In the spring of 2011, as he did every year, Stefan returned to Sweden for his annual bike tour with his friends and to visit with family. Back in Houston that summer, a Boston law firm contacted him, and he began working part-time as an expert witness, reviewing documents from a lawsuit involving a large pharmaceutical company. At $450 an hour, the opportunity made for a lucrative side job. Then in the fall, Stefan's newest study came out in the *Proceedings of the National Academy of Sciences*, on estrogen receptors and prostate cancer.

As busy as he was, Stefan still made time for friends. When Ran Holcomb was again diagnosed with cancer and returned to Houston to be treated at the MD Anderson Cancer Center, Stefan walked through Ran's door daily to keep him company. The two men talked about Ran's treatments, Stefan researching alternatives to advise his friend, and they laughed and reminisced about old times, when they were neighbors in Dallas.

Christmas Eve 2011 marked Stefan's one-year anniversary at The Parklane, and he took his car to Dallas to attend Annika's traditional Swedish holiday gathering. When Stefan and his old friend Mark Bouril arrived too early, Annika shushed them out the door, saying they were distracting her from her cooking. The men drove around Stefan's old neighborhood and talked until he spotted a homeless man on the street, alone on the holiday. Stefan lowered his window and called out to the man by name. The rest of that afternoon, the three men sat together in a Starbucks, where Stefan bought the bedraggled man coffee and sandwiches and talked to him as if they were old friends.

After his chilly beginning in Houston, life again appeared to be opening up for Stefan Andersson. As much as he'd bemoaned the change, the move had been a good one for him. On their frequent calls, Annika heard joy and excitement in her friend's familiar voice.

Everything would have undoubtedly ended differently for Stefan if in August 2012 he hadn't walked into The Parklane's lobby and happened upon a woman named Ana Lilia Trujillo. At the time, it seemed a lucky meeting. On the surface, Ana appeared everything Stefan told friends he'd fantasized about in a partner. Beautiful and lithe, with long, dark hair, a warm manner, a ready smile, and expressive brown eyes, she was the embodiment of the "hot Latina" who could salsa dance and teach him Spanish.

"I've got a real tiger by the tail," he told a friend a month or two later. "And I'm having fun."

Of course, there was no way for Stefan Andersson to truly comprehend who Ana Trujillo was on the day they met, or perhaps even in those first weeks of their relationship. When he ultimately did understand, the revelation would be terrifying.

Chapter 5

If Stefan Andersson carried the scars of his father's ill temper, Ana Trujillo's experiences, some dating as far back as childhood, molded her as well. Later many would be perplexed by their romance, two people from such disparate worlds. But who can explain the human heart? And were they truly so different? In social position and education, but examining their pasts and their personalities, their liaison wasn't as shocking as some would have thought. In each the other saw something appealing, perhaps the embodiment of what they most lacked. In each, the other initially found a savior of sorts. Only later would it all turn out to all be misimpression and camouflage.

The first and perhaps most obvious similarity between Stefan and Ana was that they were both immigrants who came to the U.S. and ultimately settled in Houston for opportunity. Both fell in love with the city, a blend of Cowtown and oil town, a pin-striped business center, a highly diverse milieu that thrives on the edge, applauding risk takers.

That first day in The Parklane lobby, chance brought Stefan and Ana together. Afterward, it would seem the proverbial perfect storm, two temperaments so diametrically opposed as to render one helpless and embolden the other to pure evil.

As a child, Ana's mother, Maria "Trina" Godinez, migrated with her family from Atotonilco El Alto, east of Guadalajara, in the Mexican state of Jalisco, to Arizona. Life is hard for those who arrive from across the border with little money, and by eight Trina worked chopping cotton. The family settled in Gila Bend, bordering the Sonoran Desert, south of Phoenix and near the Indian reservation, an hour-and-a-half drive north on Highway 85 from the Mexican border.

Married at sixteen, Trina returned to Mexico in early 1969 to give birth to her first child. The Vietnam War raging, her husband feared that a son born in the U.S. might one day be drafted into the armed services. That child was, however, a girl, Ana Lilia Trujillo, by all reports a bright-eyed, golden-skinned child whom her parents transported back to Arizona when she was four months old.

In the years that followed, Trina had three more children, but the marriage wasn't fated to last. Later, Ana would say that when she was eight, her father left the family to start a new one, and Trina became a single mother. Ana took what she saw as her father's desertion particularly hard. "I admired my father and felt abandoned by him," she said. "It was devastating. I couldn't understand why he didn't want to be our father anymore."

At times, Trina, a tall, broad-shouldered woman, worked two jobs to support her brood. Out of necessity, from a young age Ana took on much of her mother's responsibility with the three younger children. Trina had to earn money to pay for rent, food and clothing, and that meant that there were long hours when she was absent from the family. When Ana went to school, she dropped the youngest children off with an aunt, only to pick them up again in the afternoons. Those who knew her would later say that at the time Ana rarely complained. In the summers, Trina sent all four children south to Mexico, to live with family.

From early on, Ana had a flair about her, a wide smile and an almost contagious enthusiasm, along with an artistic bent, drawing, coloring, painting, picking and arranging wildflowers. "She always had a project working, and she loved beautiful things," said one relative. "That was just Ana, a sweet girl."

The family began as Catholics, but over the years Trina converted to Jehovah's Witness, a devout religion that takes exception to mainstream practices, including blood transfusions for the sick or injured and celebrating holidays such as birthdays, Easter, and Christmas, arguing that they have pagan roots. Particularly known for their dedication to active evangelism, members circulate through neighborhoods, house to house, ringing doorbells to hand out literature and share their faith.

Over those early years, Trina began as a hotel cleaning lady, eventually earning a management slot at a Travelodge. Later, she held a series of positions at the Wally Door factory, progressing from stacking wood to running a finger joiner machine that processed twelve pieces a minute. Ultimately, her industriousness led to the title of quality-control manager.

At the door factory, Trina met the foreman, Russell Gene Tharp, an ex–navy man who'd gone to Chico State College in California and once worked as an installing engineer for Georgia Pacific. Also a Jehovah's Witness, Gene, too, was raising four children. In Trina, he found a good match. An upright woman who made a good impression, she shared his faith and his family values. He admired that despite their modest means, Trina and her children were clean and well dressed, the house orderly.

Gene and Trina married when Ana was eleven, and from that point on she, along with Gene's oldest, cared for the six younger children. "There were four brown kids and four white kids," said a family friend. "Gene and Trina worked, and Ana was like a little mother, watching over them. Very loving. They all called her 'Sissy.'"

Even then, as a child growing up in a recently blended family, one where the parents had to work long hours to support their young, Ana seemed somehow to be looking for more in life. From the beginning, friends would remember how she loved expensive things. "Ana wanted what she couldn't afford," said a relative. "Even when she had no money, Ana found a way to dress well. And in that small town, she took risks, wearing things the other girls wouldn't." On the playground, Ana stopped and polished her patent leather shoes or fixed her hair bow, not wanting to have anything out of place. Far from a tomboy, yet strongly built, she disdained being dirty.

After their marriage, Trina's children all called Gene, "Dad." Their own father absent in their lives, they took to their stepfather. It might have helped that their mother was the disciplinarian and Gene the parent who more often agreed to their requests. In many ways, Ana was a good daughter, but despite her parents' devotion to their faith, Ana rejected their beliefs. "Even as a child, she didn't want to go to church," said a relative. "She refused, and she resented her parents' religious practices."

By middle school, Ana was an outgoing young girl, one who exuded energy and, despite her trials, happiness. With her bright smile, she was beautiful. In high school, she was voted best dressed and most popular. There was something else about Ana that would resonate decades later. From childhood on, Ana showed an intense interest in a world she couldn't see. As a child, she played with a Ouija board in the house, despite her mother's objections. Ana appeared fascinated by the possibility that there was a way to communicate with spirits.

Yet day to day, it was the physical world, occasionally unfair and too often painful, that surrounded her. Over the years, the Tharps moved their family to Cleveland, Texas, and to Orange County, California. While in California, Ana would later say she felt the sting of prejudice. In response, Trina sent Ana back to the Phoenix area to finish high school.

As she moved into adulthood, Ana was not just a pretty girl; she appeared to have something about her that naturally drew people. When she went to garage sales with family

members, strangers approached them and wanted to touch
Ana. She played with babies and fawned over small children. Habitually arriving at family events late, she hugged
family members, focusing intently and asking about each
person's welfare.

By the late eighties, Trina and Gene had moved the
family to Waco, Texas, where they worked at a small
furniture-manufacturing company. After high school, Ana
joined them, stacking wood part-time, while she attended
a paraprofessional education program at nearby McLennan
Community College, wanting to be a teacher's aide. There,
a friend introduced her to John Marcus Leos. In December 1990, when Ana was twenty-two, they married. Four
months later, Ana was pregnant, and in 1992, their first
daughter, Siana, was born. From the beginning, the marriage was volatile.

"I don't think Marcus was ready to settle down and have
a family," Ana would later say. His relatives admitted the
same. Leos, a stocky man with a round face, worked for
a mobile-home builder. When he hurt his back, his employer moved him into a desk job, which he eventually lost.
"Marcus didn't like to work," said a relative. "He went from
one job to the next and couldn't hold them. . . . Ana supported him and the girls."

While Trina had become a U.S. citizen years earlier, Ana
hadn't wanted to do that, preferring to remain in the country
under permanent resident status, often referred to as having
a Green Card. A practical person, from youth on, with the
example of her mother to draw from, Ana understood hard
work. During those early years of her marriage, she had a
position as a teaching assistant for emotionally disturbed
children at a small private school. The school sent her for
an in-service class in Austin, where she went out to bars
in the evenings with friends, drank socially, and laughed.
Among her acquaintances, Ana was popular, a lively and
warm, caring personality.

As the main breadwinner in the family, Ana carried the

bulk of the responsibility outside the home, but family members said that she had little help from Leos with their daughter or their small house. Years later, Ana described her first husband as "clinically depressed," perhaps explaining his behavior. One of his aunts stepped in, Margie Sowell, who cared for Siana in her own home, weeks at a time, treating her as if she were her daughter. The marriage was troubled, and one late afternoon, Sowell walked to the front door to drop off Siana and heard Ana inside yelling at Leos. "I work all day, and what do you do? You're just getting up?"

Sowell turned around and walked away, only returning later. "I didn't want Siana to hear that," she said.

Despite the trouble in the marriage, in 1997, when Siana was five, Ana and Marcus's second child, Arin, was born.

To better her lot in life, Ana looked for opportunities. A cousin who worked for the local Coca-Cola distributor told her about a job opening, a delivery slot, and Ana applied and was hired. At Coke, she drove a truck, unloaded deliveries and built displays, working on placement in stores. The pay was good. Meanwhile, her marriage to Leos continued to falter. Later she'd say that he stayed out partying with friends, and that at night she'd often wake up to find him gone. "I told him I couldn't live like this anymore," she said, explaining why she filed for a divorce.

Around that time, Ana's family suffered a devastating tragedy. One of her brothers, Sergio, had an ongoing drug problem, and the family grieved the day he was found dead from an overdose. Ana, a friend would say, seemed to take it particularly hard. She'd been more mother than sister to Sergio, and the loss weighed heavily on her.

Around the time of the funeral, Leos temporarily moved back into the house to help with the girls. Later, Ana said that while he was there, he called her and threatened to kill himself. When she arrived home, she found him trying to hang himself from a bedpost. She cut him down with a knife, then called his parents. After his release from the hospital, she claimed that he broke into her house and held her hostage for six hours. "He moved me to the bedroom, and he raped me," she said. Initially, she pressed charges.

"We all convinced her to drop them," said Sowell. "We didn't want to see Marcus in prison. Ana agreed. I thought later that changed her, and we shouldn't have asked her to do that."

Describing how Ana contended with the alleged rape, Sowell said that Ana had a way of blocking from her mind what she didn't want to acknowledge. "If Ana could push it down, she didn't have to deal with it," she said. "If she didn't feel it, it was like it didn't happen."

Despite the chaos in her personal life, Ana thrived at work.

At Coke, she entered contests and won special-edition Coke memorabilia and trips. She moved up the job ladder, from delivery to a merchandising slot, where she was given a route handling larger stores and worked developing new business by helping to place Coke machines in office buildings and stores. As part of her new position, Ana drove a company car that came with a gas card to keep its tank full. Many of her coworkers had college degrees, and she was proud. Later, she'd describe it as "very tough" being both Hispanic and female in what was for the most part a male world. "I did very well," she said with a smile.

The court thought so, too, and when the divorce from Leos finalized in May 2000, the judge gave Ana custody of Siana and Arin.

A single mother with young children, much as her own mother had once been, Ana moved to a one-story house that backed up to a grove of trees in nearby Bryan. She dropped Marcus Leos's last name and went back to her maiden name, Ana Trujillo. Despite her claims that Leos had attacked her, she continued to drive the girls to Waco to see their father, and would later say she believed he was basically a good man.

That same year, 2000, Jim Fox, a pharmaceutical rep who called on neurologists, walked through a hospital in Temple, another of the small cities not far from Waco, and saw Ana wearing little makeup, her Coke T-shirt, and slacks, her long, thick, dark hair pulled back in a ponytail. "Can you help me?" he asked, saying he had to find a particular doctor's office. "I'm lost."

"Sure," she said. They walked together, and before they reached the doctor's office, he'd invited her out to lunch.

They dated for a year. Later, Fox, a quiet, tall, slender man with brown hair who at thirty-three was a year older than Ana, would describe her as working hard to care for her family. Yet perhaps there were signs from the beginning that it wouldn't be a lasting match. Jim Fox liked things orderly. When he picked Ana up at her house for dates, Siana and Arin ate Cheerios on the floor and dishes were stacked high in the sink. "But Ana was so kind," said Fox, divorced with a son who lived with his mother in Houston. "She loved her kids. Ana was a great mom, and in the beginning, she made a great wife."

After the marriage in July 2001, Ana's girls lived with them in a brick one-story on a tree-lined street. They settled into married life, both going to work. As there often are in blended families, life wasn't without challenges. While Arin, Ana's younger daughter, then just three, adjusted easily, calling Fox "Daddy," the older girl, Siana, then nine, seemed to resent him. "She didn't like it when I told her to pick up, or what to do," said Fox, who described himself as finicky about keeping the house in order. "There was a lot of tension."

For the most part, they lived a quiet life. A homebody, Fox enjoyed staying in on weeknights. On weekends, they sometimes went out to dinner or with friends. When they did, they drank socially. If there was music, Ana loved to dance. And there were those nights when he wanted to leave, and she argued that they stay and close up the bar.

At the house, she decorated with her artwork, paintings and drawings she did on her days off. Jim paid for the house and other expenses, and Ana was responsible for the gro-

ceries. More often than not, however, she ran out of funds
before the end of the month. "She'd take the girls shopping,
and she'd be overly generous," Fox said. "She went through
money. After a while, I understood that it was just Ana, the
way she was."

Along with the heated discussions over money, there continued to be tension between Fox and Ana's oldest, Siana,
who would later say that she found her stepdad to be "anal."
Admitting that he could be fastidious about the house, Fox
said his relationship with Ana's oldest was strained, and she
would later describe it as the two of them "bickering a lot."

For the most part, Fox got along well with Ana's family.
He liked Trina, Gene, and Ana's siblings, and they quickly
meshed. When his son visited, Ana worked hard to connect
with the boy, taking him places with her girls. When he left,
she was generous with him as well, coaxing Jim into gifting
his son with $20 for his wallet. "She was a good woman,
always concerned about others. She didn't cook much, so
I did. Things were really normal," Fox said later, thinking
back to their marriage and trying to put the Ana he knew in
context with the future that awaited her. "There are things,
well, yes there were problems, but the way she changed,
that's something I still don't understand."

Yet there were those issues from her growing-up years
that seemed to haunt her. At times, Ana talked about all she
believed she'd missed out on from such a young age, charged
as she was with looking after her younger siblings, saying
she'd been robbed of a childhood. On Sundays, Jim took the
girls to church, but Ana refused. "Ana hated churches," he
said. "She talked about being a Jehovah's Witness, and how
she wasn't even allowed to play sports, how she said she was
shunned by the other kids. Never celebrating holidays, even
Christmas or her birthday. She said it ruined her childhood."

Perhaps, then, it wasn't surprising when four years into the
marriage, in January of 2006, when Jim Fox said he wanted
to move to Houston to be closer to his son, Ana decided

to make changes as well. Once his transfer was approved, they drove the two hours into the city to find a home. On the shores of Lake Houston, Ana fell in love with Summerwood, a heavily treed subdivision cut from the forest, half an hour northeast of the city. The area was under construction, a brand-new development, and they picked out a lot on Baron Creek Lane. For the house, they chose a plan for a 3,100-square-foot, four-bedroom, two-story. The design had a stately look, with a column leading to a high arch over the front door.

Their home under construction until the fall, Ana didn't wait to give notice at Coca-Cola. Later, she said, "I'd worked all my life. My girls were getting older, and I wanted to be more flexible. I wanted a stress-free environment."

For his part, Fox agreed to the plan when Ana laid it out. She'd been unhappy for months, complaining about one of the men at work. "I thought it was a little odd. She'd been at Coke about ten years," Jim Fox said. "But I didn't push."

Rather than work at Coke, she enrolled in a school to become a massage therapist, her plan to open a studio close to their new home. "I want my own business," she told Fox.

When he considered it, he decided it could work well for his wife. "I thought she was a caring person, so I thought she'd be good at it. I wanted to support her."

That spring, Jim Fox rented an apartment near the new house, under construction on Baron Creek. They chose white brick for the exterior and inside a white-tile floor in the entry, all white walls and white carpeting. Meanwhile, they put the Bryan house up for sale, and Ana continued to live there while she attended the Healing Handz Massage Academy.

The program at Healing Handz was just opening, and Ana enrolled for its first session. Housed on a horse ranch, the owners offered a three-hundred-hour curriculum that satisfied all the state licensing requirements. The owner, Susan Hartzog, would later describe Ana as friendly and warm, always trying to help others. "I don't remember all my students, but I remember Ana," she said. "We have a disabled son, and Ana was kind to him."

Thursday and Friday evenings and every other Saturday, Ana arrived at the school immaculately dressed, her long hair pulled back in a ponytail, ready to work. Throughout the sessions, she talked about her family's plans, excited to be moving to Houston. The house in Bryan remained on the market, but everything seemed to be falling into place. At the school, Ana wore scrubs, but when Susan happened upon her in town, she noticed how well dressed Ana was, nearly always wearing stylish high heels. "She looked like she came from money," Hartzog would recall. "I always assumed that her parents were upper-class."

Ana training at massage school
(Courtesy of Susan M. Hartzog)

That May, Ana completed her course work, on everything from business practices to hydrotherapy, and she and the girls moved with Jim into the apartment, where they watched over the new house as it was built. One day walking the lot, looking at the house rising on its foundation, they met Jon Paul and Ruth Espinoza, an attractive and affable young couple expecting their first child building a one-story on the adjacent lot. Their Realtor had told them that the Foxes, their new neighbors, were "a nice family with two girls."

The Espinozas initially believed the Realtor's assess-

Ana at her massage-school graduation party
(Courtesy of Susan M. Hartzog)

ment: that the couple living next door was an average, happy family, one without secrets. But before long, their opinions of Ana Trujillo Fox changed. "I got the impression there was something strange going on over there," said Jon Paul. "Things just didn't seem right."

As fall arrived, Jim and Ana and her two daughters, Siana and Arin, moved into the Baron Creek house. Unusual in suburban Houston where interiors tend toward the traditional or have more of a country Texas flare, Ana decorated the all-white insides—walls and floors—with contemporary black-and-white furniture: in the living room, black-leather couches with a white-marble table, black bookcases, and black-granite kitchen countertops. One room in the four-bedroom house was Ana's art room, and she stacked her paintings against the walls in Jim's office.

By then, Ana's mother and stepdad ran a secondhand furniture store in Waco. At times, they bought better pieces in good condition. Once Ana and Jim moved in, Trina and Gene brought two bedroom sets from the shop for their granddaughters' bedrooms.

Baron Creek was larger and more affluent than any house Ana had ever lived in, and she seemed happy, at least at first. "Ana saw what money could buy. With her second husband, she lived a life she hadn't known before," a relative said.

At first, all seemed well on Baron Creek Lane.

Jon Paul Espinoza, an insurance salesman, and Jim became friends, stopping to chat outside, sometimes cutting each other's lawns when one or the other was on the road. On the weekends, the two families waved when they pulled into their driveways to unload groceries, or flowers to plant in their yards. "At first Ana seemed very nice," said Jon Paul's wife, Ruth. "But before long, a little odd."

One day, when Jon Paul asked Jim where Ana worked, he explained that she had just quit her job at Coke to become a licensed massage therapist. Saying that she had a traveling table she could bring with her, Jim said Ana was making appointments in private homes and offices until she had a studio set up. Jon Paul liked Jim Fox, and little Arin, by then nine, who rode her bike on the street and seemed a happy, friendly girl. Both the girls were pretty, young images of their mother. Quickly after they all moved in, Jon Paul began feeling uncomfortable around the woman next door. "Ana was very attractive, but it was like she knew it," Jon Paul said. "She was a flirt."

Before long, Ruth, too, began wondering about her neighbor. One day, Ana stood outside in a see-through shirt, without a bra. "Did I just see that?" Jon Paul asked when they walked inside.

"I don't trust her," Ruth responded. "I think you should stay away from her."

When Jon Paul was outside, however, Ana made it difficult to avoid her. At times, it was as if she lurked, waiting for him, ready to approach him asking for favors, like moving objects in the yard too heavy for her to carry. He helped, but then quickly walked away. Ruth's suspicions only increased that October. For Halloween, the girls and Ana elaborately decorated the house then answered the door in costumes. For the occasion, Ana dressed all in black and wore makeup and a pointed hat, portraying a sexy witch. "The word seductive came to mind," Jon Paul said.

"I didn't like the way she dressed around my husband," Ruth said. "I didn't get a good vibe."

When the Espinozas welcomed their first baby, a little girl, Ana's daughters came over often. Siana and Arin appeared fascinated with the infant, wanting to hold her. Ana's girls were sweet and kind, and Ruth at times worried about them, wondering about their mother. The longer they lived next door to Ana Fox, the stranger she seemed to Ruth.

One day, Ruth stood at a window and watched for what seemed like a very long time as Ana walked in circles in the street in front of their houses. Wearing a spaghetti-strapped top and a long, flowing skirt, in sandals, Ana flounced over the concrete, twirling, holding her skirt in her hands, as if she were dancing. "It just looked so odd," said Ruth. "She did that for a while, went inside, then came out and did it again."

On Sundays, the Espinozas saw Jim take the girls to church, without Ana. When Jon Paul, a deeply religious man who holds weekly Bible studies at his house, mentioned it, Jim explained that Ana had been raised a Jehovah's Witness and had fallen away from practicing religion. What Jim didn't mention was what he'd found his wife doing in the house, laying out tarot cards, attempting to read them and predict the future. When he'd asked her not to do it in their house, that it was against his Christian beliefs, Ana agreed, but soon he discovered she hadn't truly stopped.

Meanwhile, Ruth grew increasingly annoyed with the behavior of her next-door neighbor, watching through a window as Jon Paul cut the grass and Ana stood nearby, waiting to talk to him. When he stopped the mower, Ana rushed over, said something to him, then gave him a hug. Taken aback, Jon Paul quickly walked away.

"What was that about?" Ruth asked, once he was inside.

"She asked me for money," he said. "She said she lost her wallet. I told her I didn't have anything on me."

"Please stay away from her," Ruth said, yet again. "I don't have a good feeling about that woman."

Thinking about what his wife had said, Jon Paul agreed. Something about Ana Fox bothered him as well, and he'd come to think of her as the type of woman who could have power over a man. "I wasn't attracted to her, but I thought, if a man was, she could control him."

Yet with all her flirtations, when Jim and Ana were together, Jon Paul thought that Ana appeared threatened by other women. "I knew the type," he said. "Always jealous and upset."

There were times when Jon Paul felt uneasy looking at the house next door. The place appeared increasingly sinister to him, as if something lurked inside. One evening, he noticed the rooftop of the Foxes' house covered by a flock of black crows. "It just felt like there was something evil," he said. "I had an eerie feeling that I can't explain."

In 2007, as they approached their first anniversary in their house, the Espinozas realized all wasn't well next door, where they heard Jim and Ana argue loudly at times, especially getting in and out of their car in the driveway. To Jon Paul and Ruth, it sounded as if their neighbors' marriage was in grave trouble.

What they weren't aware of was that the situation was changing quickly within the walls of the Fox house. "That was the bad year," Jim would later say.

That summer, Jim helped Ana lease a studio, paying the first two months' rent, in an older office building on Main Street in downtown Houston. In one of the busier parts of the city, the building was just half a block from the Rice

Lofts, apartments in the renovated historic Rice Hotel, and within blocks of skyscrapers that housed major oil companies and the courthouse district, filled with lawyers, judges, and office workers throughout the workweek.

Excited about opening her massage salon, Ana decorated, bringing in art for the walls, a couch, massage tables, plants, and a sound system to play soothing music to set the scene and help relax clients. Once settled in, she hung her framed license on the wall and sent out circulars to the surrounding offices, hoping to attract clients. From Jim's perspective, it didn't appear to go well, Ana making so little she had to ask him to continue paying her rent. But that didn't mean that Ana was home. Instead, once she began working in downtown Houston, she disappeared much of the day and late into the evenings.

"She changed like flipping a switch," he said.

The year wore on, and Jim became increasingly upset at his wife's behavior. At first since he often traveled, he wasn't aware of what was happening at home. But then nights cropped up where he went to bed alone, Ana remaining downtown long past midnight. "I trust you," he told her, at first.

As time passed, however, her arrivals came later and later, until he awoke at 2 A.M. and found her side of the bed empty. "I didn't know if you were dead in a ditch somewhere," he told her, when she walked in hours later, saying he'd been up much of the night worrying.

"Just go to bed. I'll be fine," she responded.

The first time Ana stayed out all night, she claimed to have slept at the studio. "You can't do that," Jim said. "You have to come home."

The second time, he told her, "If this is what it's going to be, we're going to get a divorce."

When he mentioned a divorce, Ana appeared surprised, then promised that she wouldn't ever stay out so late or all night again, that she'd go to the studio, take care of her clients, and drive the thirty miles home to Baron Creek Lane to be with Jim and the girls. "I'll do better," she said, giving him a kiss. But it didn't happen. Before long, Jim routinely went to bed alone, Ana's all-nighters commonplace. "It kept building and building," he said.

"Find a studio closer to the house, so you can come home at night," Jim asked.

"I love the atmosphere downtown," she told him. "I don't want to be in the suburbs in my rocking chair. I don't want to be a housewife."

Before Christmas 2007, Jim looked through a stack of paperwork in the house and found divorce papers Ana had filled out. She returned home that night, and he asked, "Weren't you going to talk to me about this?"

• When Ana said she'd been frightened to tell him, Jim responded by suggesting that perhaps a divorce was best for both of them, saying, "It's okay. This isn't working out. You aren't coming home."

"I don't want to be a wife or a mother anymore," Ana said. "I just want to go out and have fun."

A little more than a month later, in February 2008, Ana Trujillo Fox filed for divorce. By then she rarely came home before 3 A.M., and most often not at all. To save expenses during the divorce, Jim moved to an upstairs bedroom, and Ana stayed in the master downstairs. With Ana rarely home, Jim felt like a single dad. The tension rose, and before long, Arin asked to move to Waco to live with her father.

In Waco, Ana's family struggled with what they saw unfolding. "It was like she was doing the same thing her father had, abandoning her children," said a relative.

That summer, 2008, Jon Paul Espinoza returned home late one evening, and walked past the Fox house on his way to the community mailbox. When he did, he felt a sense of foreboding and someone watching him. He turned, looked back, and in the glooming thought he saw an apelike creature staring down at him from Jim and Ana's rooftop. He turned away, then back, and it was still there. The second time, it was gone. "I never even told Ruth," he said later. "I didn't think anyone would believe me. I didn't want people to think that I was crazy."

Not long after, Jon Paul's and Ana's paths crossed at a Shell gas station. While he filled his car tank, she came up to him dressed in a sexy top and short shorts. At first, he didn't recognize her. "I don't have cash to pay for gas for my car, and I can't believe I left my wallet at home," she said, flirting. "I'll pay you back."

Jon Paul gave her the money, and hurriedly left. Later that afternoon he heard Jim and Ana arguing. When Jon Paul again talked to Jim, he said that Ana had moved out for good. On a day months later, Jon Paul suddenly realized that "the crows were gone, and the house didn't have that cloud over it anymore. It was like it had never happened."

On June 19, 2008, their divorce became final and Jim and Ana Fox's seven-year marriage officially ended. In the division of assets, Jim kept the house, they retained their individual retirement accounts, and Ana received money and her 2003 black Toyota 4Runner. At one point, she returned to the house and tried to persuade Jim to start over, one more time, saying that she'd made a mistake and wanted to reconcile and become a family. After so much heartache, he said no. "You know we've been through this," he told her. "You made your promises. If this is the life you want, just go for it. Just go."

After the divorce, Ana moved into a nearby apartment, so Siana could finish high school. Yet quickly, Ana Trujillo Fox dropped her suburban wife-and-mother role and moved into downtown Houston, the big-city nightlife calling her, intent on having the freedom and fun she insisted she'd been cheated out of as a child.

It was then that Ana's life took an even more bizarre turn.

Chapter 6

"I'll never forget the first time Ana walked into my shop," said Teresa Montoya, the owner of a hair salon housed in a downtown Houston office building. A shapely, motherly woman with a kind smile and long, highlighted, dark hair, Montoya paused for a moment, before continuing. "Ana was all dressed up, like she always was, in a long, flowing skirt, a sexy top, and big heels. She had this air about her. I thought immediately, she had something special about her."

"Is there a Teresa here?" Ana asked, a mischievous glint in her eye.

"Why is that?" Teresa answered.

"I heard if I want to be successful in my business, I have to meet this lady," Ana replied.

"What?" Teresa responded, drawing out the vowel with a slight laugh in her voice.

Later, Teresa would say that it was Ana's confidence that grabbed her. "I wanted to get to know her."

During that first encounter, Ana had a pedicure in Montoya's salon, and they talked. From that day forward, the women became the best of friends. Partly it was timing; Montoya had just lost someone close to her to cancer, and she felt a void. "Ana came in like a ray of sunshine and made me happy," she remembered.

When Montoya went to see Ana's studio, she found her just down the street on the seventh floor of an aging low-rise office building in an older corner of Houston's ultramodern downtown. By then, Ana had added a small stocked bar, to offer clients drinks with their massages. There were things Montoya noticed early on about her new friend. One was the way Ana wooed people, flirting and playing up to them, winning them over. The other was that Ana had the ability to quickly change, to mesh with different people. "She had so many sides to her," said Montoya. "Ana was like a drug. Once she walked in, the party was on. She took things to a higher level. She was dramatic, and when she focused on someone, she made them feel special."

The two women quickly realized that they had a lot in common. They were both in the beauty industry. And they were both opening new chapters; Montoya had recently married, and Ana appeared excited about the direction her life was taking. "Ana was beautiful," said Montoya. "I don't care if she put on a rag. She looked like a million dollars. When you have a body like that . . ."

The first time Ana gave her new friend a chair massage, Montoya came away impressed. Although just five-foot-five and 120 pounds, Ana had a muscular body. "And she had strong hands," said Montoya. "For a woman, Ana was very strong."

One testament to Ana's physical prowess was that evenings she worked as security at Venue, an upscale hip-hop bar on the first floor of her office building. "I watched for individuals who could cause problems," she said, describing her job there.

That statement would later prove ironic as others saw her own actions spiral out of control.

The days unfolded in a haze, from lunches where the two women laughed and drank wine, to happy hours at downtown restaurants, swank establishments busy with a mix of patrons unwinding after a day's work. In Houston, Ana Trujillo Fox quickly made a stir. Out on the street, in restaurants, she stopped and talked to people. In the bars at night, she danced. It soon became obvious that Ana enjoyed having the eyes of the crowd on her, especially men's. "Ana got a lot of attention when she danced," said Montoya. "Ana was fun, just a little bit wild. And everyone wanted to be her friend."

Ana dancing in a downtown bar

One day early in the friendship, before Ana and Jim Fox's final split, Ana brought Montoya to the Summerwood house. The hairdresser noticed Ana's paintings, many stacked around the floor. One was of two women standing on high rocks, one figure holding a cross. In Ana's explanation, she was one of the women, and in the painting she was trying to find her way. "I wish I'd been on a high rock like that, so I could see where I was going," she said.

"Why haven't you hung them?" Montoya asked.

"I'm not sure I'm staying," Ana replied. That day she told her new friend that her first marriage had been a mistake and that she'd married Jim Fox because she needed a stable home for her girls. When they talked further, Ana said that she'd been a housewife since she was a girl, first watching over her younger siblings, then caring for her husbands and children. As she eyed the years ahead, that part of her life was ending.

"Downtown Houston was blossoming," said Montoya. "It was becoming a scene, and Ana wanted to be part of it. She was ready, after never having any freedom, to enjoy her life."

The trouble, however, started early, the first ripple two months before the divorce papers were signed.

The center of Ana Trujillo Fox's Houston quickly became the area in and around the Rice Lofts, trendy apartments built in a historic hotel on Texas Avenue. On the national registry of historic places, the Rice had a colorful past, including the big-band-era nights when Tommy Dorsey and his orchestra played in the second-floor Crystal Ballroom, with its impressive chandeliers and a wide balcony that looked out

The Rice Lofts

onto the city streets. After its glory days, the hotel closed, and the building fell into disrepair, until in downtown's rebirth it was refashioned into expensive apartments occupied by professionals. On the street level, the Rice's first floor housed popular nightspots and restaurants.

On that evening in April, Ana patronized one of the Rice's tenants, Azuma, a posh sushi restaurant and a popular happy-hour spot. The restaurant was hosting an AIDS fund-raiser, and Montoya stopped in briefly and saw Ana holding a glass of champagne at the bar, surrounded by men. "See you tomorrow," the hairdresser said on her way out.

Later that evening, Ana was parked in her black SUV facing north on the shoulder of the southbound lanes of one of Houston's busiest freeways. She'd apparently been driving against the traffic. The police officer who arrested her smelled alcohol, and in his report he said her speech was slurred and her eyes bloodshot. When he shined his flashlight into Ana's still-running vehicle, her blouse was unbuttoned, exposing her breasts. "Close your shirt," he told her. After repeating his order three times without Ana taking any action, he saw a shirt in the backseat, grabbed it, and threw it at her. "Get dressed!"

On the scene, Ana refused the breathalyzer, and at the station the officer said she became argumentative and unco-operative when he ordered her to stand on one leg. She was read her rights and booked and spent the night in a jail cell, but the DWI charge was later dropped due to insufficient evidence.

Ana Trujillo Fox's 2008 booking photo

The first year after Ana's divorce, Montoya often looked out her salon window and saw her friend walking briskly toward the bars in late afternoon. Off and on, Ana stopped to talk to strangers, dining outside on days when the weather permitted, striking up conversations, laughing and carefree. When she saw a homeless man on the street, she bought him a sandwich, or gave him a few dollars, then stopped to talk. The more people Ana met, the more she became a part of the fabric of the city, cultivating friendships. One of them soon spawned an opportunity.

A young professional couple Ana met had a large apartment at the Rice, and they made an offer that Ana happily accepted. Traveling for business and rarely at home, they sublet a section of their loft to her for her massage business. The move not only gave her a more prestigious address but cut Ana's rent, and placed her closer to Montoya's salon. Soon the two women worked together, the hairdresser spreading the word about her friend the masseuse, and Ana telling her clients about Montoya's salon. When a client wanted a back massage, Montoya called Ana, who had a chair set up at the salon. If they wanted a full-body massage, Ana took care of them in her studio. "We made a lot of money, it was great," said Montoya. "At first, it helped both of us."

With Ana's business taking off, Montoya later estimated that her friend pulled in up to a thousand dollars a day with her massage business. In the evenings, they drank at one of the Rice restaurants, like Sambuca, a well-known hot spot in the Rice's corner slot that had live music. One night, seated outside, Ana handed a homeless woman who approached a twenty-dollar bill. "You act like you know her," Montoya said.

"I met her in jail when I got my DWI," Ana explained, as if it were a completely natural occurrence. "They had us in the same cell."

To Montoya, it appeared that her friend had a big heart, always looking out for someone who needed a hand. "In her mind, she was always helping somebody," the hairdresser said. As time passed, however, she saw another possibility. "The truth? Ana was the one who needed help."

The longer they knew each other, the more Montoya realized that much of Ana's self-esteem centered on her ability to lure men. "Her whole self-image was based on her sexuality," said Montoya. "What men wanted, she would do."

Early on, Ana dated a wealthy physician, who lived in the Sugar Land area, a prosperous suburb far west of Houston.

To be accessible, Ana kept extra clothes in her 4Runner, and when the man called, she turned to Montoya, no matter what they were doing, and simply said, "I have to go."

Through her new landlords, Ana soon made a second contact that would prove important in her new life, Christi Suarez, a fast-talking, dark-haired woman with expressive eyebrows, a producer for a local public-access TV show and an events coordinator. As she had with Montoya, Ana clicked immediately with Suarez, and they, too, soon frequented Houston's clubs and bars. Through Suarez, Ana met Raul Rodriguez, the host of a public-access program that showcased local bands.

At night in the clubs, Suarez and Rodriguez watched as Ana flitted from place to place, talking to one man after another. At times, she moved with the music and gave one or another of the men a rose. "She danced for them, and the men loved it," Suarez said. "She played up to them. Everything was based on her sexuality."

The people Ana met were doctors and lawyers, oil executives, stockbrokers, and other professionals. Dressed in lace and skintight skirts and jeans, circulating through the bars, she sought those who appeared well-off. "Ana found out what they did. Then she made up names of companies that weren't real, and talked about how she could help them," Suarez remembered. "Some became obsessed with her. They'd buy her anything. Give her anything."

At one point, one admirer moved Ana into a suite at the Four Seasons Hotel, bought her clothes and gifts, and she called friends to join her. She stayed for days, lounging around the pool, until she finally grew bored. "She really wanted attention," said Suarez. "And she wanted someone to love her."

"He's obsessed with me," Ana told another friend about one admirer. "It's not my fault if men want to be with me and do nice things for me."

Raul Rodriguez saw the same things. Looking back, he

would later say that the men were Ana's downfall. "She was too free with herself, and that caused problems. She did whatever she wanted to do."

In addition to her massage studio and her job in security at the club, downtown Ana met a lawyer, and before long, she worked part-time in his office as a translator for his Spanish-speaking clients. He'd later say that the clients liked her and felt comfortable with her, and that she appeared caring toward them.

Looking back, Suarez considered how it all came together, and said, "I think part of it was that the Rice wasn't a good place for Ana. It was after she moved in there that things started going crazy."

The rumors of dark occurrences on that particular piece of downtown Houston real estate had begun decades before the current building was erected. The land was initially the site of the Republic of Texas capitol building, before statehood, when Texas was its own country. When the republic moved its headquarters, the building became the Capitol Hotel. The tragedies dated back to 1858, when the republic's fourth and last president, Anson Jones, shot himself in his room after dinner while a guest at the hotel. That building was razed in 1881, and the first Rice Hotel was erected by Houston oil magnate William Marsh Rice in 1881. That building was later torn down to make way for the current hotel in 1912.

Over time, witnesses reported strange occurrences at the hotel. Some claimed to have seen an ethereal woman in white who rattled doorknobs. Around a second-floor bathroom, the visage of a homeless woman sometimes appeared, a friendly spirit only seen by women. At other times, downtowners reported seeing the figure of a man jumping from an upper story over and over, a sight perhaps linked to the 1929 stock-market collapse when devastated investors across the U.S. took their lives.

One of the more common alleged sightings occurred off and on in the seven-thousand-square-foot Crystal Ballroom, with its columns and sparkling chandeliers, a popular venue for weddings. At times, guests reported floating balls of light and couples in Victorian dress on the dance floor. When carefully eyed, the figures lacked feet. One theory was that the ballroom floor was raised at some point in the building's history, and the ghostly revelers twirled on the original surface.

In more modern times, on the day of his assassination, President John F. Kennedy rested in a room at the Rice before boarding his fateful flight to Dallas. Through the years, when that room was empty, some reported hearing a man's voice.

When Ana moved her studio into the Rice, Montoya said, "That was when all hell broke loose."

From the beginning, Ana made no secret of her interest in the spiritual world. The first time she met Raul Rodriguez at a party, she spent much of the night talking about her beliefs, explaining that she'd turned her back on traditional religions, especially the Jehovah's Witnesses of her childhood. In particular, she expounded on her worship of the sun. As he listened, Rodriguez thought Ana sounded like a Wiccan, someone who thought of herself as a witch, as she described harnessing the power of the sun through her fingers and eyes.

While Rodriguez wasn't particularly concerned, he was surprised at Ana's enthusiasm. "There's always been an interest in spirituality in the Latin culture," said Rodriguez. "But Ana talked and talked about it, unusually so."

In Rodriguez's experience, many Hispanics believed in what he described as "white magic," the use of crystals, herbs, and the like, to heal. On his part, Rodriguez believed in Karma and that some people, *curanderos*, Spanish for folk healers, had special abilities. Yet Rodriguez never spent an evening with anyone quite like Ana, who seemed consumed by it. Bubbly and fun on one hand, she became intense when she talked about her interest in developing what she described as her powers.

At the party, Ana circulated, approaching people, holding their hands, turning them over and reading their palms. On a table, she fanned out a deck of tarot cards to predict futures, her eyes flashing with excitement much as they may have decades earlier when she'd shown an interest in such things as a little girl.

When Ana was a child, Trina objected when her daughter used a Ouija board in the family house. At night, without her mother's intercession, friends would later say that at the Rice Lofts, in a site some believed haunted, Ana, intoxicated after a night drinking in the bars, returned to her studio and again took out a Ouija board, calling on spirits, attempting to open a portal connecting the physical world and an invisible one. "A lot of Spanish-descended people believe in white and black magic," said Montoya. "I didn't think anything of what Ana was doing at first. But then bizarre things kept happening. It was as if she had no boundaries."

Much of what happened wouldn't seem out of step with the new Ana, the once suburban housewife who danced for men in bars. Montoya marveled at the changes in her friend, like the day she showed up at Ana's studio in the Rice and found her in a sexy outfit with a low-cut top, showing off her cleavage, standing on a stool, posing in front of a window.

"What are you doing?" Montoya asked.

"Just fooling around," Ana said, explaining that a friend had called and asked her to stand in the window, so he could take pictures of her from the building across the street.

Later that afternoon, Montoya walked into a club and found a group of men, one with photos displayed on a laptop, erotic photos of Ana. "Does she know you took these?" Montoya asked, only to learn that they were the photos Ana had modeled for at the window. When Montoya told Ana that the men had been ogling her photos, Ana looked not angry but pleased.

"Well, really, did you like them?" she asked Montoya. "Are they good?"

Montoya laughed, thinking it was all crazy, that she'd been upset about the photos, when Ana obviously felt flattered.

But the voodoo doll truly caught Montoya's attention.

"Look what I have," Ana said one day. Out of a small casket-like wooden box that also contained a chicken bone, Ana pulled a primitive doll fashioned from sticks and rags. She told Montoya that she'd bought it in New Orleans, and that she'd used it to put a spell on a man she worked with at Coca-Cola, one she claimed harassed her. True or not, what Ana said was that the man had died.

"Get it out of my shop," Montoya told her, not wanting anything to do with the totem.

Laughing, Ana said, "It's only a toy."

A voodoo doll similar to the one Ana Trujillo Fox carried

For the most part, on the surface, nothing seemed different about Ana Trujillo Fox. The Rice sponsored happy hours in a community room for residents, and Ana went often, sexily dressed, standing in her stilettos, holding a glass of wine, chatting to the mainly young professionals gathered. Some thought that perhaps the woman with the massage studio talked a little too loud, or insinuated herself unwelcomed into conversations, or touched them when they preferred that she keep a distance, but for the most part, she was a colorful addition to the parties.

As she became ever more enmeshed in the downtown night scene,

Ana continually reinvented herself, at one point hanging out with a group of rappers who drove in limousines and took her to extravagant parties. At other times, Montoya walked in and found her at the pool at the Four Seasons Hotel with a group of lawyers, getting some sun. "She moved with a wealthy crowd," said the hairdresser. "She fit in with anyone, changing depending on who she was with."

To her friends' surprise, Ana brought a young homeless woman into her studio, allowing her to stay. She had a sad story of being involved in drugs and losing custody of her child. When Ana's friends warned her of the dangers of taking in people off the street, Ana scoffed. In response, she claimed exceptional abilities that protected her and expressed no fears.

"I have powers," Ana told Montoya one day. "I can do things with my mind."

"You don't," her friend replied. Over the years, Montoya had run into people who thought they were able to manipulate others by claiming a connection to the spirit world. That led her to the conclusion that any powers they had were granted by those who accepted their abilities as real. "The only way you have powers is if someone believes in you, and I don't believe."

Before long, Ana started telling friends that she had a mentor, someone she encountered in downtown Houston who advised her on spirituality. When Montoya met the man, he was a bike messenger, delivering paperwork and packages between office buildings. The well-spoken young man said that he had a degree in theology but hadn't been able to find a job. "We talk about different religions," Ana told a friend. "He's teaching me."

Later, it would seem that Ana became what some in the mystic community called "a jumper," a person who took bits and pieces from many religions, cobbling them into her own beliefs.

As vocal as Ana was, many took note of her new interests. Montoya's friends began referring to Ana as "your

witch friend," and the hairdresser worried that perhaps Ana
had crossed some invisible line and lost control of her life.

In February 2009, Ana failed to take a class required
by the state and her massage license lapsed, yet she continued to practice. Late that month, Montoya threw her friend
a fortieth birthday party with champagne, balloons and
chocolate-dipped strawberries. Halfway through the happy
event, Ana suddenly sobbed. When Montoya asked why,
her friend said, "I've never had a birthday party. My mother
didn't believe in them."

That year, Montoya watched as Ana fell in love with a
younger man, one she showered with gifts and trips, even
taking him skydiving. Handsome, tall, well-spoken, he
talked of marriage. Then he left on what was supposed
to be a short work trip and never returned. She called
and called, until his phone was disconnected. She'd gone
through much of her money from her divorce settlement,
including her 401K, and the man she'd showered it on left
her without a word.

"Maybe he's dead," Montoya said, as Ana cried, de-
spondent.

Watching her friend suffering, trying to find her place
in the world, Montoya felt ever closer to Ana. Yet the
hairdresser's friends voiced alarm, worried about the as-
sociation. "You need to get away from that woman," one
cautioned her. "She's dangerous." Not yet ready to heed the
warning, Montoya held tight to the friendship, exhilarated
by Ana's zest for life.

Then something happened that changed Ana. Two versions
would later unfold surrounding the events of May 15, 2009.

Months earlier, Montoya had introduced Ana to a man
named Brian Goodney, who worked in the oil business and
had a loft in the Rice. They'd met off and on, going out to
dinner or drinks, but there wasn't a romantic connection.
What they would later agree on was that on that evening,
Goodney had a small dinner party in his apartment, and

Ana arrived rather late, as the other guests were leaving. Goodney walked his final guest to the parking garage, then returned to the apartment, and he and Ana were alone.

When explaining their connection, Ana later contended that she believed she and Goodney had a professional relationship, that they had plans to work together in the furniture business. In her account, he returned and she tried to leave, but for some unexplained reason, he blocked her exit and grabbed her by the shoulders, struggling with her, pinning her against a wall.

Later, Ana told Montoya that in the struggle, she grabbed a candlestick and hit Goodney on the back. In anger, he followed her down the long hallway to the door and pushed her against the wall. She fell and hit the floor, hurting her head. "She called me crying, saying she was bleeding from her ear," said Montoya, who didn't care for Goodney.

"That's what you get," she told her friend. "I told you to stay away from him."

In sharp contrast, Goodney described a much different encounter.

The trouble, he said, started weeks earlier, when Ana asked him for a twenty-two-hundred-dollar loan. She refused to tell him what the money was for, and he turned her down. That set the stage for the night of the dinner party. When he walked back into the apartment, he said that Ana looked startled, as if she'd been interrupted. Suspicious, Goodney thought she may have been rifling through his things.

"Time to go," he told her, and she followed him to the door. But then, without warning, he said, she picked a candlestick up off a table and clubbed him on the back of the head, knocking him unconscious.

In Brian Goodney's version of that night, he awoke on the hallway floor, near the apartment door. Opening his eyes, he saw Ana sitting on the floor a distance from him, staring at him. Saying nothing, she simply stood up, stepped over him, and left.

The next day, embarrassed by having been hit by a

woman, Goodney called her to ask why she hit him, but she didn't answer, Unbeknownst to him, by then Ana had filed a police report, claiming that he had pushed her to the floor, and she'd hit her head. For some reason, the police never talked to Goodney, but the following weekend, a man who identified himself as Ana's attorney called and threatened to file a felony assault charge against Goodney unless he paid Ana thousands of dollars. Goodney refused, and from that point on, he said he kept his distance from Ana.

Whatever happened with Brian Goodney, Ana's friends noticed that she'd changed. What backed up Goodney's version was that by then Ana had financial problems. In June, a month later, a legal complaint was filed against her for a seventy-six-dollar bounced check.

From the night of the altercation with Goodney on, Montoya thought she saw physical changes in her friend. "Ana said she heard ringing and that she had headaches. She held her head and rocked and said it hurt," recounted Montoya. "And she was upset because she said that he got the better of her. She became angry."

The new Ana Trujillo Fox's outrage along with a sense of entitlement seemed to be percolating just under the surface, readying her to pounce at any provocation. One evening with Montoya, Ana pulled into a space in a downtown garage. Montoya pointed out a NO PARKING sign, but Ana waved it off and kept walking away from the car. Fifteen minutes or so later, the women emerged to find the 4Runner gone. Montoya wanted to call the towing company's number on the sign, but Ana said, "I know how to handle people like this."

Moments later, Ana confronted the attendant, a small, aging Hispanic man, screaming at him. She grabbed him and pulled his hair, yanking at it. In Spanish, she shouted, "You get my car right now, or I will put a curse on you and your entire family!"

Terrified, the elderly man sobbed and hurried away, quickly returning with the SUV.

"Get in the car," Ana told Montoya.

"No, you're crazy," she replied, walking to the curb, where she hailed a cab.

Yet despite Ana's bizarre behavior, Montoya had to admit that it appeared that her friend's anger and sex worked to her advantage. That day, Ana got her car back without paying the tow fee, and Montoya watched as the men Ana flirted with gave her whatever she wanted.

Still, the new Ana frightened Montoya, backed up by what she'd heard from her family and friends. "Your friend Ana gets unpredictable after a few drinks," a restaurateur friend told Montoya one day. "With her, you never know what will happen."

Chapter 7

Beginning in 2010, it would be obvious to many around her that Ana Trujillo Fox had entered a downward spiral.

Early that year at the Rice, Ana, who'd let her apartment go and routinely slept in her studio, returned drunk late one night and spray painted the walls and hardwood floors. When her landlords saw the damage, the couple ordered her to leave. Her few possessions, including her massage table, were moved to the lobby, and she was told to arrange to have them picked up. Her couch went into Montoya's salon, along with her massage table. Despite so many who'd told her to rid herself of Ana, Montoya helped her paint a back room at the salon to use as her new studio.

Yet Ana rarely came into work, the massage table empty. "She'd end up leaving with a man," said Montoya. "I wouldn't see her until the end of the day, when she'd want to go out for a drink."

During those evenings, Ana was full of plans. She proposed collaborating on an image company with Montoya, one to advise men on how to dress, on grooming, on how to improve their self-images and become more confident. At the same time she talked of helping men become more successful, Ana was technically unemployed and homeless, her children scattered, her younger daughter, Arin, living with her father in Waco and Ana's older daughter, Siana, out of school, working, and living on her own. Meanwhile, Ana circulated from man to man, living with one then another. At times, she confessed to strange sexual encounters, including one with a wealthy middle-aged man whom she said choked her during sex. "I don't like to do it," Ana said. "It scares me."

"Don't see him," Montoya urged her. "You're going to end up dead. You're playing with your life now."

After months passed, Ana said she had ended the relationship. By then she lived with another man, one she said took care of her. While in his home, Ana began studying how to heal her body, to rid herself of headaches she claimed plagued her since the night with Brian Goodney. For therapy, she turned to her art, building what she referred to as installations, combining found objects like sticks and rocks with paper and paint. "I would create displays," she said later. "And I worked on developing hydrotherapies for my body, to use water and salt to bring out the pain and bruising."

While Teresa Montoya doubted that Ana had any spiritual powers, Christi Suarez, the TV producer, came to another conclusion. When they talked, Ana interpreted Suarez's dreams. A Pisces who read her horoscope religiously, Ana expressed a fascination with such visions.

When sober, Ana talked to Suarez, too, about companies they could start, including one to recycle computers. When Suarez mentioned that such companies already existed, Ana quickly moved on to the next idea, or pronounced that it didn't matter because her company would be better or different. Meanwhile in the bars at night, Suarez sometimes saw Ana pull the raggedy voodoo doll out of her bra and play with it, rubbing it on others. People became angry, telling her to put it away, but Ana just laughed or stood in a corner holding the doll, closed her eyes, and whispered, as if cursing the person.

More and more, Ana Trujillo Fox appeared immersed in another world. Increasingly, she drove to one or another of the yerberias, eclectic stores scattered throughout Houston, a city with the second largest Latino population in the U.S. next to Los Angeles. Once inside, she bought oils and herbs the purveyors claimed had the power to make a man fall in love or a woman more sensual, others that could cure diseases of the heart, liver, or kidneys, or some rumored to bring fame. Displayed on shelves, candles bore depictions of saints that legend said had the power to grant favors. Amulets and incense could be used in rituals to curse enemies. A mélange of Christianity, paganism, and folklore, the stores blended cultures and beliefs.

Inside a yerberia

One afternoon, Ana bought oil to burn that the proprietor said brought money, and another that would make her a better lover. And she drank, each night, in downtown restaurants and bars. Alcohol appeared to be taking over Ana's life. "She was out of control," said Montoya.

On April 19 of that year, 2010, Ana was found slumped backward with her eyes closed in her car parked in a lot

near Interstate 59, Houston's Southwest Freeway. A tow-truck driver followed her after he saw her run a red light, stop for a green one, and jump a curb. She smelled of alcohol, and the police officer who responded called in the code of a "person down" when he failed to awaken her. When she did come to, she was uncooperative but talkative. She failed the sobriety test and was eventually fined $200 and sentenced to one year's probation.

As part of Ana's probation, she had to submit

Inside a yerberia

Ana Trujillo Fox's 2010
booking photo

to random drug tests. After she once tested positive for pot, she was jailed and spent twenty days behind bars. From that point forward, Ana smoked a concoction stocked in some yerberías and smoke shops, a so-called synthetic pot consisting of herbs and plants sprayed with chemicals that didn't show up during routine tests. Sold as potpourri, packages warned against human consumption, but the ten-dollar bags were known to give a substantial high.

That year, Montoya worried about her friend's odd behavior. They argued about religion and Ana's beliefs whenever Ana brought up her powers. "If you're going to be doing black magic, I can't have anything to do with you," Montoya said one day. That year, she pressured Ana into going to a service at a Lutheran church, but afterward her friend struck out in anger.

"Don't preach to me about religion and the Bible. I know more than you do," Ana snapped, quoting scripture. "My parents pushed religion on me my whole life. And I've pulled away from it."

By then, Ana kept a distance from her family. When Trina Tharp called and asked Ana why she rarely visited or kept in touch, she said, "Mom, I want to tell you things that are constructive. I want to make you proud. When I'm not proud, I can't call you."

Just three years earlier, Ana Trujillo Fox had a good job. Two years earlier, up until the divorce in 2008, she lived in an impressive, well-furnished suburban home with a husband who loved her and supported her and her two daughters. But by the summer of 2010, she was homeless, without a car after she totaled her 4Runner on a freeway ramp. Over the months, Ana circulated in and out of different homes, mostly owned by men, some just friends, others brief sexual liaisons, spending a few nights, taking her suitcase, and moving on. One evening, she dropped in at a party at Raul Rodriguez's house and stayed for three days.

Eager to return to downtown Houston, in August 2010, for $600 a month, Ana rented a second-floor room in the Londale Hotel on the corner of Prairie and San Jacinto, a short walk from the Rice Lofts. The rooms were small but serviceable and shared community bathrooms off a hallway. When she registered, Ana told the manager, Jim Carroll, that she was a masseuse and a legal assistant. A bargain in downtown Houston where a single night in a hotel routinely costs hundreds of dollars, the three-story Londale was the oldest hotel on the same site in the city. Built in 1905, at its opening, its first street-level tenant had been Houston's original Ford Motor Company showroom.

A quaint, squat, neoclassic building with a colorful past that included rather seedy intervals during which it was rumored to have drug-dealer and prostitute tenants, the hotel catered to those who needed downtown lodging on a strict budget. At the time Ana moved in, the building was newly renovated, and the owners were bringing in a more respectable clientele. The first floor housed a bail bondsman and a restaurant, with the hotel rooms on the second and third floors.

In room 202, Ana Trujillo lived simply out of a few suitcases. One of the larger rooms in the hotel, Ana's had a sink, a television, and the linens were changed daily. To Montoya, the Londale represented a shabby lifestyle, and it seemed sad that her friend had fallen so far. Each morning, she picked Ana up, and the two women drove to have breakfast with Montoya's father. In ill health, he was considering moving

The Londale

into a nursing home, and Montoya suggested that there was another alternative. "Ana could move in the house with you. She could watch over you."

"I don't trust that woman," her father said. "I don't want her anywhere around me."

Even with that scathing assessment, Montoya continued to go out with Ana, circulating between the restaurants and bars, taking a toll on her business.

Meanwhile at the Londale, when not with other friends, Ana went out evenings with Carroll, a wiry grey-haired man with a slight paunch and round wire glasses. Carroll liked Ana, who laughed often and seemed always ready to party.

At the Londale, Ana's days fell into a pattern.

In the mornings, she slept in, then popped her door open and trudged down the hall to the bathroom, eventually making her way to Jim Carroll's room, behind the small office in the building's corner, the only room with a balcony and its own bathroom. Carroll let her use the bathtub in his room. While she bathed, unconcerned, he sat on the bed and they talked. At times, he washed her back when she asked. Or they sat on his balcony and smoked and talked. Carroll was white, and Ana explained that many of her boyfriends since the divorce had been African-American. "She told me she liked to have sex with young black guys, but that the older white guys paid her bills," said Car-

An unidentified woman, Jim Carroll, and Ana in 2010
(Courtesy of Jim Carroll)

roll. "I told her she had more game than the Parker brothers, and she laughed." Carroll wasn't surprised then when Ana showed up on rent-due days with a white man on her arm, usually middle-aged or older, yet the men he saw her partying with at night were young, tall, well built, and African-American.

On some of those afternoons when they talked, Ana told Carroll, who'd had a rough past, about her spiritual powers. At the time, Carroll was reading the Bible and rekindling his belief in Christianity. Describing herself as an atheist, Ana said she saw things other people didn't, things she interpreted as symbols from spirits, including pyramids rising from the Londale's carpeting. Carroll didn't know what to make of her claims but shrugged them off. When she told him that she felt a connection to the spiritual world, he did have a response, however, describing a room tucked between the hotel's first and second floors, the entrance plastered over and only accessible through a staircase in a storage closet.

"I call it the ghost room. The place gives me the creeps," he said.

The ghost room
(Courtesy of Jim Carroll)

That Sunday morning, about eleven, he took her there, and he leaned against a wall while Ana walked around talking, but not to him. "Hello. I'm Ana," she said. "You already know Jim. Are you here?"

At first quiet, then they heard a *ping*, like a fingernail tapping a crystal glass.

"Can you understand what I'm saying?" she said, then another *ping*.

When Ana asked if the spirit wanted anything, Jim heard a woman's voice answer, "Yes. Leave." Moments later, Carroll thought he heard the word, "Water."

Shaken, Carroll urged Ana from the room. Only later did

he return alone with a glass of water he left sitting on the floor.

In downtown Houston that year, there'd been a rash of killings in the area, and three women were found dead over a period of months. At times, the men Ana showed up with at night bothered Carroll. One brought her home after the bars closed, in the early-morning hours, and Carroll saw them on the surveillance camera. The man walked a nearly unconscious Ana upstairs. He propped her in a chair, while he unlocked her room, then took her inside. Moments later, Carroll heard a loud *thunk* from her room. He called 9-1-1, and police dispatched officers and a paramedic. When they knocked on Ana's door, she appeared unhurt.

Not long after, she and Carroll talked on the sidewalk in front of the hotel, Ana telling Carroll about a confrontation she'd had late one night with a man outside the Rice Lofts. "I'm worried about you," Carroll told her. "You should buy some pepper spray or something if you're going to be walking around downtown alone at night."

"No one is going to fuck with me," Ana said, frowning. Then she bent down and pulled off one of her shoes, a black stiletto with a thick platform and a long, slender heel. In a statement that would later seem prophetic, she said, "If they do, I'll get them in the eye with this."

While Ana's situation continued to decline, a new opportunity opened up for her that summer. Her TV producer friend, Christi Suarez, had noticed Ana's enjoyment of being the center of attention and that the camera liked her. Off and on, Suarez began using Ana to host public-access programs, mainly local festivals and events. It paid nothing, but Ana enjoyed the notoriety. The two women had become friends, going out together some evenings, calling back and forth during the day. At times, Suarez, who believed in Ana's powers, still asked her to interpret dreams.

While living at the Londale, Ana happened upon a home-less man on the street, one who'd been badly beaten. Later, she called Suarez to tell her about the meeting, describing the man as an artist, bemoaning his circumstances, and wishing she could help. Suarez suggested they throw an art show as a fund-raiser, to help the man get off the street.

That evening, at a swank downtown club, Suarez brought together a wide-ranging group of Latino artists. On the handbills she circulated announcing the event she'd dubbed "Unscripted Thursdays," she promised live music, art, a happening of sorts that would continue on into the night. The background was a painting of Eve handing Adam the forbidden apple.

The club hopped the night of the fund-raiser, art-ists spreading their canvases out across the vast, opulent space, music pounding, and crowds circulating. When Teresa Montoya arrived, she found Ana lying naked on a table, a body artist trans-forming her. When the man asked Ana what she wanted to be, she said, "Make me a snake."

Embarrassed at seeing her friend exposed in front of hundreds of strangers, Mon-toya asked, "Why didn't you tell me?"

"What?" Ana responded, not at all self-conscious.

Wearing only white bikini briefs and bandages over her nipples, streaked with a sau-rian pattern of green, black, white, and red paint, Ana pranced through the crowd,

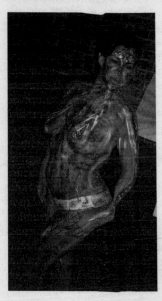

Ana painted as a snake 2010

stopping to talk to partygoers. At times, she introduced herself to the artists, talking about her own work, her installations, and spontaneously formulating suggestions for other events they could throw to promote the Houston art scene. "That would take money," one artist told her.

"I know a lot of people at Coca-Cola," Ana responded, excited. "The people at the top. I'll get them to do it!" From there she went on to claim that she knew people high up in the corporate world who controlled funds that could be funneled into large-scale art events. "We could start an artists' collective. I have experience in marketing."

"Ana was the wild child at the events," said one of the artists. "She was out there, brazen, showing off, full of ideas."

The fund-raiser a success, Suarez planned a similar event for that October, this time to take place in the Rice Lofts, billed as Haunted Hollywood. The placard had black-and-white photos from *Psycho* of Janet Leigh screaming, Peter Lorre, Vincent Price, and John Kennedy, fitting since his spirit was rumored to be one of those that occupied the old hotel. "Art Exhibition and Live Body Art," the handbill read. It began at six and ended at midnight, with a twenty-five-dollar open bar.

The venue was jammed that night when Ana showed up looking retro in a burgundy-satin bustier, a black-lace skirt, black-patent stilettos, and dark makeup under her eyes that gave her a ghostly appearance Not long after she arrived, she stripped and again was painted; this time she wore only a short black ruffle around her waist over a thong. The burgundy bustier discarded, the artist painted a black bustier that laced up, and laces climbing her bare calves from the stilettos. In photos taken that night, Ana stood proudly, her head thrown back, exposing herself to the world, defiant.

In the weeks that followed, enthused by her entry into the Houston art scene, Ana spent more time with Suarez, who'd been told by a psychic she knew that Ana was indeed

Ana at the Haunted Hollywood party
(Courtesy of James Jimenez)

gifted. "But she doesn't use her powers for good," the seer said. "She uses them for her own purposes. She knows how to manipulate you, and she finds her way into your dreams."

A rift developed between the two women, Ana pushing to become more involved in Suarez's work, something the producer resented after she'd heard Ana presenting herself to patrons at the events as if she were the coordinator. "She took credit for all my work," said Suarez. "I told her no, that I didn't need her help. Ana was furious, and she slapped me, twice."

Suddenly silent, Suarez thought back to that day. "I tried to help Ana, to give her a chance. I felt sorry for her. But from that point on, I kept a distance. I'd see her on the street, and I'd feel bad about how things had gone for her. Sometimes I'd have her host off and on, but for the most part, I stayed away."

To friends, Suarez described Ana as a wolf in sheep's clothing, saying that she looked like a kind, warm woman but could quickly become something very different, a woman capable of violence.

That Christmas, for her annual party at the salon, Teresa Montoya asked Ana to dress as Santa Claus. The outfit wasn't as Montoya imagined, when Ana arrived scantily clad in red velvet and white fur, wearing a garter belt. "I told you to wear a costume, not come as a stripper," Montoya said to Ana, who appeared pleased with the way the other guests stared.

At the end of 2010, two and a half years after her divorce, Ana's fortunes had sunk so low she had difficulty paying the Londale's $600 rent. Over her months there, she'd befriended another of the tenants, Frank Moore, seventeen years older, who worked in the oil business. The two of them went out as friends in the evenings, Moore giving Ana rides since she no longer had a vehicle of her own. The first time their paths crossed, Ana carried files to the attorney's office, where she still worked off and on as a translator. "She seemed like a really nice person," said Moore. "She was a pretty lady, and I liked being seen with a pretty lady."

Spending time with Ana, Moore's drinking escalated, and although they were just friends, they slept together. Ana suggested they share a room at the Londale and that he pay. Moore agreed, but the hotel's owners turned down the idea, and instead Moore rented an apartment in Montrose, a quaint and eclectic section of Houston near the Museum District.

Once they lived together, Moore offered to bankroll Ana, putting her back in business as a masseuse by securing a nearby storefront for a studio. She agreed, and he moved her in. She had a new set of cards printed with photos of her in scrubs giving massages, but before long, Moore understood that she rarely worked, preferring to sleep late, then wander the streets during the day and circulate to the downtown bars at night. "We'd spend three to four hundred on a weekend on booze," he said, recalling those months. "I'd call her beautiful, and she'd laugh, and at night, she'd dress up and wear those stiletto heels. She looked great, and I'd pay the bills."

When Ana drank, Moore noticed she changed. One night, Ana threw a beer at a waitress when she decided the woman didn't serve her fast enough. "Ana just turned evil at times," said Moore. "Sober, she was fun and giggly, but after a few drinks, she could turn mean in a snap. When she was angry, her eyes got dark and cold, and she looked like she was possessed."

Rather than embarrassed, Ana appeared proud of her exploits. Over the months, she told Moore of other nights in bars when she lashed out at patrons or the staff, including an incident in which she was thrown out of a bar after choking a woman. "It took two men to pull me off," Ana boasted, with a laugh. At times, she offered to curse people for Moore, which he declined.

"Is this stuff you're into Santeria?" he asked, referencing the Afro-Cuban religion practiced in parts of the Latin world.

"No, Wicca," she said, smiling, her eyes flashing. "I'm a witch."

Although she never attacked Moore, he grew to fear her. Ana was strong, with muscular arms, and she needed little or no provocation to turn on someone. One night in bed, he awoke and saw her sitting up next to him, on top of the blanket, her back rigid, her hands on her knees, her eyes closed, chanting in a strange language he didn't recognize. He didn't know if she was asleep, in a trance, or awake, but Moore grew frightened. He stayed quiet for more than an

hour before Ana lay down and went to sleep. "I didn't inter-
rupt," he said. "I didn't know what could happen."

By spring, Moore had tired of the arrangement and made
plans to move to a small town in Texas. "I had to get away
from Ana, and I had to get away from the booze. With Ana,
I was out every night drinking," he said. "I told her, this
is over. I said I was moving back with my family, to get
straightened out. Ana said, kind of sarcastically, 'Maybe I
should do that, too, go back to Waco and get straightened
out.' I told her, 'Maybe you should.'"

Certainly, there were mounting indications that Ana
needed to reevaluate her life.

Around midnight on April 29, a police officer found her
nearly passed out on the sidewalk at a busy downtown in-
tersection, in Houston's theater district, at Louisiana and
Rusk Streets. She smelled of alcohol and appeared disori-
ented. In a kind gesture rather than arrest her, the officer
signaled for a cab to transport her home. Minutes later he
was bumped on his squad car radio and ordered to another
location. When he arrived, his sergeant waited along with
the cab driver, who complained that Ana had refused to pay
the fare. This time arrested for public intoxication, Ana was
put in the back of the squad car. While the officer drove her
to the jail, he heard her curse his family to death in Spanish.
"*La familia muerto!*" she seethed.

A religious man, he turned up the radio, not wanting to
listen.

Once she was released, to move her things, Ana brought
a new friend to the apartment she shared with Frank Moore.
James Wells worked at a car dealership and part-time as a
bodyguard for Beyoncé. Tall, bald, with a trim mustache and
beard, the muscular Wells had met Ana three days earlier at
Sambuca, in the Rice Lofts. Mutually attracted, they went
to his apartment, and she spent the night. Ana had told him
that she didn't have a stable place to live, and Wells agreed
to take her in.

James Wells

At the apartment she shared with Moore, Ana collected her things to put in Wells's truck. As she got ready to leave, Moore, who'd been supporting her for months, said he'd get in touch once he settled in and suggested that they could get together when he came back to Houston. Ana agreed, but when he texted her a few days later, she responded, "Fuck off."

"I figured she didn't need me anymore, now that I wasn't doing anything for her," he said. "My opinion? I didn't think she really liked older white guys, just their money."

"I wondered why she dressed so Goth," Wells said, remembering the first months he knew Ana, who by then was using Trujillo more than Fox. "She wore black all the time, had her nails painted black, and lots of dark eye makeup, kind of like Alice Cooper. But it was okay. She was cool. I liked Ana."

At the apartment, a one-bedroom in a small brick complex near the Museum District, just down the street from a convenience store, Ana massaged Wells's back, nursing him after an injury to his sciatic nerve when he fell wrestling another of the bodyguards. Kneading his flesh in her strong hands, she loosened up his muscles and before long the pain disappeared.

On Wells's bedroom shelves, Ana found books on the ancient Egyptians, leading her to buy an amulet she wore on a chain, one she used to predict the future and answer questions. If the pendant swung front and back, the answer was yes. Sideways, and it signaled no. Along with the amulet, she wore bangle bracelets and a ring in the shape of an ankh, a cross with a loop at the top, an ancient Egyptian symbol of male and female balance and eternal life.

Sporadically that year, Ana moved in and out of James Wells's apartment, an arrangement he found acceptable. A man without singular relationships, Wells had friends-with-benefits agreements with others in the past. To him, Ana was not a girlfriend but someone he cared about who he occasionally slept with and who sometimes needed a place to stay. When they went out together, Wells gradually saw that Ana had the potential to quickly transform from the warm, loving woman he knew to a violent and angry one ready to attack. One night in a club in the line to the ladies' room, he stepped in quickly when she entered into a verbal altercation with another woman. "Why are you like that?" he asked her. "Why are you always getting into it?" Ana shook her head and smiled, like it was all a joke.

Meanwhile, Ana's life spun ever deeper into an alcoholic haze, and more friends sought to distance themselves from her. After Teresa Montoya's husband complained about their partying, she stopped allowing Ana in her salon. Despite the ban that August, on a hot summer evening, Ana showed up at the office building with a man and convinced the security guard on duty to let her into the salon by saying she needed to reclaim her laptop. Around eleven that night, James Jimenez, at six-foot-two and 250 pounds, a heavyset man with long, dark hair that hung loose to his shoulders, arrived to work the night shift and heard that Ana was in Montoya's salon.

Over the years, Jimenez had crossed paths with Ana off and on, once giving her a ride. He'd grown to think of her as eccentric after seeing her body painted at one of the events and watching her raise her hands and chant, worshipping the sun one afternoon while standing in a swimming pool. There was even the day he saw her blessing the trees. A commercial artist who'd been laid off, Jimenez had taken the security guard job for the health insurance after he needed surgery for a heart ailment.

That night, Jimenez tapped on the salon window and waited. No one came. He knocked, thinking of it as a way to give Ana a heads-up, announcing that it was time to leave. When he again got no response, he opened the door and stood inside. A light went on in the back of the salon, and Ana and the man emerged, straightening their clothes. The man rushed out past Jimenez, but Ana stayed. "Ana, you aren't supposed to be here," he told her. "Let's wrap it up. You have to leave."

Stone-faced, Ana sat in a chair and stared at Jimenez.

"You have to go!" he ordered.

When she still didn't comply, Jimenez called 9-1-1 on his cell phone. As he talked to the dispatcher, Ana grabbed her purse, walking angrily toward the door, the entire time cursing him in Spanish. Jimenez followed, still on the phone, locking the salon door behind him, as Ana left the building. At that point, the dispatcher asked what the intruder was wearing, and Jimenez walked outside to take a look at Ana.

"What direction is she going?" the 9-1-1 operator asked.

Jimenez began to answer, just as Ana turned and ran toward him, grabbing his hair and pulling him down. Stunned by her strength, he fell against the building and slid down, until he angled on top of her. "She's attacking me!" he told the dispatcher, who said help was on the way.

From across the street, two off-duty Houston police officers who'd seen Ana lunge at Jimenez sprinted over and offered help, pulling her off the security guard, both holding her down. When a squad car arrived, Ana was again taken to jail.

The next morning, Ana showed up at the salon. By then the building management had ordered Montoya to keep her friend off the property. "You'd better go," Montoya said. "They don't want you here."

"What did you tell them?" Ana demanded, staring at a woman who'd once been her closest friend.

"I didn't tell them anything," Montoya said. "They have you on video."

Looking at Ana, Montoya thought that her friend even looked different. She was staring at her with such anger, and her eyes glared, like cat eyes. Montoya yelled for the man who shined shoes in the salon, and he responded and ordered Ana to leave, threatening to call police. After she did, he turned to Montoya, and said, "You need to stay away from that woman. She's going to bring you down with her."

Finally, after so many warnings, Montoya took a clear look at the friendship and walked away.

Ana's behavior became increasingly erratic, and five weeks later, another incident took place, this time in one of the Rice apartments.

Over the years, Ana had sometimes talked with Anuj Goel at resident happy hours. A software engineer, Goel become wary of the masseuse who worked in the building, the one who drank heavily and when she did, talked too much and too loud. She'd given him her phone number in case he wanted a massage appointment, but he deleted it from his phone because "she gave me a bad vibe."

That evening, Goel and his wife returned to their apartment after dinner and walked inside. Moments later, they found someone sitting in the bathroom, on the toilet. At first, Goel didn't recognize the woman.

"You need to go," he told her.

"I'm not done," she said. They waited, and moments later she stood up. Again, he ordered her to leave, but the woman shrugged and appeared to be planning to stay. After he again told her to leave, she walked into the living room and collected her things, including her purse and a notebook. Something about the way she acted gave Goel the impression that the woman had been in his apartment for hours.

At the door, the woman turned to Goel's wife, and said, "You don't know how lucky you are to have this man."

At that moment, Goel and his wife both recognized the woman as Ana, and he became even more worried; he'd heard the stories of the altercations in the area restaurants and bars. Broadening his shoulders and hardening his voice, he ordered her to leave. As soon as she did, Goel called security, who contacted police. From that moment forward, Ana was banned from entering not only the skyscraper where Montoya had her salon but the Rice Lofts.

That fall, James Wells would later say that Ana's mother, Trina, called him to thank him for taking Ana in and giving her a place to live. "She seems a little off to all of us," Wells recalled Trina telling him. "This isn't the lifestyle we ever thought she'd be living. Ana has gone totally left field."

As the year drew to an end, Ana traveled home to Waco for the holidays. "This is not my little girl," Trina told a family member during the visit. "Something is wrong with her."

When they went to garage sales together, family members saw Ana approach strangers and rub their shoulders, claiming that she saw their auras and knew the origins of their pain. With other family members, Ana complained that her mother and stepfather didn't understand her spiritual journey, and that they had closed minds, not considering all she'd learned about channeling her powers. "They aren't supporting me in my quest to move my powers to the next level," she told one relative.

"I can fix that by laying my hands on you," she told a family member who'd had back surgery. When the woman refused, Ana said, "Why can't you all open up your minds?"

"The Ana she'd become was the complete opposite of my daughter's best friend," said Margie Sowell. "I barely recognized her."

It was in Waco on December 29, in a brightly colored Mexican restaurant, after drinking a margarita and shots of Dos Equis, that the police were called yet again. Walking from table to table, Ana talked to the guests, hanging onto the children, petting a small boy in a high chair on the head. The manager tapped her on the shoulder and offered to call her a cab, but Ana screamed at him to take his hands off her. Instead, the police were called, and days before the beginning of 2012, Ana was led off yet again in handcuffs.

Weeks later, a relative found Ana's voodoo doll at her house. Ana had returned to Houston and forgotten it. She'd shown it to her family, along with crystals she carried in her pockets that she believed had special powers. The woman brought the voodoo doll to Sowell and asked her what to do with it.

"If it was me, I'd throw it away," she said. That was what the woman did.

If the previous two years had been particularly turbulent for her, by the summer of 2012, Ana appeared to be pulling herself together. She'd largely dropped the surname Fox and, except for the occasional TV appearance for Suarez, went by Ana Trujillo, and she moved into a posh apartment in The Parklane with a fifty-year-old white businessman who lived on one of the higher floors. For a time, all seemed relatively well. They went out drinking in the evenings, circulating in and out of The Parklane, back and forth to her favorite nightspots.

It was in The Parklane that August that Ana's path first crossed with Stefan Andersson's. That day, she saw him in the lobby and perhaps sized him up to be her next conquest.

It could all have been a product of timing. Perhaps Ana suspected her liaison with the businessman was drawing to a close. Perhaps the man had already told her it was ending after the night he watched her lose control and slap a waiter at a downtown eatery. Perhaps by then her current lover realized how quickly she became irrational and even violent. Perhaps the man feared her. Perhaps Ana judged that she would soon need someone new to support her, someplace to live. Perhaps she saw in Stefan someone who could be easily controlled, someone lonely and desperate to be loved.

In the end, indecisive words like perhaps wouldn't seem relevant. For it appeared as if the pull of destiny cobbled Ana Trujillo and Stefan Andersson together. That day in The Parklane's lobby, when Ana asked one of the staff about Stefan, she undoubtedly looked beautiful, sexy, laughed and smiled, as charming as so many knew she could be. Only later would Stefan meet the real Ana. And by then, how could he escape?

Chapter 8

Life twists and turns, suddenly two strangers see each other for the first time, and from that point forward nothing is ever the same. Can either fully explain the attraction? Does anyone ever know the forces that fuse two people? In the end, Stefan Andersson's downfall would be that once he bonded with another person, he found it nearly impossible to extricate himself. He saw people with all their flaws as simply human, refusing to judge them by any higher standards. He worried about them. If they had a problem, he tried to help. Even when he should have walked away, he felt unable to turn his back.

On a hot August Houston afternoon in 2012, Stefan stood in the vast, air-conditioned lobby of The Parklane condominiums. Outside, the trees were lush green, while inside a display of orchids graced the glass entry table, as the click of stiletto heels on a white-marble floor clattered off the walls. The concierge sat behind the main desk, and at the double-glass doors stood the valet.

Fifty-eight-year-old Stefan Andersson, scientist and professor, by then had leased unit 18B for nearly two years. Viewed by the staff as a shy, quiet man, Stefan lived simply, working in the lab during the day, circulating to a handful of favorite nightspots in the evening, drinking and eating with friends. Despite his advancing age, he still dreamed of more, finding the right woman, even having the children he'd always imagined. His mind filled with thoughts of science and life, he walked into the lobby and greeted the concierge as he always did, saying simply, "Hello."

There stood Ana Trujillo Fox, her long, dark hair cascading about her shoulders, most likely wearing tight jeans or one of her long, flowing skirts with a low-cut summer top, the straps thin to show off the curve of her well-toned shoulders, along with strappy stiletto heels, the kind Stefan loved so much that friends teased him about a shoe fetish. Ana could be charming at first meetings, and on that day, she undoubtedly eyed the white-haired man and smiled broadly. Their eyes met. They talked.

"Would you like to go out for lunch?" Stefan asked at some point in the conversation.

In truth, as disparate as their lives were, they had a lot in common. Both had rejected traditional religion and worshipped the sun, albeit in different ways: Ana in a pagan sense, seeing the sun as a deity of sorts; Stefan simply for its ability to give light, something he'd so missed growing up in Sweden. Both were immigrants from other countries. Even Stefan's apartment suited Ana's tastes, with its white walls and carpet and black-leather furniture echoing the decor she'd chosen for her last true home, the Houston house she'd shared with Jim Fox. The apartment must have looked familiar to her on that first day she walked through the doors.

Instead of lunch, they shared a table for dinner. Later, Ana, who at forty-three was fifteen years younger than Stefan, would say that he was an exceptional listener. He told her about his work in the lab, his training as a scientific researcher, his role as a professor who lectured medical students. In turn, she described herself as an artist and a hostess in an art gallery, perhaps for her brief stint with Christi Suarez at the downtown art happenings. Based on her interests and theories, she said that she was conducting research of her own, investigating ways the body could use natural therapies and art to heal.

At that juncture, was there any reason for Stefan to assume she was lying?

"I've met a woman," Stefan told Annika soon after that first encounter in the lobby. On the phone, Stefan explained how they met, and that Ana Trujillo had been living with another man in the same building. "She was moving off from the other man, and one of the staff at the condos told me that she was asking about me."

As they talked that day, Annika wondered about the woman, concerned about the man Ana had been living with in The Parklane. Would he come looking for her, and could Stefan end up embroiled in their drama? "Is he going to be possessive about her?" Annika asked.

"No," Stefan answered. "She doesn't have a place to stay. She's moving in with me."

"And this other man is okay with that?"

"He's fine," Stefan said, brushing it off.

"So this man she was living with is okay with her moving into your apartment?" Annika repeated, rather surprised. It all seemed odd to her, but Stefan sounded happy, and of that she was glad. He'd had a rough transition to Houston but had found an apartment he loved, friends to go out with, and now a woman he was interested in.

A short time, perhaps weeks later, when they talked again, Annika asked, "Well, how's it going with her living there?"

"Well, I'm not getting much work done at home," he said, worrying about an upcoming trial where he was scheduled to be an expert witness for one of the pharmaceutical companies. He had research to review, and having someone else in the apartment offered distractions. Still, he sounded excited at the prospect of having a beautiful woman in his life, concluding, "It is working out better than I thought."

In the days that followed, Stefan had similar discussions with other friends he kept in constant contact with, including Ran Holcomb, the accountant, whom he told about Ana and her "hot Latin blood."

Others, too, worried about Ana's former lover, and if he would be miffed at Stefan for moving into Ana's life. "I don't think you should date her," one woman friend from Dallas said. "What if this man comes after you?"

Laughing, Stefan said, "It's just fun. I'm having fun. Be happy for me."

"You shouldn't see this woman," his friend said, having the overwhelming sense that Stefan was somehow in danger. "This is not a good relationship for you."

Labor Day week, Annika went bird-watching, starting in the Hill Country, finally working her way to Galveston. It had been a glorious trip during which she photographed 121 species, including four lifers, ones she'd never before seen, the most unusual, a black-necked stilt. Her favorite, however, was a type of warbler, a yellow-breasted chat. She'd been so excited, only later when she looked at the photo did she notice a Texas ribbon snake poised directly behind the bird.

In the past when she arrived in Houston on Saturday, she would have stayed at Stefan's for a night, sleeping on the couch. But because her old friend now had a woman living with him, Annika dropped in briefly, still wearing her bird-watching clothes and covered with sweat and bug spray. Eager to get home, she might not have stopped at all, but she'd brought samples from the lab in Dallas for the joint research she still worked on with Stefan, investigating how hormones regulate the function of the cervix. Stefan had been running late with his end of the research, a situation he attributed to pressure in the University of Houston lab to work on other projects instead of his own.

At the door, Stefan greeted Annika warmly and invited her in. They talked about mutual friends, laughed, while for most of the brief visit Ana stayed cloistered in the bathroom, dressing to go out to dinner. She and Stefan had reservations at a new Southern comfort restaurant he had discovered, Lucille's, in an old, converted house. When Stefan invited Annika to join them, she declined. "I can't go like this," she said, indicating her shorts and T-shirt. "And I need to get home."

Glancing about, Stefan's apartment looked different to

Annika. In the past, his living spaces had always been fastidious, but now she saw Ana's things scattered across the living room, and her makeup cluttered the vanity. It was very un-Stefan, but Annika thought little of it other than that the new woman in his life was changing him, perhaps for the good.

When Ana joined them, she wore a tight, off-the-shoulder, short ruby-red sequined dress and stiletto heels. Her long hair fell about her shoulders, and she had dark shadow on her eyelids. The two women exchanged greetings, and Stefan suggested, "Let's open a bottle of champagne."

"Not for me, Stefan," Annika answered. "I have a long drive." So instead, Stefan walked to the kitchen to open a bottle to share with Ana.

Earlier, Stefan had told Annika about a trip he'd made to Waco with Ana, to visit her parents. During it, to ease any qualms the Tharps might have had about Ana and Stefan staying in the house together, Ana told Stefan to tell them they were getting married. He did, and while there he met Arin, Ana's younger daughter, who played softball on her high-school team. Stefan, who'd always been impressed by athletic endeavors, said the girl showed a lot of discipline. Ana's older daughter, Siana, had moved out on her own, but during the visit, Ana told Arin that she wanted her to relocate to Houston, to live with her and Stefan. Describing the scene to Annika, Stefan said the girl looked like a deer in headlights, frightened by having to uproot.

To allow the girl to explain what he suspected she wanted, Stefan asked her, "Would you rather finish up in Waco? With your friends?" Arin replied with a relieved yes.

While the two women were alone, Ana talked about that encounter and Stefan, remarking about the kindness he'd shown her daughter. "He's really supportive," she said. Annika, who knew how much Stefan loved children, wasn't surprised.

When Stefan rejoined them, he and Annika talked, Ana saying little. Annika thought perhaps Stefan had told Ana that for a brief time years earlier he and Annika had been lovers. If he had, she thought Ana must have looked at her in her sweat-streaked garb and decided she wasn't a threat, for she seemed not at all concerned. In fact, Annika thought Ana appeared bored by the conversation, perhaps because they talked of colleagues and friends Ana had never met.

When Annika left that evening, she wasn't worried about Stefan but happy for him, hoping the match would be a good one. In her brief interaction with Ana Trujillo, Annika hadn't noticed anything to worry about. Even later, in hindsight, she'd think of nothing from that meeting that should have set off warning bells.

Early the following morning in Dallas, Annika got out of bed and poured herself a glass of juice. When she turned on the computer, she had an e-mail from Stefan about their research project that he'd sent at 2 A.M. Annika knew Stefan habitually went to bed at ten or eleven and rose early to see the sunrise. Surprised, she wondered why he'd sent an e-mail in the middle of the night. She responded, and asked, "What the heck were you doing up at 2 A.M.?"

"Voodoo," Stefan responded.

Annika had never heard him use the word before and wondered what he was talking about. Then, thinking little of it, she laughed and assumed it was some kind of a joke, a moment of silliness.

That same day, Stefan stopped at the concierge desk and asked for an authorization unit admittance form, the paperwork needed to give someone access to the building and his apartment. He was given one, and he filled in the name of the person to be admitted as Ana Trujillo Fox. The authorization gave Ana the right to come and go from The Parklane and Stefan's apartment as she pleased.

Around the same time, Ana ran into Teresa Montoya. The women had seen little of each other except in passing since the night a year earlier when Ana had been removed from Montoya's hair salon and in response attacked the security guard. "I miss you," Ana said, and Montoya replied that she had missed Ana as well.

The two women went out to lunch, as they had so many times before, and ended up drinking wine. Ana told Montoya about Stefan, describing him as intelligent but saying that she was bored and not attracted to him sexually. "He's so much older than I am," she said, dismissively. "But I'm going to try to work it out."

Later, Stefan pulled up in his Mercedes to drive Ana home and waved at Montoya. She thought he looked handsome with his white hair, and as he drove away, she found herself hoping that the relationship would become her friend's salvation.

"**A**na wants to get married," Stefan told Annika after he and Ana had lived together for a month or so. If it was Ana's idea to marry, to Annika it sounded as if Stefan was considering the proposal. Although surprised, Annika had assumed that the relationship was going well. On the phone when they talked three or four times a week, Stefan's conversations were sprinkled with references such as "Ana and I are going . . ." or "Ana and I did . . ."

"Well, is there something to this?" Annika asked. "Are you thinking about it?"

"You never know," he said.

"Well, be careful. Hold your horses here," she said. "Stefan, you just met her. There's no rush. When the initial charm wears off, it may be different."

There seemed little doubt that the initial charm Annika referred to featured a heavy dose of sexual attraction, at least on Stefan's part toward Ana. Other men had found her intoxicating, and Stefan wasn't immune to her charms. In fact, Ana fulfilled all the requirements he'd told his friends he looked for in a woman, when he'd described the "hot Latina" who could salsa dance and teach him Spanish.

Near the end of September, perhaps six or seven weeks

into their affair, Ana would later say that Stefan brought her to Houston's Galleria, a sprawling shopping center complex of expensive stores just outside the West Loop. "He bought whatever I wanted," she said. "He told them to bring me their best stilettos." There, she'd later say, he gifted her with two purses and two pair of shoes, including a fifteen-hundred-dollar pair of Christian Louboutin heels, with their distinctive red soles. In the apartment, she walked around nude, wearing only the shoes. Later, she said that she convinced him to return the Louboutins, saying she worried about spending so much money. But as she described it, the shoes were part of their mutual attraction. "That was our sexual play. That was his pleasure," she said. "I wanted to please him and do whatever he wanted."

Ana in the September 27 iPhone photo

So much in Ana's mind focused on her sexuality, the pull she had on men. Years earlier, she'd been a working mother, a wife, but now all that was gone, and she'd become a woman who relied on her body for survival. She so identified herself through her sexuality that during her time with Stefan, Ana would become the star of her own scrapbook, having him frequently snap photos with his iPhone of her in provocative poses. One was taken on September 27, of Ana in Stefan's black-leather chair, wearing a bustier, a jeweled mask, and black stilettos with a row of nails on the heels, her head thrown back.

Who could fault Stefan for being attracted? Friends had noticed years earlier how Ana changed based on the person she was with, how she found a way to transform herself in a bid to seduce men who could be useful. At that juncture in Ana's life, Stefan supplied what she most needed, a place to stay. Perhaps he didn't mind. He'd helped others before, without ever looking for anything in return. Yet Ana wanted more than shelter; she'd gone through everything she had, and she needed money. On October 8 of that year, 2012, at 7:17 P.M., nearly two weeks after the cell-phone photo, Ana and Stefan signed a hand-written contract she wrote that read: "We are entering to-gether in an agreement. I, Ana, will return $7,000.00 to Stefan on 7/7/2013."

Both signed the agreement, and Stefan gave her the money.

Whatever the money was intended for, perhaps as a loan to finance the many projects she bandied about, at The Parklane, little seemed to change. Days still drifted past with Ana experimenting with her own image and Stefan acting as her chronicler, manning his iPhone as he took photos of his lover in various costumes, including one where she dressed like a Muslim woman covered head to ankle, including a scarf drawn over her face. In another, she wrapped the scarves like a sash and halter top. Without crisp resolution, Stefan's photos were moody and cool.

As intense as their relationship had been at the inception, before long, Ana's constant presence must have grated on Stefan. Or it was possible that he simply found her needs exhausting. For not long after, Annika asked about his live-in lover. "How's it going?"

"Well, she's not really . . . she doesn't leave me alone because she doesn't have a job right now."

Ana in two of Stefan's iPhone photos

When Annika asked about the jobs Ana said she had, including hosting at an art gallery, Stefan said, "She had a hard time keeping the hours."

Yet if Stefan found being with Ana distracting, he must not have minded enough to cause any second-guessing when he assessed the viability of the relationship. Late in October, Stefan called Stan Rich in Dallas, and asked, "Do you know where I can get a prenup?" When Rich asked why, Stefan said that he'd met a woman. "I'm in love with her, and I want to marry her. I just need a prenup."

Concerned, Rich told Stefan it was too early to consider marriage, only knowing Ana for a few months. "I've been alone for seventeen years. I don't want to be alone anymore," Stefan answered, when Rich advised him not to rush.

"Wait until you have everything in order. In the meantime, live together," Rich suggested. "You won't be alone." Afterward, Rich believed that he'd calmed Stefan down and that his friend wouldn't move ahead without giving marriage more thought.

With others, Stefan talked about buying a house in suburban Houston with Ana, moving outside the city, something his friends had never thought he'd consider. And he mused about the possibility of becoming a father. At forty-three, Ana claimed that she'd been pregnant the year before and lost the baby in an ectopic pregnancy, suggesting she could conceive. With the help of modern fertility treatments, something Stefan understood well, he must have envisioned that there was the very real possibility to finally have the family he'd always wanted. "I want one while I'm still young enough to enjoy the child," he told a friend.

At first, Ana blended into Stefan's life. She entertained herself while he went off to work at the university lab in the morning. The apartment's staff grew used to seeing her walk out to the golf course and the trees surrounding the high-rise. Hours later, she returned carrying sticks and leaves she described as materials for her art installations. "I'm going to have a show in a gallery," she told one woman who worked at the condo.

In the evenings, Stefan and Ana circulated between his favorite restaurants. They both enjoyed going out for cocktails, and it wasn't unusual to see them seated at the bar in Bodegas drinking tequila, wine over dinner at Lucille's or one of Stefan's other haunts. At times, they joined the tight circle of Stefan's friends.

On some of those nights, Stefan's friends left wondering what he saw in his new woman. Todd Griggs and his fiancée, Bessie Garland, first met Ana when Stefan brought her to a party in The Parklane hosted by mutual friends. That evening, Ana monopolized the conversation, talking about herself, her spiritual beliefs, and at one point wanting to read Bessie's palm. Uncomfortable, Bessie pulled her hand away. Off and on, Todd saw Ana flirt with the host, in front of the man's wife. "We'd all just met her, and it seemed strange," said Todd.

Fairly early, Stefan made an excuse to leave, but Ana wanted to stay. The others were so uncomfortable with her presence that they coaxed her out the door with Stefan.

Just as rocky was their second encounter with Stefan's new woman. On that night, Stefan brought her to meet his friends at Lucille's. As on so many other nights, they sat at the bar. Todd talked to Stefan about the stock market, as Ana zeroed in on the other men, flirting. When she came up to Stefan to say she wanted another drink, he didn't instantly respond, and she became furious and loud. "Quiet down, please," he asked, but Ana only yelled louder.

Upset, Stefan guided her outside. Through the window, his friends watched Stefan talk quietly to Ana, as she continued to scream. When she finally calmed, they walked back into the restaurant to rejoin the group.

Yet nothing major happened until a Saturday night in late October, when Stefan found water pouring onto his kitchen floor. At just after ten, he took the elevator to the concierge and reported that Ana had cut the line going to the refrigerator's icemaker. A maintenance man was dispatched, who had a difficult time shutting off the valve. When Stefan attempted to help him, Ana laughed, ordering him to let the man do it. "He can just deal with it. It's his job!"

The water finally off, the maintenance man and Stefan mopped up the kitchen floor with towels. When asked why she did it, an intoxicated Ana mumbled about hearing the refrigerator making a sound and interpreting it as "an entity" talking to her.

Days earlier, Stefan had spent $665 to buy Ana a ticket to visit her family in Mexico, flying into Guadalajara, telling friends he needed her out of the apartment so he could work. She left soon after the refrigerator incident. While she was gone, The Parklane manager, Lil Brown, invited Stefan to her office. "If you have a few moments, I'd like to visit with you," she said.

A matter-of-fact woman, Brown, who'd been at The Parklane for nearly three decades, brought up the refrigerator incident and two other matters involving Stefan's live-in guest, the first that a maintenance supervisor on the property described Ana as flirting with men working on the property, and the second a complaint filed two weeks earlier, in which a resident said Ana approached his son in the elevator. The father, who was with the toddler at the time, told the concierge that Ana had been overly friendly, frightening the child by saying things like, "Oh, you're so cute. I'm going to take you away from your daddy."

Terrified, the boy, maybe three or four, hid behind his father, crying.

At the meeting with the building manager, Stefan defended Ana. The instances with the men on the site and the child, he explained, were simply examples of her friendliness. Yet he did admit that something needed to be done. "I will talk to her," he said.

Later, when describing that meeting, Lil Brown would say that after the official part of the meeting, she took a more personal stance. With the door closed, she pantomimed taking off one hat and putting on another. "Now I'm going to take off my manager hat and put on my friend hat," she said, to a man she'd known in passing for a couple of years.

While in the beginning of the conversation she'd told Stefan she wouldn't advise him on his personal life, she now felt obligated to clearly lay out the situation, to make sure he understood. "Mr. Andersson, I'm going to talk to you as a friend," Brown said. "If I were you, I would take the incident with the refrigerator seriously or the situation could escalate into something major down the road."

When she stopped talking, Stefan sat quietly, and The Parklane manager thought he'd paused to consider what she'd said. When he spoke again, Stefan explained, "I worry about her. I don't think she has anywhere to go. What should I do?"

"If it was me, I would do everything I could possibly do to distance myself from that young lady," Brown said, her voice sober.

A few days later, Brown asked Stefan for further clarification of Ana's status at The Parklane, to which he responded that she was there temporarily, while he tried to help her. On her report, Brown wrote: "Management to monitor activity of this young lady on property."

For the two weeks Ana was in Mexico, Stefan worked and perhaps thought about what Lil Brown had told him. While Ana wasn't here to distract him, he tried to get caught up in the lab and on his research for the upcoming legal testimony.

Three months after they'd met, Stefan had received his first warning about Ana Trujillo and was apparently feeling at least somewhat suffocated by having her hover over him in the apartment. And there was something else, although not exactly troubling, that might have raised Stefan's concerns.

"Ana gets rough," he told his accountant friend, Ran Holcomb. "She gets a little rough sometimes."

Assuming Stefan referred to during sex, Holcomb thought that his friend sounded excited by being with a strong, younger woman. He never considered that his good friend could have been in danger.

Chapter 9

In November of that year, 2012, an artist she met at Christi Suarez's art happenings saw Ana at an event in downtown Houston. At first, he didn't recognize her. She looked different, rougher than he'd remembered. As they talked, he thought she seemed odd, sounding at the same time anxious and almost in a dreamlike state. "She was really intense and strange," he said. "She kept talking about media reports on the end of the Mayan calendar that December 21, and how some said it could be the end of the world. Rather than ending, Ana thought that the world would have a new beginning. If that happened, she said she wanted to go into the Mexican wilderness to live simply, like her ancestors."

In her purse that day, Ana had a notebook, one she told him held ideas for her future. When she opened it to show him, he saw scribbles, concentric circles and spirals with a smattering of words. "It's a blueprint for all things," Ana said, as if voicing some profound truth. She then brought up Native American shamans and seeing the spirit world.

"I thought she was searching for something," the artist said. "And I sensed there were a lot of things changing inside her."

"How's Ana?" Annika asked Stefan that month.

"She gets disruptive when she drinks," Stefan told her. From there, Stefan recounted Ana's behavior in the weeks since she'd returned from Mexico. In addition to the problems at The Parklane, some of Stefan's friends complained about Ana. At dinner one night, Ana looked at one of Stefan's friends, and told him, "You could do a lot better than her." The "her" she referred to was the man's wife, who at that moment was seated beside him. Afterward, the woman wanted nothing to do with Ana.

"It's not going well," Stefan admitted.

As the year drew to a close, the tension between Ana and Stefan mounted, perhaps not in evidence anywhere as much as at the Hermann Park Grill, where Stefan had been a regular for more than a year before he brought Ana with him. In the casual restaurant on the edge of the golf course, they sat together, the Golf Channel on the overhead screens, Ana playing on her laptop, while Stefan reviewed reports or read articles, or talked to the golfers coming in after their rounds, asking about their games. When they inquired if he played, Stefan said he didn't, but he was curious about the game. Initially, Ana and Stefan seemed happy together. He ordered his veggie omelets with mushrooms in the morning, and they both enjoyed the catfish buffet on Fridays. About noon on the days he didn't go to the lab, he ordered his first five-dollar glass of merlot, while Ana drank chardonnay.

On temperate days, they preferred the outside, where Stefan sat in a chair with Ana nearby on the grass, her legs crossed and tucked yoga style, her arms extended, soaking up the sun. One day, she bought a bucket of balls on the driving range and entertained herself by swinging at them with a borrowed club, missing much of the time. When the golf pro explained that to go out on the range she had to pay, Ana did. He later found her sitting beside a pond on the course, chanting.

At first Erika Elizondo, who worked in the grill, thought that the woman in Dr. Andersson's life could be good for him. Elizondo had always worried that her regular customer seemed a bit lonely. But then things started to happen. The first was late that fall when Stefan and Ana occupied an

The Hermann Park Golf Course with The Parklane in the background

inside table. That day, Ana flirted with younger men in the grill, golfers, and Stefan appeared embarrassed. When he whispered something to her, Ana became angry, and Stefan looked even more distressed but said nothing.

One afternoon during a lull in their work, Elizondo and a coworker watched golfers hitting balls outside the grill, wondering if one of them could smack it into the window and break it. Just then she heard Ana shout: "You are not going to fuck me the way he's going to fuck me!"

As on so many other days, Ana and Stefan were at a table together. Her hands on the edge as she shouted at him, Ana jerked backward, stood up, and stalked toward the door, where a younger man waited for her. They left together. After Ana's dramatic departure, Stefan sat quietly at the table, head bowed. He waited awhile, then left.

Another day at the grill, when the golfers circulated in and out picking up lunch, Ana shouted, "I'm not going to do that! I'm going to do what I want!" Elizondo didn't know what she was referring to other than just moments earlier Stefan had been talking quietly to her.

Perhaps the incident that caused the biggest stir in the grill happened on a day Elizondo wasn't there to witness it, an afternoon when Ana and Stefan talked together at a table. For some reason, Ana became upset and began arguing with him although no one but Stefan could hear what she said. Abruptly she walked to a table where three African-American men, regulars in the grill, played cards. In a swoop, Ana bent over the table and swooshed her hands over the top, scattering their cards onto the floor. One of the men jumped up, and shouted, "What is your problem?"

"Just leave me alone," she said, seething. "You're all just niggers."

"You need to get that woman out of here," one of the men, understandably upset, told the clerk in the pro shop. "She's a woman, and I won't put my hands on her, but if she were a man . . ."

The next day, when Elizondo came in and heard about the incident, the man who described it to her said, "What a shame. Ana is a beautiful woman, but she's going to be the death of Dr. Andersson."

The evidence mounting that the new woman in his life wasn't as he'd pictured her, instances of her bad behavior becoming too numerous to ignore, in mid-November Stefan apparently asked Ana to leave his apartment, for at that time he signed an order rescinding his permission to allow her to enter. Yet that didn't mean that they stopped seeing each other. In fact, that Thanksgiving Stefan and Ana drove to Waco to spend the holiday with her family.

Whatever happened on the trip, Ana must have been convincing, perhaps promising to change, to not act out in public. Once back in Houston, Stefan gave the relationship another chance. For when they returned home, he told a friend that she had moved back into The Parklane with him.

This time, however, he wasn't as patient. "I need her to move out," he said just days later.

In December, Stefan traveled to the East Coast to consult with lawyers involved in the trial for which he'd prepared. Despite his declarations to friends that he'd asked her to find somewhere else to live, Ana remained in his apartment. When he departed for the airport that morning, she promised to leave in a few hours and lock the door behind her. Apparently accepting that she'd do as she promised, perhaps because she didn't have a key, Stefan agreed.

Later he must have thought better of the situation, for Stefan called a friend in the building and asked him to make sure Ana had left and locked the door. When the friend reached 18B, he found the door closed but the latch taped, so that it wouldn't lock. When he nudged the door open, the apartment smelled of pot.

Just weeks later, it was proving more difficult than might have been expected for Stefan to get Ana Trujillo out of his life. Although he'd banned her from his apartment when he returned from his trip, just before the New Year, on December 29 at seven thirty in the morning, Ana walked into The Parklane yet again, this time not with Stefan but with another man who had an apartment in the building.

It would seem later that the man served a purpose, to get her inside the building so that she could get to Stefan. At one o'clock that same day, the man stopped at the front desk, confused, asking if he'd arrived with someone when he'd returned that morning. Apparently he'd been drinking, brought Ana home with him, then fallen asleep, and when he woke up, Ana was gone. "Yes, Ms. Fox," the concierge confirmed.

"Where is she?" the man asked, perplexed.

The concierge said that she didn't know. "She came in with you."

The man walked off, and the following morning he wasn't the one who logged out when leaving the apartments with Ana. It was Stefan Andersson.

That year, 2012, drew to a close, and despite the fears surrounding the end of the Mayan calendar, the world didn't end, didn't change, but continued on. Something else, however, was ending—Stefan's grant money. It dwindled down in the fall until in January he had only enough remaining for a few months. As he had in the past, Stefan wrote letters and applied for grants, but he was distracted, still complaining that at UH he wasn't given time to do his own work, instead helping with other research.

Unlike late 2009, when he'd left Dallas, however, this time Stefan didn't panic. In January, he traveled back to the East Coast to give a deposition, which went well. Not long after another law firm, one representing a Canadian pharmaceutical company, contacted him offering similar work. At $450 an hour, the potential earnings from serving as an expert witness offered an exciting opportunity. After more than twenty-five years chasing research grants, Stefan appeared excited about the change. Although he'd reached another fork in his career's path, this time he saw the future opening up clearly in front of him.

The only troubling development was that Ana Trujillo refused to vacate Stefan Andersson's life. Yet there seemed little doubt that he wanted her out.

On December 30, not long after Ana was seen with him walking from the building, Stefan again dropped a note off at the concierge desk, explaining that he wanted Ana barred from entering his apartment. An incident report was typed up, and the staff was notified.

Somehow, however, she must have convinced him to let her back in. For five days later, on January 4, Ana took a cell-phone photo of her feet wearing blue-suede stilettos, shoes that would soon become infamous across the world, propped up on Stefan's glass coffee table, a television playing in the background, with two crystal champagne glasses and a shot glass containing a small amount of an amber-colored liquid beside her.

The January 4, 2013 iPhone photo

As 2013 began, Stefan, perhaps spurred on by the changes in his employment, considered his future. When he thought about where he wanted to live, he contemplated moving to France, and he reapplied for his Swedish citizenship, hoping to have dual standing with the U.S. "I think I'll walk around with a baguette under my arm," he told a friend. "I can drink wine in the cafes and meet beautiful women."

As Stefan pictured a departure to live in a small village in France, Ana saw no such parting in their future. "He's in love with me, and he wants to marry me," she told Teresa Montoya, who was happy for her friend. "I'm not attracted to him. I hate it when he touches me. But I'm trying to make it work."

On January 12, it appeared that she'd convinced him either that they still belonged together and that she deserved another chance or that she needed help and had nowhere else to go, for on that day Stefan signed another consent form allowing her into The Parklane and his apartment. Again, the arrangement would prove a brief one.

Weeks later, Stefan walked downstairs to the complex's garage and found his beloved Mercedes dented on all four sides, the paint scratched, the bumper crooked. Ana had taken the car for a joyride one night while he slept and gotten into an accident, deploying the air bags and scraping and bashing the car. When he confronted her, however, she later laughed repeating to a friend what she had told him. "I didn't drive it. That was you!" she said. "You were drinking, Stefan. Don't you remember having the accident?"

Perhaps she shouldn't have laughed and been so bold with her answer, for Stefan didn't believe her. The car repairs cost $6,000, without doing all of the cosmetic work. From that night on, he hid his car key and wallet, afraid to leave them out where she might find them.

"You really need to get rid of her," Bessie told Stefan one night at a restaurant. The nurse was there with her fiancé, Todd, who'd been telling Stefan the same thing about Ana for months. "No one likes being around her," said Bessie, who found the way Ana told Stefan what to do offensive, ordering him around like a child. "We're worried for you."

When Annika called Stefan, he sounded nervous. "Ana's here, and she'll get angry," he told her. "She doesn't like it when I talk on the phone."

"I thought you were through with her," Annika said, losing patience with him. Although she understood that Stefan had a difficult time saying no to anyone, especially a friend, this Ana continually wormed her way back into his life. "Why are you with her?"

"I am trying to get rid of her, but she keeps showing up," he said. "I go out, and she's there. She knows where I go. If I talk to someone on the phone, she makes a scene."

In early 2013, Ana moved in and out of Stefan's life like a dark cloud that hovered over him, often spending nights in his apartment. On January 20, he took yet another photo of her, this time on his balcony, her top falling down to expose the tops of her breasts, her hair tousled, as she wore black leggings and a black tank top, necklaces with turquoise pendants, and her Ankh ring clearly visible.

The January 20 iPhone photo

"Well, you know, Stefan and I had a fight," Ana said the afternoon of the same day the photo on the balcony was taken when she turned up at James Wells's apartment. Christi Suarez had dropped Ana off, telling Wells that she had nowhere to go. Wells agreed to take her in, at the time thinking that Ana reminded him of a little sister who constantly needed help.

Although it had been nearly a year since she'd moved out, Ana and Wells had seen each other in passing at the clubs. In the meantime, one of Wells's old friends, Chanda Ellison, who'd relocated to Houston from Ohio, and her nine-year-old daughter had moved in the previous September. Wells was giving Ellison and the girl a place to live, and as when Ana lived there, there were mutually agreed to friends-with-benefits privileges.

That day, Wells, who by then drove a tow truck, explained the situation to Ana and introduced Ellison, who at four-foot-eleven was a short, round, strongly built woman with dark cropped hair; neither Ellison nor Wells asked what brought on the fight with Stefan. Ana appeared to dismiss the situation as merely a temporary setback, saying he loved and wanted to marry her.

From the beginning, Chanda Ellison wasn't particularly fond of Ana Trujillo. "She was very sexual," said Chanda. "James is pretty laid-back, the kind of guy who sees good in everyone, and pretty nonjudgmental. But I thought, nah, there's something wrong here."

When Ellison asked Ana why she wasn't working, the response confused her: "Money isn't important to me." Yet the new woman in the apartment bragged about her boyfriend, Stefan, who she said gave her anything she requested. When Ellison asked why she'd left such a generous man, Ana said, "I get so mad at him, and we fight."

"I think maybe he's violent with her," James said to Chanda, who worked out of the house screening self-pay patients for hospitals. "Maybe that's why she stayed with him."

"I don't believe it," Chanda said. "I think there's more to this than that."

Chanda Ellison

"If I marry Stefan, he'll buy me whatever I want, and I'll never have to work again," Ana boasted. "But he's old, and sometimes he drinks. He promises me things, then he doesn't remember . . . It's annoying."

At Wells's apartment, Ana slept in mornings until nine or ten, then left for the day. Off and on, Wells saw her on the street, wandering. One of her favorite places was an art installation not far from the medical center, tucked into a pocket of land adjacent to a parking lot, across the street from a pawnshop. A semicircular structure covered in a Mayan-inspired pattern of ceramic tiles, in the middle was a planter, where Ana sat, arms raised, worshipping the sun.

On another day, Wells saw Ana out on the street, standing on a feeder road near one of the expressways, making triangles with her hands as she stared up at the sun. "Ana!" he yelled, but she didn't answer, instead turning and running toward downtown Houston. Wells attempted to intercept her in his tow truck, but when she didn't stop, he drove home instead.

In the apartment, Ana accumulated boxes of what she referred to as her work, binders and folders of papers she'd drawn shapes on, many circles, and jotted down phrases or single words. Although the Mayan-calendar scare ended the previous December, she still talked as if the world would soon end. In the evenings, she took out her tarot cards to tell her future, one day showing Wells a card with a man holding two swords pointing down.

"That means death will be upon us," she said. "That's what I was trying to tell you."

Despite Ana's assessment of their relationship, Stefan Andersson must have seen the situation very differently. For the day after he told Ana to leave, he again signed papers barring her from The Parklane, and this time he went so far as to have the locks changed on his apartment.

That didn't prevent her from trying to get inside. "Ana, Mr. Andersson's former guest, showed up, and she is not allowed to his unit per his request," read a report filed the following day. According to The Parklane records, just after noon, Ana had walked in, and the concierge told her she had to leave.

"Stan, I think Ana has a drug problem," Stefan told his friend one afternoon.

"If that's true, you need to get away from her. Just let her go," he said. "Stop all contact with her, Stefan."

Stefan sighed. "I'm trying," he said.

Stan Rich then listened as Stefan described how hard it was for him to avoid Ana. She knew his favorite places, where he met his friends in the evening for dinner. On mornings when he went to the Hermann Park Grill, Ana showed up, spent the day eating and drinking wine, then left him to pay the check. Rich understood how Stefan hated change and relied on familiarity, going to the same places night after night, needing the relationships he'd built with friends to fight his bouts with depression.

"Get a restraining order," Stan advised. "Get rid of her. Don't answer her phone calls or her texts."

"I know you're right," Stefan said, sounding heartbroken. "The problem is that I get so lonely. I have a couple of drinks, and she shows up, and I end up with her staying the night. I can't seem to help myself."

Perhaps that was what happened, for before long Ana was again circulating in and out of Stefan's apartment. By then, Stefan's friends had tired of listening to his excuses about why he simply couldn't turn his back on Ana and allow her to fend for herself. Some stopped asking about Ana, and others, when Stefan brought up his troubles with Ana, said they didn't want to hear.

Yet Stefan kept trying. On February 20, he again signed papers barring Ana and had the locks changed for a second time. For weeks, he had avoided places he thought she might go. Then on the twentieth, he had lunch with his fellow scientist and friend Anders Berkenstam, this time at one of Stefan's regular places, Bodegas. The two men sat together at a table eating tacos when Ana walked into the restaurant. In the lively lunch crowd, it was unlikely that anyone else noticed her as she approached Stefan, smiling.

When she reached him, Ana Trujillo bent down, as if to kiss him. "Owww!" he yelled. When Stefan pushed Ana away, she had blood on her lips, and blood trickled out of a bite on his cheek.

Frightened, Stefan crouched and covered his face, as if to

prevent her from doing it again. Calmly, Ana walked out of the restaurant.

Anders ran for help, and the restaurant manager brought liquor to disinfect the wound. The embarrassment, pain, and fear must have been welling up inside Stefan. The two men left Bodegas and went to another restaurant, one where Ana wouldn't know to look, and once there, an embarrassed and frightened Stefan cried. "I'm a grown man," he said, confiding how he'd tried to push her out of his life. "Why can't I just say no and tell her to leave me alone?"

Although he'd already signed paperwork to ban Ana from The Parklane, three days later, on the twenty-third, Stefan feared that there might still be some way for her to get inside. Frightened, he went to the concierge and asked her to check two things, first the number of passkeys issued in his name, in case Ana had managed to have one made without his consent. His second request was that they check with the man Ana lived with prior to moving in with him, to find out if he ever gave her a passkey to the building. The management said they would, and later reported that they had no record of Ana's having any passkeys.

Somehow, that didn't appear to truly protect him.

"What happened to you?" Erika Elizondo asked one day, as she served Stefan his breakfast at the Hermann Park Grill. His eye was blackened and the bruise was an angry one, difficult to miss.

"Oh, nothing," he said with a nervous laugh.

When Stefan was at the golf club, Ana still routinely walked in, smiling, greeting him, claiming a chair at his table or one nearby, leaving him with the bill. When Annika called, he whispered, "Ana's here. I have to hang up."

"Just tell her to leave you alone," Annika said, like so many others frustrated with Stefan's inability to ban the woman from his life. She didn't know about the bite, or the black eye, and she understood how Stefan had always struggled with telling anyone no, but even to her it seemed that he'd let the situation continue far too long. "Stand up to her!"

Embarrassed, Stefan didn't answer but hung up the phone, afraid of a scene.

After the incident in Bodegas, Stefan started quietly confiding in those who would listen about Ana and what happened when they were alone. Some heard stories about how she came up behind him, grabbing him by the neck, pulling him down. "I thought she'd strangle me," he told one friend in a restaurant. Then he looked around, and said, "I need to stop talking about her. I'm afraid she'll come in and hear me."

In restaurants, when Stefan showed up with Ana beside him, Bessie Garland mouthed, "No!" and shook her head at him. Stefan laughed nervously, but as soon as she edged him away from Ana, Garland whispered, "You have to get away from her." Stefan looked sheepish and didn't answer.

When he arrived alone, Stefan sat off to the side and asked Garland and her fiancé, Todd Griggs, to look out for Ana and warn him if she walked in the door. "She follows me," he said. "I can't get away from her. If you see her, please tell me, and I will hide. Don't tell her that I'm here."

Later, Griggs wouldn't remember exactly when it happened, but one night in a restaurant, Stefan turned to him, fear clouding his eyes, and said, "Ana held a knife to my throat."

"Stefan, you have to stay away from her," Griggs said, not knowing what to do to help his friend. In the years he'd known Stefan, he'd always appeared happy, always had a smile, but now he looked tired and troubled. "Break it off, now."

"I know you're right, but it's hard. She follows me. It's hard to get away," he said. Appearing ashamed, he said, "You cannot tell anyone."

"But you need to get away from this woman," Griggs warned. "Please, you need to end this."

"I know you're right," Stefan said. "But it's not so easy."

"I can't go out, she's there, wherever I go, she shows up," Stefan told Annika one evening, more worried than she'd ever heard him. His job at UH was ending, and while he had the expert-witness job, for the first time he worried about money. When Ana found him, she shadowed him through the evening, drinking, leaving him with the checks. His alternative was to stay home, but that left him alone, without the companionship he so craved.

"She's taking advantage of you. Don't pay," Annika said.

"I can't do that," Stefan said, an answer Annika expected from Stefan, who always felt compelled to do things for others.

In April, Ran Holcomb returned to Houston for cancer treatments. "I'm going to tell Ana you're here for a couple of weeks, so she leaves me alone," Stefan told him. Still his phone rang six to seven times a day, calls from Ana. At first, Stefan wouldn't pick up, but before long he'd give in and answer.

"I'm going to get rid of her, Ran," he told his friend, his voice strained yet determined. "I am going to get Ana out of my life!"

Chapter 10

In early 2013, Stefan dined in one of his favorite restaurants and struck up a friendly conversation with a teenage girl at the next table. Moments later, her mother, Janette Jordan, walked in. A striking woman with shoulder-length dark hair, Jordan had emigrated to the U.S. from the United Kingdom, and still had her British accent. She worked in sales and marketing for a large restaurant corporation, and had three children, the teenager at the table, who was a student at the University of Houston, and two others in their twenties. That day, Jordan and Stefan talked, and found they had much in common, from an interest in history to their European roots. Jordan understood Stefan's penchant for spending evenings out, reminding her of Britain, where a nightly stop at a pub was customary for many.

From that point on, they began seeing each other on occasion, meeting for dinner and drinks, or a Sunday brunch. When Stefan told her he was fifty-eight, Jordan, who was more than a decade younger, was surprised. From his appearance, the white hair, his slightly hunched shoulders, his somewhat frail look, she'd assumed he was older. Yet when they talked about books or life, when he discussed his work and science, his expression brightened, and she found him charming. They took walks in the parks, and he brought her to a gathering at Houston's Museum of Fine Arts. She watched him with waiters and doormen, always kind. "He was just that guy," she said. "A true gentleman. Good to everyone. Stefan dressed well, and had beautiful blue eyes. And he had a real zest for life."

At times, Stefan tried to talk to Jordan about his ex-girlfriend, Ana, but Jordan cut him off, not wanting to hear it. It seemed ill-mannered to complain to the new woman in his life about his former lover, like a man complaining about an ex-wife. When Jordan objected, Stefan dropped it. What he did tell her was that the woman was capable of showing up at any moment. "She makes things difficult," he said. "She's kind of crazy."

"They're all crazy," Jordan said, making a joke of it.

"No," Stefan said, serious. "This one truly is."

Stefan continued to see Jordan, and talked to friends about how much he enjoyed being with a woman who wasn't "high-maintenance." He seemed buoyed by the relationship, for the first time in months enthusiastic. Although they didn't talk about their exes, Stefan confided in her, discussing his views on life, as in March during a Sunday brunch, when he told Jordan about a funeral he'd attended for a Houston friend.

"They can take you at any time," he said. "Who knows how much time we all have?"

"I'm taking Janette to places Ana doesn't know," Stefan told Annika when he explained that he'd met a new woman. "I don't want a scene. And I can never be sure what Ana might do, where she'll show up."

That day, as he had for months, Stefan stressed that he wanted Ana gone from his life. What he didn't tell Annika was that despite everything Ana had done to him, he continued to routinely backtrack, exposing himself to danger. Rather than report the violence to police, Stefan told only a few close friends that he was being abused.

In significant-other violence, this unfortunately isn't an unusual cycle. According to U.S. government statistics, less than half of all incidents of domestic violence are reported to police. The most common reasons: fear of retaliation and humiliation. Perhaps it was doubly hard for Stefan, a man, to admit he was being abused by a woman, partly because domestic violence is rightfully most often viewed as a crime against women committed by men. In the U.S., 85 percent of the victims are women but they are only 2 percent of the abusers.

Increasingly isolated, Stefan must have felt weak and incapable. Those who knew him best, like Annika, understood. Describing his own upbringing as abusive, Stefan had vowed never to be like his father and avoided conflict. And Stefan had a big heart, the kind that made it hard to turn his back on anyone, especially a person he'd once loved.

In early March, Stefan again walked into The Parklane with Ana. The concierge clocked them in at 11:13 A.M. When Annika visited weeks later, on her way home from her spring bird-watching trip, Ana's possessions in bags were stacked in Stefan's apartment, which had otherwise returned to its pristine pre-Ana condition, everything in its place. "Ana won't pick them up," he complained. "She said she doesn't want them in bags."

Years earlier, others had noted that Ana had a habit of leaving items in friends' homes, places where she wanted to return. For months, she'd used the same tactic on Stefan. "Put it in paper boxes and leave them downstairs with the concierge," Annika advised him. "She can pick it up there, and it's not your problem anymore."

Stefan nodded that he would, but Annika doubted that he would follow through.

For the most part, Stefan seemed well, his life back to normal. They talked about Janette Jordan, Stefan assessing her as focused and accomplished, and "normal," things he by then understood that Ana Trujillo was not. Everything went well throughout Annika's visit despite the shadow of his relationship with Ana, until a text message beeped on his phone.

"It's her," he said.

"**A**na and I had a fight. She doesn't live here anymore," Stefan told Ana's friend Christi Suarez, when they talked a few weeks later. Suarez was trying to find Ana, who had promised to host an upcoming public-access TV show at a crawfish festival in Victoria, Texas, two hours south of Houston. When Ana complained that she had nothing to wear for the gig, Stefan had bought her cowboy boots and a hat.

"She tried to choke me. I had to pry her hands off my neck. And then she slapped me," he said, sounding afraid. "I'm too old for this, and I threw her out. I'm done with her."

As they talked, Stefan told Suarez that he cared about Ana and worried about her, but that he couldn't have her in his apartment. Instead, he tried to see her only in public places, to avoid any more violent incidents. "I've put her things in boxes, and they're at the concierge desk," he said. "Please, come pick up for her. I can't have her here. I'm afraid of what she might do to me. When she drinks, she gets crazy."

Having been slapped twice by Ana herself, that was something Suarez had no problem believing.

Days later, Stefan admitted something similar to his CPA friend, Ran Holcomb, who was in Houston for another round of cancer treatments. "Ana hits me," Stefan said, rather sheepishly.

"Make her go!" his friend responded.

"I am trying," Stefan said, with a shrug. "She just won't leave me alone. She follows me."

Days later, Ran called Stefan and found him at the golf course grill with Ana. "You have to be kidding me," Ran said. "What value does she bring you?"

"None," Stefan acknowledged. "I don't invite her, she just comes. She won't leave me alone. I have to get rid of her."

"**I** hate it when he touches me," Ana told Suarez when they talked on the phone later that week. "He's an old man."

Suarez had only met Stefan once but liked him. She'd

hoped that the relationship would work out and give Ana stability. Over the years they'd known each other, Suarez had witnessed Ana's life crater around her, watched her make one bad choice after another. Ana had even begun looking different, her complexion rough and her hair straggly, perhaps from all the alcohol or the herbal pot she still regularly smoked. Or maybe it was something else, the witchcraft and the communing with spirits Suarez knew Ana was involved in. After she'd met Stefan, Suarez advised Ana to stick with him, to let him help her. Now she knew that Ana was physically abusing Stefan and that he was afraid of her.

"Stefan gave me a bunch of money to marry him," Ana said, perhaps referring to the seven-thousand-dollar loan he'd made to her the previous fall that was coming due in two months. Ana laughed, and said, "I spent it all. It's gone."

Once she tracked down Ana, Suarez made arrangements to drive her to the crawfish-festival show. The night before the trip to Victoria for the taping, Suarez tossed and turned, nervous about seeing Ana again. In Suarez's dreams, Ana appeared as she'd been painted at the first event, as a snake.

The following day, Suarez's friend Raul Rodriguez, the host of the show Ana was appearing on, and Suarez drove to James Wells's apartment to pick up Ana, who dawdled getting dressed. Then they drove to The Parklane, picked up Ana's things from the concierge, boxes and suitcases, and put them in the back of the SUV, along with the video equipment. On the way to the festival, Rodriguez thought Ana looked out of it. He'd spent nights at restaurants with her when she was drinking, but was surprised that she was so foggy when sober.

Quietly, he said to Suarez, "You shouldn't have brought her. What if she does something crazy?"

It would turn out that he didn't have to wait long.

In Victoria, as he unloaded equipment, Rodriguez heard Ana ask for her things. With equipment to move out of the way first, he ignored her for just a minute. "I want my suitcases!" Ana shouted.

When Rodriguez turned, Ana had her hand raised and appeared ready to charge at him. "She had the most horrible look on her face," he said. "Her eyes were just dead."

"You'd better not do whatever you're thinking about doing," he warned, glaring back at her. "I'm *not* going to let you beat me up."

Instantly, Ana backed off, but Rodriguez couldn't forget what had happened, how she'd suddenly snapped. "I wondered why she was so filled with rage," he said.

Despite her strange behavior, once cameras rolled, Ana performed well, lively and animated. After the festival, Rodriguez drove the two women back to Houston, dropping Ana and her possessions at James Wells's place.

"Things were getting really strange at the apartment," Chanda Ellison later explained. "I thought Ana was jealous, that she wanted me gone. But I wasn't going anywhere. James didn't want me to leave, and I didn't want to go. But James didn't want to kick Ana out, either. With Ana, James didn't want to see it. He liked Ana."

From early in the year, shortly after Ana moved into the modest brick apartment complex eight blocks from The Parklane, there were incidents. One was the afternoon Ana told James that her laptop was broken, and Chanda was responsible. It wasn't true. On another occasion, Ana returned to the apartment and, for no apparent reason, walked over to Chanda and grabbed her prescription sunglasses off her face. "Give those back," she said.

Smiling, Ana twisted and broke the frames, while staring contemptuously at Chanda. "Are you talking to me?" Ana demanded, drawing out the question like an accusation. When Wells broke up the ensuing argument, Chanda retaliated, taking a box of Ana's things and abandoning it outside on the curb. Vagrants wandering the area quickly moved in and rifled through the box, claiming what they wanted. While Ana was upset, it eventually blew over.

To Chanda, it appeared that Ana Trujillo thought every

man was in love with her, coveting her body. One day, Ana called a psychologist she'd met, talking on the phone with the man. When she hung up, she said, "He has the hots for me, too."

Some of the male adulation, Chanda had to admit, might have been more than Ana's imagination, however, as with the therapist, who sent sexually explicit texts to Ana that she showed to Chanda and Wells.

Even odder were the rituals Ana's two roommates witnessed, not knowing what they were seeing. One night, Wells walked in on Ana surrounded by burning candles, chanting, in the living room in the middle of the night. "What are you doing?" he asked.

"I couldn't sleep," she answered.

When alone in the apartment, Ana left the door open, saying she had to because the apartment was possessed. When Wells asked her to explain, she said that one night when she was alone, she heard a pop and saw a figure she described as reptilian. At first she said the figure in the vision was Wells, then a neighbor; finally, she said, "It was Stefan."

Out at night in the clubs, Chanda saw Ana, who carried a small scissors, snip off pieces of hair from people she was angry with when they weren't looking. Later she burned the strands and chanted. And Chanda, like others, noticed something odd about Ana's eyes, that they turned yellow when she was angry.

When she heard Ana talking, Chanda often thought that their new roommate had a sense of entitlement. "She saw herself as beyond reproach," said Chanda. "No one could tell her anything to do. No one."

"My parents have closed minds," Ana complained to James Wells. "They don't want to understand that I have powers."

So many questions circulated around Ana. At times, Chanda and Wells both wondered why Ana spent the days with Stefan but never the nights. "I just thought it was odd," he said. "I mean, Ana said he loved her."

Although Ana lived with them for months, Chanda and Wells only met Stefan on a few occasions. Twice, Chanda went out with Ana and Stefan, including on May 11, for his fifty-ninth birthday, to a trendy club called Bar 5015, one of Ana's favorites, a low-slung building with a long bar and white tufted vinyl barstools.

That night, Chanda was surprised that he'd chosen that bar, thinking it wasn't a place "for an old white man" to be. The crowd was more young urban with an edge. But Stefan was in a good mood, ordering a bottle of champagne and buying drinks. Chanda watched as Ana flitted from one man to the other at the bar, flirting, but Stefan didn't seem disturbed. At one point, he said to Chanda, "I care about Ana. I love her. But she's a handful, and I can't deal with her."

Frequently, Ana worked her way back to the table to ask if Stefan wanted anything, and to have him order her another glass of wine or a shot of tequila. Then, as Stefan and Chanda talked and listened to music, Ana wandered off to chat with another man.

Late that night, James Wells drove up in his tow truck to pick up the women, and Stefan stood outside with them. Ana fumed, complaining that the security guard at The Parklane had refused to let her into Stefan's apartment the night before.

"I told him, when you see me, you better let me in!" Ana said. "The man said if someone said not to let me in, he couldn't!"

"He's just following orders," Wells told her.

As the others talked, Stefan said nothing. Instead, he put his hands in his pockets, turned, and walked away.

That night, during the birthday celebration, Chanda told Stefan not to worry about Ana, that she and Wells would watch over her. But just weeks later, with Ana's odd behavior escalating, with the pacing, the chanting, and the strange rituals, Chanda knew she couldn't keep her promise. One of them had to leave. If Ana stayed, Chanda would have to move on.

"What is that?" Chanda asked Ana the night they sat in the apartment watching television, and Ana poured salt to draw a star inside a circle on the floor. What Chanda didn't know was that in some pagan rituals, salt was used to symbolize the sea, the womb of the goddess, and blood. As Chanda and Wells observed the strange ritual, Ana placed candles on the star's corners and lit them. She then sat rigid, legs crossed, next to the pentagram and chanted. When Wells asked what she was doing, Ana claimed that it was a ceremony to remove evil spirits from the house. Ana's roommates didn't know that in some occult practices such rituals were done at times for protection and at other times to conjure spirits.

The bizarre episodes continued, and Chanda Ellison felt anxious. It seemed to her that something was building with Ana Trujillo Fox. At night, Chanda heard the other woman prowling the apartment, rarely sleeping. "Her behavior took a toll on me," said Chanda. "James always gave Ana the benefit of the doubt, but I didn't like what I was seeing."

On May 25, 2013, a Saturday five months after Ana moved in, Chanda had an intense feeling that something bad was going to happen. In that circumstance, she did what she usually did: She attempted to walk off her worries. Leaving the apartment, Chanda strode on the sidewalk at a brisk pace. As she hiked, she noticed a three-foot-long branch, the thickness of a broomstick. She picked it up and used it as a walking stick as she continued on. In the apartment, she placed it to the side, propping it up against a wall.

That night was even edgier than usual, as Chanda lay in bed listening to Ana through the apartment walls. The smell of candles wafted in from the living room, and Chanda heard chanting. By the following morning, Chanda battled a crushing apprehension. To be alone, she stood in the closet, and she prayed. "Lord, if there's anything evil in her, please, remove her because I don't know what you want me to do. Show me what to do, Lord. Help me."

That same afternoon, May 26, Stefan sat at a table in the Hermann Golf Course Grill when Ana arrived. At about three, she called James Wells and he drove to pick her up. When he arrived, Stefan was gone, and Ana asked Wells to buy her a glass of chardonnay. He did, then waited for her to drink it. Once she finished the glass, Ana began muttering.

"Are you drunk?" he asked. Wells interpreted the look Ana shot him in reply as, *why are you asking me that?*

On the drive home in the truck, Wells, who didn't see himself as romantically involved with any of the women, mentioned that an old girlfriend was stopping by. At that, Ana's mood shifted drastically, and she became angry, asking why the woman was coming. "She's just a friend," Wells said. Jealous, Ana kicked the stand Wells anchored his computer to inside the truck.

"You're being silly," he said.

In the apartment, Chanda lay on the bed watching television, and Wells joined her, sitting in a nearby recliner. He looked up and saw Ana glaring at him from the doorway "looking at me all evil but not saying anything."

Instead, she walked toward him, puckering her lips, and Wells thought that they would kiss and make up. He leaned toward her. She bent down, her lips meeting the top of his bald head. At that instant, searing pain shot through him, and he realized that she'd bitten him. He pushed her back, opened his hand, and slapped her in the face.

After falling toward the door and hitting the back of her head on the doorjamb, Ana mocked, "Ho, ho, ho! You're a dead man!"

The hair on the back of his head prickled at the hard tone of her voice. "Ana, you're a devil," he said, reining in his anger, and standing up. "You have to leave this house right now. I am mad enough to kill you. Before I do, you have to go."

To remove himself from her, Wells walked from the room, but instead of backing off, Ana followed him into the kitchen and came up behind him, slapping him in the face.

As he'd warned he would, Wells slapped her back. To stop the fight, for the second time, he attempted to walk away, and again Ana followed. This time, Chanda wedged between them.

"Let me handle this," she told Wells. "I don't want you in trouble."

At that moment, a text came in for a tow job, and Wells nodded at Chanda, then turned and left.

Inside the apartment, the two women were alone, and Chanda watched Ana carefully, judging by the look on her face that she still seethed. In a fight between a man and a woman, Chanda suspected police would automatically believe the woman, making it a dangerous situation for Wells. To be sure Ana understood, she said, "I don't want James to go to jail. Got it?"

"Oh, you're talking to me?" Ana replied. With that, she charged Chanda, grabbing her. The women struggled and fell over the couch. When Chanda saw the stick from her walk the day before leaning against a wall, she grabbed it and attacked, hitting Ana hard across her body, swinging it at her head and face.

"Stop!" Ana finally yelled. "Stop!"

Chanda did.

"Ana, you need to go over there and sit down," Chanda told her. "This is ridiculous. We don't need to fight like this."

"Nobody is going to tell me what to do!" Ana shouted. The women argued, Ana charging, "You're just mad because James loves me."

As before, Ana pounced on Chanda, who again struck back, pounding Ana with the stick. They fought until Wells walked back through the door and physically pulled them apart. Both women were bruised, but Ana had taken the hardest hits. Yet when he looked at her, Wells saw that she had a smug look on her face, like she'd won. "I thought she was psychotic or demented, or just plain evil," he said.

Another call came in, and Wells, afraid to leave the two women alone in the apartment, took Ana with him. In the tow truck, she cried throughout the run, complaining that Chanda had beaten her. "Ana, you are going to have to decide what you are going to do with your life, but you can't stay with me anymore," Wells said. "The devil is in you, and I want you to leave."

"I'm going to go home to Waco, to my family," she responded between sobs.

"That sounds like a good idea," Wells said.

At the apartment after the tow, Ana kissed Wells on the cheek, then took her backpack and some of her clothes in a suitcase and left. "I'll be back for the rest," she said.

Wells nodded, as she walked out the door.

That afternoon, Ana called friends, all of whom turned her down when she said she needed a place to stay. Ultimately, the only one who opened a door for her, the only one to reach out to help Ana, was Stefan.

Years earlier, he had told a friend that he knew his time on earth was brief, and that whenever he could, he felt compelled to help someone in need. As often as he said he wanted Ana out of his life, yet again, he took pity on her. It would prove a tragic mistake.

Chapter 11

Bruises covered Ana, from a bright red contusion forming a ball on her chin to angry welts scattered across her face and body, and a knot on the back of her head suffered when she fell against the doorjamb. That afternoon as she walked into his apartment, Stefan must have been horrified by the damage. The following morning at seven thirty, he took pictures with his iPhone, documenting the injuries. In one, a photo of her naked back and shoulder, part of a frowning Stefan's image would be recorded in the reflection of the bathroom mirror.

That same day, Stefan accompanied Ana to Park Plaza Hospital, near the Houston Museum of Natural Science just across Hermann Park, to be treated. While there, the nurses took a statement and a doctor assessed her injuries, then police were notified of what Ana described as an assault, claiming she'd been attacked by Wells and Ellison. The weapon listed on the report was a stick. When she left the hospital, she took with her prescriptions for a narcotic pain reliever and a drug to help with muscle stiffness. On a scale of one to ten, Ana gauged her pain as a six. Despite the heavy bruising, her X-rays revealed no broken bones. When Ana described how the fight started, she claimed she'd accidentally bumped her boyfriend's head with her teeth.

Later that day, Ana stopped at Wells's apartment to get more of her things. She used her key to unlock the door and walked inside. Glancing out the window, Wells saw Stefan in

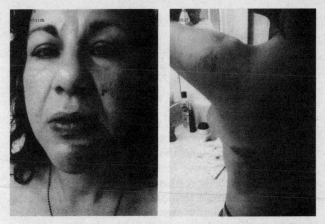

Two photos of Ana taken the day after the fight, with Stefan visible in the mirror in the left upper corner of the second photo

the Mercedes waiting for her. Wells asked her to stay and talk, but Ana refused, saying, "I'm not here to talk to you."

"Why not?" he asked.

"Because you beat me up."

"Is that what you think happened?" Wells asked, and Ana said it was.

"That's not what happened, and you come in here with that attitude," Wells said. "This isn't you, Ana. You're not well. You need help. Something is wrong."

When she asked for her things, Wells agreed but not until she returned his key. For some reason, she wasn't willing to do as he asked at that time. "I'll be back later in the week," she said, and quickly left.

Hours later, Chanda noticed a police officer in a squad car outside the apartment. By then, Wells was on a towing call, and Chanda talked to the officer, who said Ana had filed a complaint, describing the altercation from her view, that she'd been attacked and was merely defending herself. "Well, she said you hit her with a stick," the man said.

"I sure did. That one," Chanda answered, pointing at the walking stick.

When they were done talking, she got in touch with Wells in his tow truck, and he, too, recounted the events leading up to the fight to the officer. When their stories agreed, the officer said the investigation was over. "I believe you both," he said. "I'm closing this case right now."

In the days that followed, James Wells called Ana, asking her why she tried to press charges against him. She contacted police, who ordered him not to call her, explaining that Ana claimed he was harassing her. But she'd phoned him as well, and the log on his cell phone proved it. By then, Wells had consulted a Houston attorney, Allette Williams, a tall, attractive, elegant woman. Williams explained that what Chanda told Wells was right, that he had to keep a distance from Ana Trujillo.

The week wore on without more incidents until the following Thursday, when Ana called and asked Wells to have Chanda vacate the apartment the following afternoon so she could pick up her things. He agreed, but then talked to his attorney who advised him not to let Ana inside the apartment, instead to put her things outside. Friday came and went, and Ana never called and never arrived.

Finally, late that night, she called again and asked to make sure Chanda was gone when she came the next day.

"You know, Ana, I'm not doing this shit," Wells answered. "I made plans for you today, and you didn't come or call. You want me to do this again? I'm not going to be inconvenienced for you. You don't need to come in the house anyway."

By then, Chanda had again talked to Wells, reiterating what their lawyer had said, that Wells shouldn't let Ana inside or be alone with her, that he needed witnesses in case she tried to file more false charges.

In early June, attorneys from another law firm hired Stefan to review a case with an eye toward having him testify at an upcoming trial. "This is a sign people do want me," he told a friend. "And this is something I like to do."

His life appeared to be falling into place, with one exception. Since the day of her fight with Chanda Ellison, Ana continued to stay at his apartment, but Stefan saw that as only temporary as she prepared to move home to Waco in early June.

On Saturday, June 8, Ana would later say that they rose early, as she and Stefan often did, to see the sunrise. Stefan helped her move the large black-leather couch out of the way, so she could dance to welcome the day. Then she did what she called her wish for the day, asking for justice for her family.

That afternoon, Ana and Stefan ate lunch at the Hermann Park Golf Course Grill. It was to be their last day together. Ana had gotten word out that she needed a ride to Waco, where she planned to spend at least that summer. One of the staff members at the grill, Carmen Pimentel, knew someone on Texas Southern University women's golf team, which was heading to Waco to play the Baylor University team. Pimentel arranged a ride for Ana with the team at seven that evening.

At the golf course, although Stefan paid for Ana's food and drinks, they kept a distance; much of the afternoon, Stefan sat alone outside, reading, while Ana played on her computer inside. At one point a golf pro stopped to talk to Stefan, and he mentioned that he was excited about a Sunday brunch date he had planned for the next day with Janette Jordan.

That afternoon, Jordan texted Stefan asking if they were still getting together the next day. "Looking forward to it. Where do you want to go?" he responded. A flurry of texts later, they'd decided on Backstreet Café, a popular restaurant built into an old house with a large backyard courtyard.

"I'll meet you there," Jordan texted. "We'll eat outside."

Stefan agreed. A short time later, Stefan's former father-in-law, Dick Swift, texted to tell Stefan that he was eating lunch at one of their favorite restaurants, a chicken-fried-steak place in Oklahoma City. Years earlier, Dick and his wife had taken Stefan there. Despite the divorce, the two men had remained close friends.

"Are you there now?" Stefan asked.

"Yes, eat your heart out," Swift texted back with a laugh.

Although it was her day off, waitress Erika Elizondo later dropped in at the grill with her children. When Ana saw the youngsters, she called them over, and she played a video of herself hosting a public-access program. Elizondo was concerned, asking what she'd shown them. "Is that woman famous?" one of the children asked.

"I don't know, baby," Elizondo said. "But she may be one day."

After they left the grill, Ana called James Wells to tell him that she was taking a cab to his apartment to collect her things. Wells agreed, and he brought Ana's possessions outside to the curb. He had suitcases, two boxes, a chair, some pictures, and a mirror in a silver frame that was shaped like the sun. The chair was an antique, heavily carved, with a black-leather seat.

The cab pulled up late that afternoon, and James and the driver loaded Ana's property into the trunk. When everything didn't fit, they made arrangements for a second trip. The entire time, Ana never looked at Wells, avoiding his gaze.

When she arrived in the cab the second time, they finished loading her baggage. Once the cab's trunk was closed, Ana turned to Wells. For a moment she acted like she thought she had more items inside his apartment, but he told her that was everything. Finally, she got into the cab's backseat, and he stood next to her at the open window. Reaching out, she took his hand, and folded three nickels inside his palm, squeezing his hand tightly around them.

Confused, Wells said, "You don't owe me anything. We're good. I just need you to get the help you need."

"Something bad is going to happen," she said, looking up at him.

"Ana, don't do anything stupid," he told her.

"Put the nickels in the cupboard, or something bad is going to happen," she said.

Wells frowned at her, and replied, "Ana, I'm not going to do that."

Apparently angry that he would defy her, she reached for her seat belt, as if to unbuckle it and get out of the car saying, "You know, James, if you don't fucking do it, I'll do it myself."

"All right," he said, trying to calm her. "Okay, I'll do it."

Moments later, she drove off. Inside his apartment, Wells never did as he'd agreed, leaving the nickels on a counter.

At 4:22 that afternoon, The Parklane's loading-dock-surveillance cameras recorded Ana and Stefan walking toward the freight elevator.

At 5:55, the cameras again picked them up, this time with the building's valet cart covered with Ana's boxes and suitcases, her mirror and chair. They pushed the load onto the elevator and took it to the storage area, where they put everything but Ana's three suitcases. They unloaded a second cartful six minutes later, then took the suitcases up to 18B. Ana's ride to Waco was supposed to arrive in an hour, leaving Stefan free to spend the evening and the summer as he pleased. After months of being shadowed, the many times he confided in friends of his fears about Ana, he must have finally thought that perhaps it was over, that she would be gone, and he would be able to resume his life.

But all didn't go as planned.

"I'm trying to find Ana a ride to Waco," he told a friend on the phone, explaining that Ana was going to see her family. "She had a ride set up, but it fell through."

Early that evening, Carmen Pimental called to deliver the bad news; Ana's scheduled ride to Waco had to be postponed when the car filled up quickly, leaving no room for her and her luggage. Instead, Pimental had made arrangements for Ana to drive up the next morning with the coaches, at about seven. Stefan, apparently unhappy with the delay, tried to find another ride for her but ultimately failed. That meant he had one more night with Ana before she left Houston.

At seven fifteen that evening, the lobby cameras recorded Stefan and Ana walking off the elevator, dressed to go out for the evening. They both wore jeans, Stefan with a loose black shirt with a tequila logo embroidered on it and Ana a double black belt, a black-lace tank top, and a pair of cobalt-blue-suede stiletto heels.

On what was to be their final night together, Stefan took Ana to one of her favorite places, Bar 5015, where a month earlier they'd celebrated his fifty-ninth birthday. In the crush of the busy bar, they drank and hobnobbed with other patrons. Stefan quietly watched one of the televisions behind the bar, listened to the live music, and talked to a few of those seated around him, while Ana acted as if she were the guest of honor at a party, dancing on her barstool, flirting with the men around her, laughing loudly, smiling broadly, and fighting to be the center of attention.

At Bar 5015, the liquor bottles displayed on shelves behind the bartenders, a wooden deck with tables circling the building from which The Parklane was visible just blocks away, Stefan and Ana lingered for hours, sharing a twenty-five-dollar bottle of wine followed by six shots of Don Julio Silver tequila at $12 each. Stefan didn't like vodka, but Ana rounded out her evening with four eight-dollar shots of Absolut.

As the night wound to a close, at 1:37 A.M., Stefan called Yellow Cab, to arrange a ride to The Parklane. He then settled up the bar bill, which totaled $129. As was customary for him, he generously tipped $30, for a total of $159 on his credit card.

At that same time, Rosemary Gomez, a plainspoken woman with broad features, the mother of four grown children, looked for her final fare of the night. Beside her in her cab sat her common-law husband, Reagan Cannon, who re-modeled houses. Weekdays, Gomez covered the area around Houston's Intercontinental Airport, but the tips were better on weekends, shuffling revelers home from clubs and bars inside the city. As a woman, Gomez often didn't feel safe alone, and she sometimes brought Cannon with her, riding shotgun. On this night, dispatch tagged her at 1:37 for a pickup at Bar 5015, where a Mr. Andersson needed a ride.

Arriving at Bar 5015, Gomez pulled into the parking lot along the side of the building. With the club nearing clos-ing time and clearing out, many of the spaces were already empty. A white-haired man waited, she lowered her window, and he came forward. "Are you Mr. Andersson?" she asked.

In his soft Swedish accent, Stefan answered, "Yes, can you give me a minute? I need to go get my friend."

Gomez agreed, and as Stefan went inside to collect Ana, the driver pulled forward and turned the cab around, point-ing the front toward the street for an easy exit. Then she and Cannon waited.

From where he sat, Cannon, who had the feisty manner of a man who didn't mind a good fight, and Gomez looked out at the double doors leading into the bar. Stefan disap-peared inside, then walked back out to the cab. "I'm having a little problem with my friend," he said. "Can you wait?"

"Okay," Gomez said.

Again, Stefan walked toward the bar, this time stopping to talk to a woman who'd come out with a man and stood near the door. Gomez thought the woman at the door ap-peared agitated. "I said go get a fucking cab!" Gomez heard the woman shout.

"I have a cab. It's here," Stefan replied.

With that, he approached the cab for the third time. "Can you wait one more minute? I'll pay you if you start the meter."

Thinking the man looked embarrassed, Gomez agreed. Moments later, Stefan finally walked toward the cab with

Ana beside him. He opened the driver's-side back door, and she got in. Then he walked around, got in the cab, sitting behind Cannon, and gave The Parklane's address: 1701 Hermann Drive. Gomez started punching it into her navigation system, when Ana suddenly shouted out directions, attempting to tell the cabbie which way to turn and how to get to the condo.

"All I need is the address," Gomez said. "I'll put it in my GPS."

In the backseat, Stefan remained calm, and Gomez asked one more time for the address to put it in her system. He began to recite it, but was cut off by Ana shouting, "Shut the fuck up! You don't know where the fuck you're going. I'll tell you!"

When Gomez again asked for the address, Stefan patiently told her, while Ana mumbled and cursed under her breath at Gomez. "I told you which fucking way to go," she said, then turned to Stefan. "Aren't you going to tell the fucking bitch anything?"

"What do you want me to tell her?" he asked. "She's not doing anything wrong. Let's just get home."

At 1:53, eight minutes after the cab arrived at the club, Gomez pulled out of the bar's lot. For the next nine minutes, Stefan apologized as Ana continued to berate the cabbie and complain, charging that they were being taken on a circuitous route to run up the bill. "Please, just be quiet," he asked her, but Ana, slurring her words and drunk, wouldn't stop.

At 2:02, the cab pulled under The Parklane's porte cochere, and Gomez barely had her brake on when Ana attempted to jump out of the cab. The door was locked, something Gomez habitually did until she'd been paid her fare.

It was then that Stefan announced, searching through his wallet and pockets, "I must have left my credit card at the bar. Ana, do you have any money?"

"I gave you my money," she said.

"What, three dollars?" he responded.

"Let me out!" Ana shouted, yanking on the door handle. "Let me out of this car! Open this fucking door right now! Come back tomorrow, bitch, and he'll pay you. You can get the money then."

Frustrated, Gomez turned to Stefan, and said, "Mr. Andersson, I'm sorry, but I'm calling the police."

"Please don't," he answered, pulling another credit card from his pocket and offering it to her. She took it and unlocked the doors.

"If my wife calls the police, your wife is going to jail," Cannon said, fuming over the shouting woman in the backseat. At that, Cannon jumped out, walked around the taxi, and swung open the door for Ana, shouting, "You act like a damn slut! Get out!"

Ana did, but still angry, she kicked at one of the taxi's doors. Cannon looked, didn't see a dent, as she stalked off toward the condo lobby. As she passed him, Ana grinned at Cannon, as if to say, "I got my way."

While his wife handled the bill, charging it to Stefan's card, an angry Cannon walked back around the cab and asked Stefan to get out. Once they stood face-to-face, Reagan asked, "Man, what are you? Are you a man or a mouse? Why do you let her treat you that way?"

"I can't do anything with her," Stefan answered, apologizing.

"Then you need to get away from her. It shouldn't be this way. Get her out of your life."

Stefan agreed. Gomez joined them and handed him his receipt. For the seven-dollar fare, he gave her twenty dollars. Irritated by the confrontation, Cannon paced, but Stefan and the cabbie stood together as he again apologized. "I don't know you, and you don't know me, but be careful," Gomez warned. "Your friend is out of control. You could get in trouble, or something could happen."

"I'll be all right," Stefan said.

"Your friend is not in her right mind," she said. "Be careful."

Stefan held her hand and squeezed it, thanking her. But then she took both of his, and asked, "Can I pray for you?"

In the driveway in front of the condo, under the overhead lights, Rosemary Gomez prayed for a stranger, asking God to protect him. Stefan, although an atheist, respected her beliefs and appeared grateful for her compassion. When she finished, he hugged her.

"You're a very kind lady," he said. "Thank you."

Inside The Parklane, Florence McClean sat behind the concierge desk watching the drama unfold outside. She saw the cab pull up, then heard the loud voices as Ana exited the cab. While not able to make out what was being said, McClean sensed the tension.

Working the night shift at the condos, McClean monitored the security cameras and oversaw the front door and the valets. She'd picked up the night job to make some extra money, to augment her earnings from her day job with the county education department. During her time at The Parklane, she'd grown used to seeing the quiet professor with the talkative girlfriend. Ana often stopped at the front desk to tell McClean about her art projects. One day, she brought in a small stick she said she planned to use to make an art installation on Stefan's coffee table. When they came and went, McClean had noticed how patiently Stefan held the doors for Ana, and how he waited while Ana talked to others in the lobby.

On this night, the valet, Roland Ouedraogo, opened the door for Ana as she stalked inside from the cab, and once in the lobby, Ana made a beeline for the concierge desk, visibly agitated. "What's wrong?" McClean asked. Outside, she saw Reagan Cannon pacing, back and forth, as if fuming about whatever had happened in the cab.

"We're having a rough night. The cab driver is trying to rip us off, driving us all over town!" Ana responded, standing at the desk. Although he couldn't have possibly heard her through the glass, she then turned, and shouted, "Stefan, come inside!"

For the next few minutes, Ana walked back and forth between the desk and the door, opening it and shouting again, "Stefan, come inside!" Watching her, McClean thought Ana looked jumpy, aggressive, and irritated at Mr. Andersson. The concierge wondered why Ana was at The Parklane. McClean knew that Stefan had filed a request to have Ana banned from the property. But he was with her, so that must have been rescinded. Something must have changed.

"Stefan, come here, now!" Ana shouted.

Outside, the cab driver talked to Stefan, holding his hands, praying for him. "Ana, go upstairs," Stefan shouted back. She shouted at him again, and this time Stefan waved at her, indicating that he wanted her to go upstairs. Ana turned and walked away, disappearing into the hallway where she got onto the elevator to the eighteenth floor.

"Hi, Mr. Andersson. How are you doing tonight?" McClean asked Stefan when he walked into the lobby just mo-

A surveillance-camera image of Stefan, on the left, walking toward the elevator

ments later. Usually he would have smiled and said hello,
but tonight Stefan didn't answer. Instead, he walked slowly
past the concierge desk, his eyes cast down, appearing over-
whelmed and defeated.

Moments later, the elevator door opened, he got inside,
and the door closed behind him.

In apartment 18D, Karlye Jones roused from her sleep. A
bang on the wall above her head woke her, and she immediately looked over at the clock: 2:13 A.M. She glanced at
her husband who slept peacefully beside her, apparently
undisturbed by the racket. To her, it sounded like someone
moving furniture, a couch or a bed. The noise was so loud
the wall and the pictures hanging on it shook. *At this time of
night?* she thought. *What are they doing?*

Just home that day from their Caribbean honeymoon,
Jones had lived in 18D for three years. A grad student
who worked on muscular dystrophy research, she liked
The Parklane. One reason: The thick walls between the
units meant Jones rarely heard anything from any of her
neighbors, except in the hallways. Jones had seen the
older man who lived in 18B sometimes, nodded hello as
she passed, said good morning, and walked on. A quiet
man, he kept to himself. Then the Latino woman began
showing up. At times Jones saw the man and the woman
argue as they got on or off the elevator. Jones didn't know
their names, only that they lived in the apartment next to
hers, 18B. Her bedroom backed up to their living room,
but she'd never heard anything from inside their apartment until the *boom* that night.

Beside her, Jones's husband continued to sleep soundly.
Getting out of bed, she threw on a robe, then walked through
the living room toward the apartment door, intent on asking
them to quiet down. But then she heard shouting, yelling,
a man's voice. At the front door, Jones paused and waited,
wondering whether or not to pound on her neighbor's door

in the middle of the night, interrupting what sounded like an argument. The voices grew softer, muffled, and she waited. The patter quieted and stopped. She heard something shuffle, then slamming doors. Again, she waited. Nothing more.

The apartment next door went quiet. Total stillness. Jones waited briefly, then turned and went back to bed.

On the way home from their night's work, driving to their house outside the city, Rosemary Gomez and Reagan Cannon heard a phone ring in the backseat. Someone had left a cell phone in the cab, not an unusual occurrence. In the passenger seat, Reagan reached back and searched, finding a small flip phone tucked into a crevice in the seat. A minute later, the phone rang again. "Ana?" someone said when he answered. It was a woman, and Cannon hung up.

After 3 A.M. at the house, Cannon searched the phone, looking at recent calls, trying to figure out whose phone it was and how to return it. Glancing down the contact list, he spotted a listing for Stefan Andersson, recognizing the name of the man who had been their final fare of the night. At 3:37 A.M., Cannon used the found cell phone to call Stefan's cell. A woman answered, sobbing, her words slurred.

"You're going to have to quit bawling and squalling if you want me to understand," Cannon growled, recognizing Ana's voice.

Instantly, she stopped crying. "Call 9-1-1," she said. "I've been assaulted."

Cannon didn't believe her, assuming it was a ruse. "Call yourself," he said. "If you can talk to me on the phone, you can call 9-1-1."

Judging it was all some kind of a sick game, Cannon hung up, wondering if the woman was trying to convince him to make a false 9-1-1 call, to get him in trouble and get even.

Miles away in her bed in her east Houston home, Christi Suarez slept. Since she'd known Ana Fox, the woman had been invading Suarez's dreams. On this night, Suarez saw Ana from the back, just her hair. They were talking, like they used to when they were good friends, before the big falling-out, before an angry Ana slapped her, twice.

In Suarez's dream, a burst of wind blew away Ana's hair, exposing her skull, covered with hideous, bleeding wounds.

Chapter 12

The call logged in at 3:41, to a 9-1-1 dispatcher. "What's your emergency?"

"I need help," Ana said, her voice garbled.

"Where are you, ma'am?" the dispatcher asked. Ana gave the address to The Parklane on Hermann Drive. Only instead of 18B, she identified the apartment as 1801. Slurred with intermittent sobs and moans, at times Ana verged toward incoherent. Struggling to understand, the dispatcher interrupted, asking her to stop crying, so she could comprehend what Ana said.

"What did your boyfriend do?" the woman asked.

"He was punching me . . . he tried to . . ." Ana said, but then her words dissolved into another moan. When the dispatcher asked if the boyfriend Ana spoke of was with her, she said that he was, but she added, "He's not breathing. I need you right now."

"I'm getting someone out to you. Are there any weapons involved?"

"No, ma'am. It's just me and him. He drinks a lot," she said, then more sobbing and unclear words. The dispatcher asked what the man was wearing, as a method for police to identify him on the scene. "No, he's in the apartment. He's about to die . . . I couldn't find the phone. Someone called me."

"So is he beating you up, or is he about to die? . . .

So what do you mean he's about to die? What's going on with him?"

Ana's voice again lapsed into undecipherable wails. "Ma'am, would you stop crying and talk to me? What is going on with him?" the dispatcher asked.

"Be quiet!" Ana ordered, but who was she talking to? Stefan? It sounded like someone on the scene with her, in the apartment.

"Hello?" the confused dispatcher responded. On the phone, Ana's voice faded away as the dispatcher heard slurping, a sucking of air, and a blowing.

"Breathe. Breathe. Breathe, Stefan," Ana said, followed by more noises. "He's bleeding all over the place. He's bleeding. He's about to die."

Unable to understand what Ana said but realizing someone on the scene was injured, the police dispatcher transferred the call to a fire and medical emergency operator, who again asked for the address. Ana answered, then pleaded, "Please, hurry!"

"Ma'am, try to calm down and speak clearly. I can't understand what you need the ambulance for. What happened? Are you reporting an assault, ma'am?"

"He assaulted me," she said. "I'm going to need an ambulance. Listen, he's about to die."

"What happened to him?"

"I told him to let me go, but he wouldn't," Ana said.

"What happened? Are you calling for yourself or are you calling for him?"

"I hit him in the head," Ana said, followed by moans and unrecognizable words. "I hit him with my shoe. I didn't know what else to do."

"You hit him with your shoe? Is he awake now?"

"No," Ana said. "He was drinking a lot also."

"Is he breathing normally now?"

"No. I don't think so. I've been giving him CPR. I couldn't find the phone, then somebody called me."

". . . Ma'am, if he's not awake and he's not breathing, we need to start CPR."

"That's what I've been doing."

The operator offered to give Ana directions, and began to do just that, but Ana talked instead, saying that she'd been administering CPR, and that Stefan was on the floor, and there was blood. Lots of blood.

"They're here," Ana finally said, and the call ended.

Chapter 13

The dispatcher categorized the emergency as an assault in progress, and Houston Police Department Officer Ashton Bowie arrived at The Parklane at 3:48, five minutes after he was bumped on his squad radio. The information was sketchy, just that the caller was a woman, that she was crying, her words muddled, and that she'd said someone was about to die. It sounded like a domestic-violence call although nothing was certain. At the same time Bowie pulled up into the driveway, another dispatcher was assigning an EMS unit to respond, but they were ten minutes out.

Working patrol from HPD's South Central station, Bowie had moved to Houston from Louisiana. His beat was District 70, the Museum District/Texas Medical Center area, a busy but relatively calm part of the city, without a lot of violent crime. As soon as he pulled the squad over and parked it, he rushed inside.

At the concierge desk, Florence McClean saw the officer walk in. "Where are you going?" she asked.

"Eighteenth floor," he said.

I wonder what Ana did now? McClean thought as she buzzed the uniformed officer through to the bank of elevators. The valet on duty, Ouedraogo, hadn't even needed to hear that the officer was headed to the eighteenth floor before he assumed Ana had done something to bring the police to their door. Like McClean, he'd witnessed Stefan and Ana's arrival that night. Briefly, Ouedraogo wondered if the cab driver or her husband had called the police, reporting the confrontation.

The elevator door opened on the eighteenth floor, and Bowie got out. It was then that he realized the error. He had an order to respond to 1801, but the apartments were differentiated by letters. Searching for the person who'd called, he circulated, wondering what door to knock on, when he heard the faint sound of a woman's sobbing behind the door to apartment 18B. He listened for a moment, then rang the doorbell. "Police."

"They're here," he heard from inside the apartment.

The door opened, and the apartment was dimly lit. The face of the woman who answered, slim with long black hair, was streaked with something dark. As the officer looked her over, he realized it was blood. Bowie's immediate thought was that she'd been injured.

"What's going on?" he asked.

"He was holding me, and he wouldn't let go," she whined, as on the phone call, her words barely intelligible. She stepped back to clear the way for Bowie to enter, and he noted that her clothes, too, were covered in blood, especially the legs of her jeans. And he smelled alcohol, perhaps explaining her slurred speech.

His hand on his gun, Bowie slowly walked in, ready in case there was a suspect still on the property, someone who had hurt the woman, the reason for all the blood. Once inside, however, Bowie saw a supine man where the entranceway T'ed off at a wall. There was a dense puddle of blood near the man's head, leading Bowie to at first assume that the man must have been shot in the head.

"Is anyone else here?" he asked the woman.

"No," she said. When asked, she also said that there weren't any guns.

Taking a few steps forward, Bowie moved closer to the white-haired man on the floor. He looked to see if his chest moved, if there were any signs of breathing. There were none. "Hello," he said. "Police. Can you hear me?"

Nothing. No response. Stefan was pale, and there was so much blood, Bowie assumed he had to be deceased. From the look of the body and the blood drying on the carpet beside him, the officer thought the man must have been dead for some time. Inspecting a thick pattern of puncture-type marks, gashes, and bruises on Stefan's head and face, Bowie asked, "Do you have a weapon?"

"No," the woman said.

"What did you hit him with?"

"My shoe," she answered.

Bowie glanced about and saw on the floor near the man's head a blue-suede shoe with a long stiletto heel, stained with blood and bearing wisps of white hair.

Ana's blue-suede, stiletto-heeled shoe

On his radio, Bowie called in and was told that an ambulance was on its way. "I also need homicide," he said. "And send someone from the ME's Office."

"I tried to give him CPR," the woman said. "Can you try?"

Bowie looked at the man, again judging him dead too long for lifesaving measures. Instead, he turned to the woman and told her that he was going to pat her down. When he did, he found nothing. He then instructed her to sit in the hallway. "I don't know what happened," she said. "We were arguing."

Off and on, the woman sobbed and wailed, but Bowie saw no tears.

At 3:55, the first paramedics ran into the apartment, before long followed by others from a second ambulance, six emergency medical personnel all converging on the scene. Glancing at Ana seated in the hallway, seeing the blood, one asked, "Are you injured?"

"No," she said.

"Who's the patient?"

"He is," Bowie said, indicating the man on the hallway floor.

Clustering around Stefan, one paramedic put on latex gloves, then bent and felt for breathing, finding none. On his chart he would later note that Stefan felt cool and looked pale, not surprising based on the blood pool and heavy spatter on the walls surrounding him. Reaching into Stefan's pants, the paramedic touched the crevice between Stefan's pelvis and thigh, feeling for a pulse in the femoral artery. He didn't find one. On his report the paramedic wrote that the body was apneic, pulseless, and exhibited multiple traumas to the head. The pool of red near Stefan's head, the paramedic noted, had been there so long that the blood was drying and coagulating.

"He's dead," the paramedic told Bowie and the others. "Looks like he's been dead for a while. At least thirty minutes."

Looking over at Ana Trujillo, they saw no cuts or bruises, just blood, streaks of blood on her face, blood covering her hands, her body, saturating her jeans. When they, too, asked if she was hurt, she claimed no injuries.

On the floor, Stefan still wore the clothes he'd had on that evening, the black shirt with Hornitos tequila advertised on

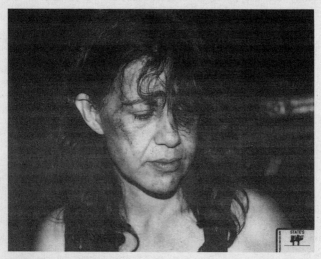

Ana's blood-streaked face

it, a pair of jeans, his white hair encrusted with blood, blood surrounding him not only on the floor but all three of the nearby walls.

At 3:59 A.M., the paramedic in charge talked with a physician, who pronounced Stefan Andersson dead.

About that time, the second officer on the scene arrived, and Bowie asked him to take Ana to his squad and keep her quiet in the backseat, while they waited for detectives to arrive. Two minutes after paramedics pronounced Stefan dead, Florence McClean sat at her desk in the lobby and watched an officer lead Ana Trujillo through The Parklane's heavy glass doors to a waiting patrol car.

They must have had a fight, McClean thought as she saw Ana escorted past her. When the ambulances left so quickly, not able to imagine the horror of what had happened, the concierge assumed Stefan remained upstairs, giving the police a statement.

Ana being taken to a squad car

Officer T. S. Miller took the call in homicide when Officer Bowie called in for assistance. "I have a deceased male, and we've detained a woman named Ana Trujillo Fox," Bowie explained. Before long, Miller was on his way to The Parklane. Like Bowie, Miller worked the eleven-to-seven shift. A former geologist who'd made a career switch, Miller had been with HPD for eight years. The first thing he did on the scene was talk to Bowie, who filled him in on what Ana had said and what he'd seen in 18B.

Armed with the basics, Miller took the elevator back to the lobby and walked out to the black-and-white where Ana sat guarded by police, to ask her to sign a consent-to-search form, to give them access to the apartment. She refused.

Moments later, the second homicide officer, Sgt. Troy

Triplett, arrived. Without a signed consent, he and Miller had no option other than to leave the scene, with Bowie protecting it, while they drove to the DA's office in the Harris County Criminal Courthouse to get a search warrant. Before they left, the homicide detectives instructed officers to drive Ana to HPD headquarters and secure her in a sixth-floor interview room, so that when they were ready, they would have her in place to give a statement.

An hour or so later, once they had the signed warrant, Triplett and Miller hand-carried it back to the apartment and entered for the first time. The scene was shocking, Stefan's body, his head covered in gruesome bruises and lacerations, the hardening pool of blood, the horrible look on his face, his right hand clenched, his arms flung over his head and covered with cuts, contusions, and patches of blood. And nearby lay the shoe, such an unlikely weapon.

Dividing up the work, Triplett took over witness statements and Miller was assigned to diagram the apartment and work with the crime-scene unit, which was on its way.

Arriving at 7:20 that morning, the forensic officers on the scene were E. P. "Ernie" Aguilera and C. D. "Chris" Duncan. Unlike in the movies and on television where crime-scene operatives carry little more than a briefcase, Aguilera arrived in an Expedition filled with equipment.

Diagnosing a crime scene is a methodical task, requiring an initial organization. Those who do it regularly have a rhythm, tackling it by using a systematic approach. Before beginning, the first thing the two CSU officers needed was an assessment from those who'd already entered the apartment. That led to a conversation with Miller and Triplett, who described the body, the wounds, and what they'd taken note of inside the apartment, bits and pieces of potential evidence. Once done, the forensic officers discussed how to split up the work. In this case, it seemed obvious. As the homicide detectives described it, the death scene was covered with spatter. Since Duncan was one of HPD's top blood men, he took responsibility for that evidence. That meant Aguilera would document the rest of the scene, including drawing a diagram and collecting evidence.

Task one: Before either man disturbed potential evidence, they needed to video the apartment to show what the scene looked like upon their arrival. Starting at the doorway, the camera running, Aguilera walked slowly down the hallway toward Stefan's body. It was such an eerie sight. Just hours earlier, Stefan had walked through the lobby. What was he thinking as he opened the door and entered his apartment? When did he realize that he'd entered a very dangerous situation? Minutes earlier, the cab driver advised him to be careful. She'd sensed something about the couple in her cab, an undercurrent of violence. So many others had warned him about Ana Trujillo.

Now Stefan lay lifeless.

The video finished, the forensic officers systematically photographed the apartment, again beginning at the doorway. As Aguilera walked toward the corpse, he took multiple images from various angles, including close-ups of Stefan's head and facial wounds and the cuts and bruises pocking his arms and hands. A group of images were also taken of the stiletto heel as they found it, near his head. Progressing through the apartment, they photographed anything considered significant, including tufts of white hair on the couch, presumably pulled from the dead man's head.

When Aguilera examined the door into the apartment, he found no signs of forced entry or damage. In the hallway, on his diagram he penciled in Ana's three suitcases. When he looked inside, he found shoes and clothes, ready for her trip to Waco. On his diagram of the position of the body, Aguilera noted that Stefan's head faced north.

As he encountered evidence, Aguilera placed yellow numbered markers adjacent to each item, then took photos with his Cannon digital camera. The bloody high-heel shoe next to the body was designated with evidence marker #1. On the record, he noted that it was a size nine and the brand was

Qupid. The heel was five-and-a-half inches, and the shoe had an approximately one-inch platform. Its mate, found beside Stefan's shoes at the wall that divided the kitchen from the living room, was marked with evidence marker #4.

Meanwhile, Duncan and Aguilera assessed the crime scene as a whole, attempting to diagnose how it happened. In the living room, they discussed the importance of the clumps of Stefan's white hair. Since they found no blood in the area, Stefan hadn't yet suffered any wounds. That led the two CSU officers to conclude that the couch must have been the site of the initial violence, during which Stefan Andersson's hair had been pulled.

Interestingly, they found no long dark hair that could have come from Ana Trujillo.

Proceeding from the couch toward the body, Duncan encountered a single drop where the living room met the entrance to the hallway. The shape was round, which meant that it had fallen vertically, while the source stood. In Duncan's mind, that drop was particularly important. Research over the years had documented that where the least amount of blood was found was usually an indicator of the location of the first bloodletting, since at that point, the source hadn't yet started bleeding profusely. That meant that if the battle began at the couch with hair pulling, by the time Stefan reached the entrance to the hallway, he had started to bleed.

At that point, Duncan entered the hallway. Walking slowly, he found forty drops of blood located six feet from Stefan's feet, positioned between that first blood drop and the body. They were round, indicating that as the blood fell, Stefan still stood upright. Nearby, four feet and six inches high, Duncan discovered a transfer stain, where something with blood on it rubbed against a wall. In his report he wrote: "These transfer stains are consistent with having been deposited by a blood-stained hand."

On a curved wall near the body, he recorded the presence of more transfer impressions. Disappointingly, none had visible ridge patterns, evidence of fingerprints, to link to a source. Methodically, Duncan followed the evidence, inspecting the walls surrounding the body. On all three, he recognized bloodstains "dispersed through the air due to an external force," in other words spatter that occurred as something hit or cut into a body, causing an injury that spewed blood. The highest hit four feet eight inches above the floor, but the majority within two feet of the floor.

Looking at the blood, Duncan analyzed a horizontal pattern high up and spatter propelled at a greater angle close to the floor. In his report, based on the totality of his observations, he came to various conclusions including that "the bloodletting event moved from the living room, down the hallway, and the source of the blood progressively moved lower" as Stefan Andersson first fell against the wall—transferring the blood—and then dropped to the floor.

Another of Duncan's conclusions, based on the scene, was that the majority of the spatter came from a source "very near the floor." In other words: Most of Stefan's wounds were suffered while he lay on the floor.

Once he'd diagnosed the blood spatter, Duncan inspected Stefan's body. Quickly, he noted clusters of puncture wounds on the scalp and the face, and on Stefan's hands and arms, what Duncan believed were defensive wounds, suffered when Stefan covered his face, perhaps in a desperate attempt to block the attack.

Since Ana Trujillo, the woman who'd been on the scene and was now waiting in an interview room in HPD's homicide department, had no noticeable wounds, the probability was that the blood had come from Stefan Andersson. But that couldn't be taken for granted. Perhaps she'd had injuries that officers hadn't seen and some of the blood was hers. To verify the source, a DNA team arrived to swab samples, ones they logged in by location, marking each by the case number to be sent to the lab.

Hours passed as the officers worked the scene. Finally,

before transferring the body to the morgue, Stefan's hands were covered with brown-paper bags secured at his wrists, to protect any evidence. If he had Ana's skin under his fingernails, her blood on his hands, it might indicate that she told the truth, that she'd struck him in self-defense.

Unaware of the drama unfolding in the next apartment, around nine that morning, Karlye Jones woke up in 18D. At breakfast, she told her husband about the noise in the neighboring apartment the night before, so loud it made the wall shake. "Didn't you hear it?" she asked. He hadn't.

A short time later, as she got ready for her shower, someone knocked on their door. "Did you hear anything last night, strange noises?" a police officer asked.

"Yes, at 2:13," Jones answered. "I absolutely did."

After Jones recounted what she heard, including the yelling from the apartment, a voice she pegged as a man's, the officer asked. "Did you hear anything from a woman?"

"No," she said.

"No screams or cries for help?"

"No," she said again. "The only one I heard was a man."

In 18B, while Duncan assessed the blood evidence, Aguilera worked his way through Stefan's sparsely furnished apartment. In the kitchen, he found nothing in the refrigerator. In the kitchen cabinets, little except Stefan's collection of unused prescription medications he'd collected over the years. The bedroom, with the bed and bookcases, appeared normal, as if nothing had happened in that room. From the look of it, whatever happened in Stefan's apartment that night played out in only two areas: the living room and the hallway, where the body was found.

In the living room, Duncan noted indentations in the carpeting, indicating at some point furniture had been moved, including the couch, which had been pushed back against a wall. Later, Ana would say Stefan repositioned it for her, so she had space to dance. Perhaps he also relocated the glass-top coffee table, placing it in front of the fireplace, along with his large black-leather chair.

What was on the glass coffee table, too, raised questions: One of Ana's art installations, a collage of dyed, crushed paper, a Y-shaped stick, a vase with water, and a stalk of lucky bamboo, her beloved bangle bracelets in a curved line, and streaks of salt.

The apartment on the morning of the killing

That seemed odd, but what piqued the officers' curiosity were notes on the table, odd writings that were perhaps the first true indicators of Ana Trujillo's troubled mind. Remembering how much blood she had on her body, her clothing, her hands, seeing no smears or streaks on the papers, the investigators determined the writings must have been done at some point before Stefan's death. Yet what was inscribed on those notes, jumbled with little punctuation and strange grammar, in the context of the killing, seemed particularly odd.

The coffee-table installation

"I ask the higher forces," pleaded one.

"I love you. May you live forever in us," read another. "Within you until all see feel you," read a note signed Ana and dated June 8, the day before the killing.

A drawing of a heart and what appeared to be a stylized swan in black marker was on another with swirls, along with the words, "Heaven and earth; tears of blood; bring forgiveness."

"May the shield of truth protect you. May the word of justice judge. Let the pen be mightier than the sword," on another.

So strange and haunting, given the reality of the lifeless man in the hallway: "Let your heart lead your way and fill your mind with beautiful memories of all of us and yours when in darkness and eyes cannot see, think of the sea water of life."

Another that seemed especially peculiar read: "I ask for you and your Spirit & Soul To be at Peace, Your Mind calm . . . your heart pure . . . Strength."

Whose heart? Stefan Andersson's? Was he the man who could not see, the one whose soul Ana Trujillo wanted to be at peace? Did that mean that even before the killing, she planned to close his eyes forever? Did she envision Stefan when she wrote the name of a song entitled "My Beloved Departures"?

As Aguilera examined Ana's purse, the scene became even more disturbing. First the CSU officer pulled out tennis shoes, then a black-and-white wallet. Lastly, he removed a softcover book. In his latex-gloved hand, Aguilera held a tarot-card book, one used to foretell the future. The page the book was open to explained the meaning of card number thirteen. An accompanying illustration pictured a skeleton on horseback, carrying a sickle.

Ana's purse/backpack with the shoes and tarot book found inside

That passage read: The "ghostly figure of a skeleton on a horse frightens newcomers because they think it signifies their imminent departure from this world. This is not so. The card simply denotes that something is going to come to an end . . . This card can mean that someone around you is coming to an end of their life."

On the morning she pummeled Stefan Andersson to death, Ana Trujillo's tarot-card book was open to the death card.

Chapter 14

About nine that morning, a rainstorm hit Houston. At her home, Jeanette Jordan texted Stefan Andersson about their brunch date, their plan to eat outdoors at the Backstreet Café. "Weather's not good. Should we meet later?" she asked. Knowing Stefan as an early riser, she thought it strange when he didn't reply. Time passed, the heavy rains continued, and she texted again: "Hey, I know you have reservations, but let's push it back and go later." Again, no response.

This is weird, she thought, assuming she'd been stood up.

At the same time at the scene of the killing, Officer Miller helped with collection, watching the CSU officers bag evidence, from the tarot-card book and the eight notes found on the glass table, to hair samples and DNA swabs. Miller, Duncan, and Aguilera would spend much of their Sunday in 18B, pulling together physical evidence to help prosecutors decide if Ana killed Stefan as she claimed, in self-defense, or committed a grisly murder.

Meanwhile, at HPD headquarters, Sergeant Triplett took an elevator to the sixth floor, homicide, where Ana Trujillo waited in an interview room. A running video camera pointed directly at her, she sat in a black office-type chair on rollers beside a long table, the off-white wall behind her corrugated to minimize audio interference. Appearing anxious, Trujillo kept her head down, her hair falling heavy about her face, wearing the same bloody jeans and black top she'd had

on at Bar 5015 the previous night. At times, she bounced her
knees together, like an impatient child burning off nervous
energy when forced to sit.

Five minutes after the camera began recording, Detective Brian Evans, who'd briefly talked earlier with Ana in
the car outside The Parklane, entered accompanied by Sergeant Triplett. The atmosphere in the room felt tense with
the memory of the brutality at the condo. Yet Evans had a
quiet, respectful, nonjudgmental manner as he initiated the
conversation. "We wanted to meet with you in hopes that we
can get your side of what happened there last night," he said.
"We need to try to . . . understand, if you could explain, your
relationship with Stefan."

Trujillo nodded. Hands wedged between her thighs, as
if to steady them, her words were somewhat clearer than at
The Parklane but still slurred, as she recounted how she met
Stefan the previous fall in the condominium lobby. Twice
she repeated her belief that, "He really liked me. In the beginning, he was very nice." They dated, then, very quickly,
"He asked me to move in."

Evans leaned forward, as if absorbing each word, while
Triplett, a veteran officer who'd worked robbery before
homicide, balding with glasses and a pale complexion,
slouched nonchalantly in his chair, tapping his pen on the
table.

The way Trujillo told it, within a month of their meeting,
Stefan Andersson asked her to marry him. In her version
of their relationship, she was the wary one, suggesting they
try living together first. While mild-mannered when sober,
when he drank, she claimed, Stefan became aggressive. "He
progressively gets out of hand, you know?" she asked, her
voice rising in a question. "He starts to get angry. He gets
real jealous. And he started to get violent towards me. And
so I said, you know, I don't want to live like this. I don't want
to live in a violent relationship."

The officers didn't know either Trujillo or Andersson,
and they listened intently. Perhaps she told the truth. Per-

haps Stefan Andersson had attacked her. The assumption was often that the woman was the victim, since in truth that was most often the case, and the man nearly always the aggressor.

As Evans and Triplett listened, Ana described herself as the kind, compassionate one, saying she'd taken care of Stefan. An artist, she said that she taught him about art and love. "I'm a very spiritual person, and it's actually ironically opposite of everything that happened," she said, referring to the night's altercation. "I showed him about spiritual love. Spirituality and poems, that's all I did. And I myself have been assaulted. He knew I suffered from posttraumatic disorder. I can't go outside, from place to place. I stay with one individual for protection."

The interview started out well for Trujillo, the two investigators appearing interested and attentive. Yet as she talked—neither of the men interrupting—she quickly digressed, her thoughts wandering to her past. The alcohol or her disturbed mind interceded, and both men appeared to struggle, trying to keep up as she queued up one painful episode after another from her past, layering one on top of the other without explanation.

When she talked about a man who'd raped her, at first Evans thought perhaps she meant the dead man. But then, no, it was the father of her two daughters, she said, her first husband, Marcus Leos. "I forgave him," she said. "I brought the girls to see him. He went to rehab or whatever he did . . . He asked me for forgiveness, and I said okay."

Although she'd just left a man's bloody body on his apartment floor and had come to the homicide unit to answer questions about what led to the killing, in the interrogation room, Trujillo rambled. Consumed with anger over the pain she carried with her from her past, she described her first husband as a good man who had drug issues. Although years earlier she'd sent her younger daughter away to live with her grandparents in Waco, Trujillo said, "I've always taken care of my girls."

The subject was supposed to be Stefan Andersson, but he appeared forgotten. Instead, Ana ruminated about her past, focusing on her history of failed relationships with men. After dramatically expounding on her relationship with her first ex-husband, she brought up her second, Jim Fox. This time, although not violent, Trujillo labeled the problem in her marriage as his demanding nature, saying he required that things were done in certain ways. That took a toll on the family and, although he loved her, she said she left him because she had to "choose between him and my daughters."

Yet how could that be, since soon after she left Fox, Ana pulled away from her daughters as well, Siana eventually moving out on her own, while the younger girl, Arin, lived with their father in Waco.

Reflecting on the way her life once was, when she worked at Coca-Cola, fighting her way up to a good job despite road-blocks, caring for her children and living for her family, Ana said sadly, "I did it all. I was a wife. I had a career. I took care of my girls. I cleaned the house. I cooked. Everything. And it wasn't enough."

Those years, however, were long past, and in her mono-logue, Ana, as she had in the preceding years, jumped from one man to another. In each case, in her interpretation of events, the men she met fell madly in love with her. Then, when she rebuffed them, they turned on her.

The first was Brian Goodney, the man she'd had the al-tercation with in the Rice Hotel. To the detectives, she de-scribed Goodney as a successful businessman and stressed that he had a friend with an art gallery, someone who could have helped her with her career. Ana claimed that from her perspective the connection was purely business; she de-signed furniture and a line of salts and minerals for massage therapists, ventures on which she thought she and Goodney could partner. But she claimed that he fell in love with her, and when she rejected him, he assaulted her. "He hit me against the wall," she said. "He wouldn't let me go."

So much of what she said about her prior failed relation-

ships echoed what she asserted happened that very night in
18B. When she talked of the moment when she tried to leave
Goodney's apartment, her shoulders rose and fell, her face
twisted in a scowl, as she dramatically acted out the confrontation for the police officers. Only to stop Goodney, to
escape him, she alleged, had she grabbed the candlestick
from the table and hit him on the head.

After Goodney, Ana brought up an unidentified man
she lived with, one who took her in and let her hide out
in his apartment, when she felt unsafe. Again, she wanted
only friendship, but the man wanted more. When she tried
to leave, he, too, she said, became violent. She claimed
he wanted her as his sex slave. "I'm addicted to you," she
quoted him as saying. "You're mine, and I'm yours. You
belong to me!"

Reciting each account, Trujillo became progressively
more animated, sometimes staring at the two investigators
with a wild gaze. As she described the men, she used terms
others had connected to the changes in her. "He looked possessed," she said of Goodney, on the evening she claimed
he attacked her. Looking importantly at the detectives, she
said, "He was trying to tell me that he was black magic."

The next man, the unidentified friend who called her his
love slave, wanted even more from her. "You're everything.
You belong to me. I want your spirit." He whispered in her
ear, "I want your soul."

Although the conversation became progressively stranger,
the two officers never changed their demeanors. Both Evans
and Triplett simply looked at Trujillo, responding as if everything she said made sense.

From the man who wanted her as his slave, Ana moved
in with James Wells. Of all the men, in her view, he seemed
the kindest. "He cared for me and he loved me, you know."

"You were more than friends?" Evans asked.

"Yes, yes." Yet again with Wells, who she spoke of long-
ingly, she said that she was unable to return his affection.
"I could not love him because I did not feel anything for

him . . . He was my friend, and he always loved me like that, but I had no love. I could not love anyone."

Wells cared for her until she first moved to The Parklane, to live with the businessman. There her drinking escalated, but she said that she drank for medical reasons, to quiet the anxiety that had plagued her since her altercation with Goodney.

After having been married to a pharmaceutical rep, she said she didn't trust prescription drugs, relying instead on alcohol to numb her pain and her art to help her find her way. "I wanted to heal myself spiritually," she said. "I met beautiful people, and the people that I love were close, and I did art. That's all I did was art and listen to music . . . I learned how to heal myself, water therapy . . . I had to treat myself . . . I had to heal myself all the time."

The morning ground on in the interview room, the woman seated at the table at times moaning and rocking back and forth as she described her life. She'd just killed a man, and these two investigators would decide if it was justifiable self-defense or murder. Rather than plead her case, however, rather than talk about what should have been the foremost topic on her mind, the taking of a human life, Ana Trujillo rambled on about her prior relationships, all the men who'd loved her, men she never loved in return. In each case, she was the victim, the one who suffered. The men became obsessed with her when she couldn't return their affections. In response, they became angry, possessive, and violent.

Yet she said she needed the men, for she was not a woman who could care for herself. This woman who'd pranced in front of TV cameras, who always wanted to be the center of attention, who stripped at parties and had her body painted, then walked through crowds while strangers stared at her, who posed provocatively for the cameras, this Ana Trujillo protested that she was shy and frightened, and that she needed to be protected. That was what the men were for, she said, to watch over her, and to expect nothing in return.

In her vision, she was an ethereal spirit, a beautiful presence to be sheltered by others. People fed her, bought her drinks because they loved her. Even the thought of possessing money, she found distasteful. "I didn't want to touch the money," she said. "I didn't want to become corrupt, and didn't want to get paid or anything. You know, my friends, they would watch over me . . . because they loved the way I was."

To compensate for her self-doubt and psychological pain, she admitted relying not only on alcohol but smoking pot. Instead of making her weak, she said, "I became strong."

"It gave you more courage and bravery?" Triplett asked.

"Yeah. Yeah," she said.

Although the hours droned past, there was no reason to rush the woman. The investigators were building rapport with her, hoping she would open up and talk to them about the killing. They needed to have her tell them what happened inside that apartment. Most of all, they needed to answer the biggest question: Why?

As Ana talked, it became evident that while she depended on each of the men in her past, in each case there was something about them that she disdained. James Wells, for instance, she said smoked too much, and his apartment, the one he allowed her to stay in, was messy and dirty. Yet out of kindness, her big heart, Trujillo said she accepted Wells and the other men as they were. Rather than being grateful for her ability to overlook their deficiencies, she said they saw her kindness as weakness.

Finally, at 10:23, nearly an hour and a half into the interview, Trujillo brought the conversation back to the man they'd gathered to discuss. Evans and Triplett appeared relieved as she said, "Stefan was older, beautiful. I like intelligence. He treated me very good, and he liked my art . . . I showed him the beauty of art, the healing."

Yet here Evans stopped her. Before Ana discussed the killing, he had something he had to do, to read her the Miranda warning: "You have the right to remain silent. Anything you say or do can and will be used against you in a court of law . . ."

Finished, he asked if she would sign a statement acknowledging that he'd read it to her, that she understood, and that she agreed to talk about Stefan's death. "Are you willing to do that?" Evans asked.

For the first time, Ana appeared concerned. "Okay . . . Are you saying I need an attorney? Are you saying . . . homicide?" After a pause, she asked, as if it had never before occurred to her, "Stefan died?"

For more than an hour, Ana Trujillo talked to police without expressing concern about the fate of the man on the floor surrounded by a pool of blood. Not once had she inquired if Stefan, a man she described as her fiancé, a man she said she loved, had survived.

"Yeah, Stefan is dead," Evans said.

For a moment, Ana was quiet, yet she didn't cry or show any emotion. Instead she said, as calmly as if talking about stopping at the grocery store, "I was giving him mouth-to-mouth."

"Right, I know that was relayed on the 9-1-1," Evans said.

Suddenly Ana, looking not sad but alarmed, said, "So, are you saying it was me?"

For the next half an hour, Ana Trujillo mused out loud, considering whether or not she should talk to the two detectives. They confirmed that what she told them could indeed end up being repeated in a courtroom, that she had the right to leave at any time, that if she didn't have funds for an attorney, one would be appointed to represent her, and that it was her decision whether to answer questions or walk away. She said she understood that she didn't have to talk to them, but, she wondered, wouldn't they be more likely to believe her if she cooperated?

To confirm nothing stood in the way of Ana's ability to make an informed decision, Evans explored her mental health, asking if she'd been diagnosed with any psychiatric conditions. She said she hadn't. Again the room fell quiet. Then, for the first time perhaps, Ana considered what had transpired. Staring down at her clothes, she asked, "Is there any way I can change my pants or anything? It's making me sick looking at the blood."

A crime-scene officer was called, and he brought a white-cotton jumpsuit to pull over her clothes. She did so, then sat and stared at the officers. When she began talking again, it was as if she'd jumped back to the prior conversation, away from the killing and into her past.

Moments earlier, she'd acted as if ready to discuss Stefan's death, but instead she rambled on about her first husband, her family, and her successful career. She talked of her years at Coca-Cola, and yet again about how she'd attempted to heal her body through her art. She'd made great strides, she said, including learning to use hydrotherapy and salts to draw out bruising. Along the way, she claimed to have developed special powers. "I have the ability to somehow, things become magnetized," she said. "So I learned how to use that energy and transfer it to heal."

Off and on to encourage the conversation, the investigators flattered her. "You're a very intelligent person," Evans said at one point.

"Why do you say that?" she responded.

"Well, I can tell . . . ascertain that you're an intelligent person. You're a very articulate person as well."

"Thank you," she said, obviously pleased.

Minutes ticked off the wall clock, and they continued to discuss whether or not she would sign the release that would allow them to talk about the matter they were gathered to discuss, the paperwork that would permit the detectives to ask her about Stefan's death. Finally, she said she would. The reason was her fear that if she didn't tell them right then, if she waited and slept first, when she woke up she might not remember what had happened, why and how she'd killed a man. As she explained it, there'd been episodes in

her past when she awoke and realized that she'd blacked out
the events of the day before.

"I don't want to block it out or anything. If I forget and
then you guys can't do anything, because I forgot . . . I don't
want to lose this." She then said what the detectives were
waiting to hear: "I will talk to you, and I will tell you."

Earlier, she'd described meeting Andersson at The
Parklane. Again she talked about how his intelligence drew
her to him. The story she told repeated everything she'd said
about the other men in her life. Initially, she saw Stefan as
only a friend, someone she viewed as a potential collabora-
tor. In her outlook, she envisioned her role as his holistic and
spiritual mentor. But he fell in love with her.

A man who'd always adored children, Stefan proposed
that they marry and start a family. Yet she said that she
lacked any enthusiasm for their sexual liaisons, seeing him
as a man with a soft, aging body. As she talked of the dead
man, she stressed all she'd done for him, for which she said
she'd received little appreciation. In her words, when they
first met, Stefan was negative, unhappy, unhealthy, and
physically undesirable. But she'd changed him. An atheist
since childhood, under her tutelage she claimed he'd not
only begun taking better care of himself but had a spiritual
awakening.

Within a span of minutes, Ana made complete about-
faces in her description of the man she'd just killed. Repeatedly she described him as a good, caring person, one who
watched over her. She said that she loved him. Then, suddenly, she talked of him as if he were a dangerous, domineering, abusive man. "He'd get up like really mad," she
said. "I was afraid of him . . . He wasn't himself."

Earlier, she'd talked about the other men, especially
Goodney, as if they were controlled by evil spirits. So many
had wondered what evil lurked inside Ana, but it was the
men in her life she insisted who'd sold their souls. That also
held true for the dead man. Stefan, she said, at times acted
"as if he had two horns coming out."

Rather than disagree with her assessment, she said Stefan admitted that at times he felt as if he had "the devil in me." That was an affirmation she took seriously, "because that's real."

Yet Stefan was generous. He bought her a four-thousand-dollar purse, and the man who loved seeing women in pretty shoes paid $1,500 for a pair of stilettos. Through it all, she expected him to take care of her, to keep her from having to become involved in the daily chore of making a living. For Ana, money was a concern to be handed over to others, those who facilitated her life. "It's a representation of how people buy people, and they kill and do whatever they want just to get a dollar."

Her relationship with the scientist cooled starting the previous January or February, Ana said, as he focused on preparing to be an expert witness at a trial. From that point on, their romance crumbled. It was then that she said her relationship with Stefan became abusive. Yet at each turn when Evans or Triplett asked if the dead man mistreated her physically, Ana said no. "Not physical, uh, mentally abusive, ugly to me."

"Just by words and how he treated you?" Evans asked.

"Yea, and the words he used. Yes."

At times, her statements had some strings of the truth. Stefan's great flaw, she said, was his lack of strength. He wasn't the man she expected him to be. "This is supposed to be my husband," she stressed.

When Ana talked about not being interested in money, Evans speculated that people became involved in relationships for many reasons, including companionship and sex. Referring to the cycle she'd painted in which men wanted more from her than friendship, had that "been the case with Andersson?" he asked. If so, had that made her angry and frustrated? What Evans was looking for was the psychology behind Ana's view of Stefan. "It may motivate you to act a certain way toward him," the investigator speculated.

"No, no," Ana said. "Not at all."

The time wore on, and the detectives remained patient, letting the woman's story unfold. Off and on they continued to flatter her, to act as if they had no desire other than to hear her thoughts. During a rare moment of brevity, she concisely described the pattern she said her life had taken, one in which men were strongly attracted to her. They fell in love, and she rejected them. Overall, Ana talked to the two homicide investigators as she might have therapists, hired to listen to her muse about her past relationships and her life.

"I think you look at things from a compassionate . . ." Triplett said.

"Yes!" she answered, obviously pleased. "Caring. Yeah!" In her opinion, she was "hypersensitive to other people's feelings." And she left no doubt that she believed she had something remarkable about her. Earlier she'd talked about an ability to magnetize things. In addition, she said she could "feel when somebody's temperature rises or their mental state changes."

At one point, she asked, perhaps in a clear moment looking about the room and pondering the turn her life had taken, "So how did I become from being so accomplished, from being so amazing, you know my family and my children, and I had everything, and it was beautiful, and I worked for it and loved it. How did I come here and be here?" As she concluded the sentence, she gestured toward the table in the interrogation room.

The conversation went on, and she talked of James Wells. Although earlier she'd described him in loving terms, her tone changed, and she claimed that he, too, wanted to control her. In detail, she discussed the fight she'd had two weeks earlier with Chanda Ellison, claiming the other woman pounced on her out of jealousy. Throughout, Ana pointed out bruises on her arms and legs, on her chin, describing them as resulting from the fight in Wells's apartment.

After she'd been kicked out by Wells, Ana said she called Stefan, and he once again took her in, letting her stay at his apartment while she healed.

Their reunion, she described as a great success; Stefan was so delighted to have her back that he offered to buy her younger daughter a car. And then came the night before, when they'd gone to Bar 5015 and drank.

At the club, she said, all went well. She and Stefan talked to other patrons, laughed, and had fun. Yet for hours, she said she tried to get him to go home. It was when another man bought her a cranberry-and-vodka drink at the bar that Stefan's mood abruptly changed. "He got real possessive," she said. From the restaurant, they took the taxi to The Parklane.

Three hours into the interrogation, Ana finally described how and why Stefan Andersson ended up bludgeoned to death. In the apartment, she tried to placate him, but Stefan became upset first about the man who bought her the drink and then that she was leaving the next day for Waco, to see her daughter. Possessive, he feared she wouldn't return.

"He starts to get out of control. He's yelling, and he's getting into a frenzy."

Frightened, she wanted to leave, a tactic she'd used in the past to allow him time to regain his composure. But he kept her from walking out the apartment door. "Did he tell you that you couldn't leave? Did he stand in front of you and wouldn't let you go out the door? Did he push you from the door? Did he pull you away from the door?" Sergeant Triplett asked.

Ana didn't answer.

Evans, too, asked how Stefan blocked her exit, but Ana seemed unable or unwilling to focus on the question. Instead, she described going toward the door to get her packed suitcases. "He doesn't like it that I don't care, that he can't stop me," she said. "He felt out of control. And he had to be in control at all times . . . And I was crying, because he was saying really mean things."

What mean things did Stefan Andersson say to her? As Ana recounted it, he said that he'd never hurt her. "I'm not like your friend. I'm not going to beat you." Rather than being comforted by his assurances, Ana pegged his words as degrading, as if he insinuated that she was "stupid for allowing somebody to hit me."

The argument escalated. Imitating an angry Stefan, Ana growled like a lion when she said he talked to her, and she wanted him to stop. "Please stop talking," she said she begged him. "He wouldn't stop talking."

In the interrogation room, Ana became progressively more enthusiastic describing how in the apartment her body trembled and her breathing became labored. "He came towards me," she said. "He goes, 'I'm not going to let you go anywhere. You're never going to leave me, ever!' . . . He grabbed me, and we started . . ."

As the detectives watched, Ana demonstrated a wrestling match. They were in the hallway when it began, and then she ran to the living room. Stefan jumped on top of her, and she cried, "I couldn't get out of it!"

Yet so much didn't make sense. She said Stefan held both her hands, but then that she grabbed her shoe and hit him, as he sat on top of her. "I was suffocating. I was hitting him to just get him away, right?"

When he lost his balance and fell over, she got on top of him. "It was like, 'Stay down Stefan!' But he grabbed me . . . He wouldn't let me go . . . And I was just hitting him with the shoe. 'Please stop. Stop! Stop!'"

When Triplett pushed for details, she said, "I hit him a couple of times and then he grabbed my hand so I lost the shoe."

At some point in the turmoil, she heard his labored breathing, but still she didn't get off his chest. Instead, she claimed he again growled at her, and as he lay dying, she pleaded with him to stop hurting her. "I realized there was more blood on the carpet. I jumped off of him. He was still kind of, he was breathing you know . . . I started mouth-to-mouth."

As he drifted off, she slapped him, yelling at him to stay

awake. She searched for the phone, found it, and called 9-1-1. "I am like, I felt sickened when I saw him. I would have panicked when I saw the blood, but I didn't care. Like a little blood, you know? Like the blood just started coming out."

When Officer Bowie arrived as the first responder on the scene, it appeared to him that Stefan Andersson had been dead so long the blood pooled beside his head, on Trujillo and on Stefan's face, hands, and arms had all begun to dry. But Ana said that couldn't have been true, that Stefan was alive and still breathing when she heard Bowie knock on the door.

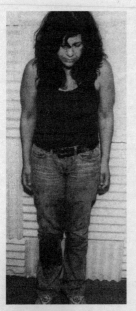

Ana in her bloody clothes in the HPD interrogation room

The final exchange in which she'd described the killing had been an emotional one, containing the information the two investigators had so patiently waited to hear. At that point, four hours into the interview, Evans and Triplett were done; they'd not only heard but videotaped Ana Trujillo's account of the final moments of Stefan Andersson's life.

Ready to move on, Triplett checked Ana's basic information, confirming her birthdate and the correct spelling for her name. He asked if she was on any medications, and she said she wasn't. "What's your mother's name?" the sergeant asked. "Or don't you want her to be contacted?"

"Yeah," Trujillo answered, apparently meaning no. "I don't think that she will take it well."

Moments later, two forensic

officers entered the room, a woman and a man, carrying a camera and evidence bags. First they took a photo of Ana against the wall in her blood-soaked top and jeans. Then they ordered her to take off her outer clothing and put her things into the bags. She did. As she removed her jeans, she pulled from a pocket the two white crystals she always carried with her, ones she claimed had the power to protect her and to heal.

Stripped down to her bra and underpants, Ana Trujillo stood against the wall as one of the CSU officers snapped photos. As he did, Ana pointed at bruises. Earlier she'd told the two investigators the injuries resulted from her fight with Chanda Ellison. Now, perhaps sensing the interview hadn't gone well, she implied they were indications of where Stefan Andersson had hit her.

Leaving her with the forensic officers, Evans and Triplett said nothing, instead turning their backs and walking out of the room. They'd had hours to evaluate Trujillo, but they knew little about her. Alone, her head hanging down, dressed in the white jumpsuit she'd been given to cover her bloody jeans, did she look like a brutal killer? Or was she telling the truth? Did they believe that Stefan was the violent one? Had Ana acted only in self-defense?

Apparently, something about her interview left the investigators with doubts about her truthfulness.

At 1:29 P.M., nearly twelve hours after Andersson and Trujillo left Bar 5015, Triplett and Evans gathered their notes on the case to take to the Harris County District Attorney's intake unit to talk to a prosecutor. After they left the interview room, the sound of metal hitting metal was heard, as handcuffs were locked onto Ana Trujillo's wrists. When Triplett and Evans left the DA's office that Sunday, they carried an arrest warrant signed by a judge charging Ana Trujillo Fox with murder.

While the forensic team combed through Stefan's apartment and homicide detectives questioned Ana, the press heard the first reports of a killing in the posh Parklane apartments, a grisly scene in which a woman pummeled an un-named man to death with a stiletto heel.

Anders Berkenstam saw the report on the television. "What if it's Stefan, and she killed him now?" he said.

Hours later, the University of Houston, where Berken-stam was a faculty member with Stefan, called to tell him that it was, in fact, his friend who had died. The news must have hit the Berkenstams hard. They were both good friends of Stefan's, and they'd been warning him for months to stay away from Ana. It had gotten so uncomfortable, that when they saw him walking down the street with her, they turned and walked away.

When a friend called and told Annika what had hap-pened, she had a hard time believing it. Although she knew Ana had been a problem for Stefan, she'd never imagined such an outcome, that the woman would actually take his life. Yet before she had an opportunity to sit down and con-sider what she'd just heard, allow the sadness to creep in, she had a task, to contact Stefan's family in Sweden and his large circle of friends.

Biking on a trail that afternoon in Dallas, Stan Rich took a break to call Stefan. The two men talked nearly every Sunday. When Stefan didn't answer, Rich left a message: "Hey, Stefan, what's happening?" Ten minutes later, Rich's phone rang.

"Did you get the e-mail?" a friend asked. When Rich said he hadn't, the caller said, "Stefan was murdered in his apart-ment last night."

Ana killed him, Rich thought, remembering back to his many conversations with Stefan.

When Annika told Ran Holcomb, the CPA was with a client. Cutting it short, he rushed home and logged onto the Internet to check the news reports. Reading them, he kept remembering all Stefan had said, including that Ana had been violent with him. "But I didn't think this was possible," he'd say later. "How could any of us have imagined that she would kill him?"

Returning from a tow job, James Wells turned on the television and saw the image of The Parklane in a news report. Turning up the sound, he and Chanda listened to a reporter talk about a gruesome scene inside the building, a horrific murder. "Please Lord Jesus," Wells said. "Don't tell me Ana did something stupid."

Then they heard: "It happened in apartment 18B."

"That's Stefan's apartment," Chanda said.

Moments later, the station ran video of Ana being taken to a squad car to be driven downtown for questioning. Wells felt his knees buckle, and Chanda wept.

Chapter 15

The following day, a Monday, at 11:06 A.M., Stefan Andersson's body lay on a stainless-steel autopsy table at the Harris County Institute of Forensic Sciences, a redbrick building with smoky glass windows slightly more than two miles southwest of The Parklane. Jennifer Ross, M.D., the assistant medical examiner assigned to the case, stood next to the table along with Officer Miller, the homicide detective who'd spent the previous day documenting the scene.

At first, Ross, in scrubs, wearing a surgical mask, a hat, and latex gloves, had no need for a scalpel, as she assessed the body before her. In her notes, she described what she saw, a man who looked his age, fifty-nine. When the body was found, Stefan's black shirt was pushed up under his arms, revealing his chest and abdomen. Once the ME pulled it down, she saw a sketch of an agave plant in green. Across it was the Hornitos tequila logo, ironically a brand from Ana Trujillo's birthplace in Jalisco, Mexico.

Before cutting the shirt from the body, Ross documented tears near the neckline, one on the right shoulder and the other in the front. White hairs adhered to the shirt, scattered about it, and Ross found more stuck to the blood coating his hands. The only apparent evidence of Ana appeared to be a few long dark hairs clutched in Stefan's right hand. Those, the shirt, and the white hairs were collected and bagged as evidence, along with Stefan's key ring and wallet.

On the autopsy table, Stefan Andersson weighed in at 180

pounds and measured five feet nine inches in height. Ross
described his body as cold, noting that was to be expected
after nearly a day in a morgue cooler. A slight purplish livid-
ity in his back indicated how he'd lain on the floor, the blood
accumulating at its lowest point after his heart stopped
pumping.

As the exterior exam continued, the physician carefully documented the obvious signs of injury. On Stefan
Andersson's corpse, that would and wouldn't be a difficult
task. "There are blunt force injuries of the head, neck,
torso and extremities," Ross wrote. The problem was not
finding the wounds; it was that there were so many. "A
cluster of approximately eleven blunt-force injuries on the
left frontal scalp, centered two and a half inches below
the top of the head." She judged that the injuries were
right-angled, full-thickness, abraded lacerations, some
L-shaped, with each "arm of the L" measuring one-half
inch in length.

That grouping finished, she examined the left side of Stefan's face, near his scalp. Here she found another cluster,
this time of approximately ten wounds. Several were verti-
cal, and she noted that some were superficial. There were
bruises on Stefan's left ear and near his left eye. On the pos-
terior parietal scalp, the crown of the head toward the back,
she found several oddly shaped abrasions, the largest measuring one-half inch.

A long list developed of cuts across much of Stefan's
head, from the crown to the cheeks, even on his eyelids and
the bridge of his nose, his lips and inside his mouth. When
Ross employed her scalpel and dissected his neck, expertly
peeling away layers of skin and tissue, she found intramuscular hemorrhaging, a possible indicator of strangulation.

Continuing on, the forensic pathologist listed the bruises
on Stefan's chest and abdomen, including three blue contusions each measuring nearly an inch on the lower left chest.
Here, unlike with the head wounds, Ross saw little bleeding.
The same was true when she turned her attention to lesions

on the right back. Opposite those, on his left back, she discovered a five-and-an-eighth-inch abrasion accompanied by minimal bleeding.

On Stefan's right arm, the physician noted more injuries, consistent with those she'd already enumerated, some up to nearly an inch long, and a small laceration to the palm at the base of the second finger, along with a bruise on the wrist.

On the left hand, Ross found fewer but similar bruises. When she surveyed the totality of the injuries to the arms and hands, she assessed them all as consistent with defensive wounds, occurring when Stefan raised his hands and arms to protect his head and face during the attack.

If Stefan had been in the room watching, the scientist in him might have been fascinated by what Ross did next, as she sectioned his body, carefully peeling back layers of flesh.

On the skull, she'd documented contusions and tissue damage, but once she reached the bone, it appeared surprisingly unharmed. Perhaps she assumed she would find cracks after such a brutal attack. The injuries were horrific to look at, leaving large indentations and gashes in the tissue, and they'd resulted in prolific bleeding, but the beating hadn't fractured Stefan's skull.

Once inside his chest, she studied his heart, noting signs of chronic high blood pressure. Yet the heart appeared relatively healthy. Inspecting the circulatory system that fed it, she found mild atherosclerosis, hardening of the aorta and major arteries, but judged it as insignificant when considering cause of death. The digestive system including the esophagus appeared normal.

Like the skull, no other bones showed any evidence of fracture.

There were indicators of fat in Stefan's liver, most likely a result of his years of overindulging in alcohol. But for the most part, Stefan Andersson's body appeared in tune with his age, typical of a man nearing the end of his sixth decade.

After the in-depth description of each region of the body, Ross broke down the injuries into categories for her report. There would be two important areas. The first were the abrasions, contusions, and lacerations to the head and neck. As she'd struggled to count, she'd stopped at twenty-five. Yet that was merely an estimate of the number of blows Stefan suffered, one Ross considered low. Many of the strikes appeared layered, suggesting one blow landed on top of another, making it difficult to know exactly how many times the dead scientist had been hit.

While noting the abrasions to the neck and extremities, especially the arms and hands, it was the torso that Ross found more important, where she'd documented intramuscular hemorrhages. The physician suspected pressure had been applied to his chest, perhaps enough to impede breathing.

Using black-and-white line drawings of a full male body, she drew the injuries, including those on the chest and abrasions found on the back. On similar drawings of the head, she marked wound after wound, sometimes writing "cluster" next to groupings. The black-ink depictions of Stefan's wounds covered the paper. She did the same with the arms, showing that both were covered with injuries.

The exam ended, but Ross wasn't ready to rule on cause of death. She had more questions. Toxicology wouldn't be completed for weeks, and she wondered if Stefan could have been drugged. She'd found no offensive wounds on his body, only defensive ones, leading her to believe that he hadn't fought back. Could Stefan have been incapable of fighting Ana off because he was somehow incapacitated?

Another question in Ross's mind was whether or not the dead scientist had been strangled. With so many injuries to the neck area, Ross wasn't sure. To find out, the physician filled out a form requesting a trauma analysis of the bones of the throat, especially the hyoid bone, a U-shaped structure at the base of the jaw that sometimes breaks during strangulation.

The autopsy diagram

That day, once Ross finished, Stefan's body was transferred to the facility's anthropology lab, in hopes that the
staff there would be able to answer Ross's question. After
its arrival, technicians stripped the remaining tissue from
the hyoid bone. Cleaned, the bone was examined by a
bone doctor, first by sight, then with a stereomicroscope.
"The specimen was unremarkable for trauma," Ross

wrote. The bone and the neighboring structures were "as expected."

Nevertheless, the intact hyoid didn't rule out strangulation. Many times, even in known cases of strangulation, the bone remained unbroken. There were physical indicators that convinced Ross that strangulation was still a possibility, including scattered petechiae in Stefan's left eye, delicate blood vessels which tend to burst during asphyxiation.

Finally, Ross had asked to see the shoe, and Miller retrieved it and brought it to her.

The pathologist had X-rays made, revealing a steel rod inside the five-and-a-half-inch heel. Black and white, the ghostly images explained why the shoe was so deadly. Comparing the heel to the wounds on Stefan's face and his shaved scalp, Ross confirmed a match, demonstrating that the shoe's heel lined up precisely with the pattern of the indentations and gashes on Stefan's head, face, and body.

An X-ray of Ana Trujillo's shoe

Weeks later, the lab report came in. When Stefan's blood was tested, his alcohol rate was noted as .13, high enough that it would have been illegal for him to drive but in someone who drank nightly, as he did, not enough to make him appear intoxicated.

No pot or illegal drugs were found in his system, but there was a small amount of gamma-hydroxybutyric acid, also called GHB. While widely known as a date-rape drug used to render a victim helpless, it was also a by-product of other drugs, including an herbal sleep aid found in Stefan's kitchen cabinet. Ross noted GHB's presence, but because it was a minute level, she discounted it as a factor in his death. In addition, the lab work documented traces of prescription drugs Stefan used, including an antidepressant.

The autopsy completed, Dr. Jennifer Ross signed the final report. Under cause of death she wrote: "Blunt force head and facial trauma." Under manner of death, she concluded: "Homicide."

Chapter 16

Tuesday morning, two days after Stefan's death, Ana Trujillo made her first appearance in the Harris County Courthouse, where she was formally charged with murder. Images
of Ana in an orange jail jumpsuit, her long dark hair curly
and loose, her wrists handcuffed, flashed across international media outlets. The story of the woman who'd killed
a man with her stiletto heel had been picked up across the
Americas, Europe, and Asia. Many reporters noted the similarity to plots in movies where stiletto heels were used as
weapons, most often 1992's *Single White Female*.

Nearly all the articles contained Ana's contention that
she struck only to ward off an attack from Stefan. "Stiletto killer claims self-defense," read some. "Woman called
9-1-1, said she was being beaten inside condo," said another.
In the courtroom that morning, Ana stood beside Lott J.
Brooks III, a Houston attorney she'd once worked for as a
part-time translator. She talked briefly to the judge, Brock
Thomas, while she was again read her rights and registered
an official plea of not guilty. "The world will be watching how this case unfolds," said a prominent Houston TV
anchor at the end of her report on the case.

After Ana was escorted out of the courtroom by a bailiff
and locked inside a holding cell, Jack Carroll, a tall, lanky,
deep-voiced Houston attorney, with a bushy mustache and

a slightly sideways saunter, walked through on his way to talk to a client, a habitual robbery suspect who'd threatened people with a knife.

"Hey, hey, I know you!" Ana shouted.

Jack Carroll in his office

Looking about, he saw a woman in the cell and walked away, disinterested. He didn't realize that they had a connection; Jack Carroll had been a client of Teresa Montoya's in her hair salon for many years.

Later, Montoya called the defense attorney and explained, saying that the woman who'd tried to reach out to him was her friend, and that Ana had been accused of murdering a professor by beating him with her stiletto heel. Once he hung up, Carroll Googled Ana Trujillo Fox on his computer, and a plethora of articles appeared from across the globe.

Days later, Carroll sat across from Trujillo in a jailhouse interview room. They talked, and Ana described the fight with Stefan as she had in the past, as a woman defending herself against an abusive boyfriend. Believing her, Carroll offered to act as her lawyer pro bono, without charge.

On multiple levels, Carroll seemed a good match for the case. He had a strong record, he specialized in criminal-defense work, and he enjoyed big cases. "I like the action," said Carroll, who started out as a corporate attorney but decided to switch to a criminal practice. Unlike in the business world, as a defense attorney Carroll handpicked his cases, and he had more control over his life. "I don't like taking orders."

A well-known Houston attorney with an office a block from the courthouse, Carroll vaguely remembered seeing the woman in the cell at Montoya's hair salon. Before he'd quit drinking and gotten married, he'd also lived downtown and had been part of the scene. When he left the jail that day, Carroll had a new and very-high-profile client.

At about the same time that Carroll met with Ana, the prosecutor assigned to the case, John Jordan, held a press conference in a courthouse hallway. With dark, smoky eyes under thick brows and an expressive face, Jordan worked as chief prosecutor in Thomas's 338th District Court.

Assessing the case, Jordan, who was known to be highly effective in a courtroom, had questions. The first and perhaps most important was whether or not what Ana Trujillo claimed was true. Did she kill Stefan Andersson in self-defense?

The question troubled Jordan; what if behind closed doors the scientist was a violent man? A mistake in this case could be costly on other levels. Convincing victims of domestic violence to come forward often wasn't easy. Jordan knew that most cases went unreported. What if he mistakenly prosecuted a woman for murder who truly was justly fighting back? That, he feared, could have a chilling effect on future cases, frightening victims into not coming forward because they didn't trust police and prosecutors.

In the past, Jordan, a former parole officer, had used the press to get the word out when he needed information. Now what he needed were statements from those who knew Ana Trujillo and Stefan Andersson, assessments of their characters from those closest to the killer and the dead man.

In front of a bank of TV cameras, red recording lights glowing, Jordan said, "It is our understanding that Ana Trujillo and Stefan Andersson were involved in a dating relationship, and this relationship was ongoing. If the public has any information on whether this relationship was volatile, whether it was good, whether it was bad, we want to know everything there is to know about the relationship."

Prosecutor John Jordan

It was pure circumstance that Jordan got the case, one that he knew would continue to draw headlines. Why? Overall, the public was fascinated by tales of women who kill, perhaps because the perception is that females so rarely do. In truth, the statistics weren't as lopsided as many believed, at least not in certain types of cases. According to the U.S. Justice Department, between 1976 and 2005, 10 percent of murders were committed by women. Yet females were involved in 35 percent of cases where the victim was an intimate partner and 30 percent of killings of a family member.

Making this particular case more press worthy, of course, was the weapon, an article of clothing many saw as a representation of ultrafeminine sexuality. Would the world press have taken notice if Ana Trujillo shot Stefan Andersson to death? Or stabbed him with a knife?

Probably not.

Sizing the situation up, Jordan also realized that if the case was in fact a murder and progressed forward, there were inherent complications. The main one: Juries were often reluctant to convict women.

What Jordan took away from his years of experience was that there was a presumption when a woman killed a man that the victim was somehow responsible. Many assumed that a woman wouldn't kill unless she was being hurt or abused, exactly what Ana Trujillo claimed. That meant the most likely outcome would be that a jury would be inclined to believe that Trujillo told the truth, a situation Jordan would have to confront in a courtroom.

In addition, if he did get a guilty verdict, Jordan had concerns about sentencing.

Punishment, in this particular case perhaps more than most others, was a wild card.

News of the case kept filtering out, bits and pieces making their way into the headlines. When James Wells heard what Ana was accused of, he worried that she'd end up on Texas's death row. "I didn't want someone I knew and cared about executed," he said.

What Wells and undoubtedly the public in general didn't understand was that, despite the brutality of the killing, Ana wasn't eligible for the death penalty. Under state law, the ultimate sentence was only an option in murders with special circumstances, such as the killing of a police officer, or a killing in the commission of a second felony. The maximum penalty Ana faced, if found guilty, was still formidable, however: life behind bars in a Texas prison.

Yet a long sentence for a woman convicted of serious crime, even a shocking murder, wasn't a given either. "A life sentence for a woman is very, very rare," said Jordan.

Years earlier, Jordan worked on the Susan Wright case, often called "The Bloody Mattress Murder." In 2003, Wright, an attractive blond mother of two and a former topless dancer, tied her husband to the bed and stabbed him 193 times, then buried his body in the backyard. In that case, prosecutors got a conviction, but despite the gore of the killing, the jury bypassed life and gave Wright twenty years. Like Ana Trujillo, Susan Wright claimed to be a victim of domestic violence, but Jordan thought that a man convicted of the same murder would have gotten a stiffer sentence.

Looking at the Trujillo case, the prosecutor assessed that it would be a battle, but he wasn't the kind of lawyer who walked away from a fight. "I believe I'm doing what I was meant to do," he said about his job. "It's what I was put on this earth for."

That same morning, two days after the murder, in London, England, the *Daily Mail* carried an article with a photograph of Stefan in his lab and a wire picture of Ana at the hearing in her jail garb, while a Reuters article that proliferated across the Net focused on Stefan and Ana's last night out. "The couple had been out drinking . . . Trujillo . . . later called 9-1-1 and said she was being assaulted." Accompanying most of the articles were photos of extreme high heels. One outlet mocked the case, calling Stefan "a fashion victim."

"Murder by stiletto," others wrote.

With such intense interest, a cable program enlisted the aid of an expert who taught women how to use high heels for defense. On the program, the martial arts aficionado demonstrated how she believed Ana used the shoe, first stomping Stefan on the face and head with it on, then holding the shoe in her hand and hitting him with the heel.

Meanwhile, reporters converged on The Parklane, cornering residents and asking for comments. "I think the killing was unintentional," a woman who lived in one of the apartments told a reporter. Ana Trujillo "defended herself with the only thing she had . . . when do you break out your stiletto heel and kill somebody?"

In the midst of the flurry of public interest, there were also those who looked behind the headlines, assessing the case on a personal level, considering the people they knew and loved. In Waco, Ana Trujillo's family struggled with the charges pending against her. They'd realized that she'd changed, but was she capable of such carnage?

On the opposite side of the equation were Stefan's family and friends. In his lifetime, although he'd lived alone, the brilliant scientist had amassed a long list of friends, from Sweden to South America, to New York, Dallas, and Houston. So many thought of the kind, gentle man they knew and wondered how he'd met such a gruesome and public end.

Others fell in the middle, including Christi Suarez. Watching the press coverage, she felt conflicted. Ana was her friend, but Suarez knew the woman charged with murder had a violent side. Within days of the killing, the television producer's psychic friend called her and said that Stefan had contacted him. "Stefan said he needs your help. He wants you to know that he didn't touch her," the man said. "He was very afraid of her."

"What do you mean he needs my help?" Suarez asked. The man didn't have an answer, and Suarez tried to put it out of her mind.

As the interest built, John Jordan, the prosecutor in charge of the case, felt certain that he had to find out more about the people involved. Only a thorough investigation into Ana and Stefan's relationship would put the rumors to rest. "In a case like this, you have to be proactive to set aside the battered-woman defense," said Jordan. "When claims are made against a victim, it's important to either prove or disprove them. The truth is that when a man kills a woman, the question people ask is, 'Why did he do it?' But when a woman kills a man, it tends to be, 'What did he do to deserve it?'"

Jordan had already made his plea for information, and now he waited. Before long, his office phone rang, Stefan's friends from around the world eager to talk about the man they knew. One of the first was Annika Lindqvist. "It just made me so mad that she was saying these things. That wasn't Stefan," she said. "And I worried that people would believe her."

"Stefan wouldn't have done that! Never!" she told Jordan on the phone. As they talked, she explained about Stefan's parents, how he'd always described his father as abusive and how he identified with his mother, so much so he avoided conflict and abhorred violence. "He was the kindest, gentlest man. He would never, ever hit a woman."

From that point on, Stefan's friends and colleagues called from across the world, wanting to tell the prosecutor of the man they knew, one who often backed down, walking away from an argument or a fight, even to his own detriment. The most convincing call, perhaps, was from Jackie Swift, Stefan's ex-wife, who told Jordan that one of the problems in their marriage was that Stefan wouldn't argue with her, that he never lost his temper.

Slowly, too, a picture in stark contrast to Ana's claims of being an abused woman showed up in Houston media. When a *Houston Chronicle* reporter visited Stefan's hangouts, he came away with an account from Lucille's of the time Stefan came in with a black eye. And when the reporter walked into Bodegas, a memorial table had been set up for Stefan, and the management was giving out free Bud Light beers and shots of Jiro tequila in his memory. "They looked like a normal couple," the manager told a reporter, saying that the staff and patrons at the bar were angry that Ana had killed Stefan, whom he called the restaurant's "customer number one."

One of those interviewed by media clamoring for any insight was Jim Carroll, the by then former manager of the Londale, the downtown Houston hotel where Ana lived in the fall of 2010. What Carroll recounted for the cameras was an account of two conversations he said he'd had with Ana. "She told me if anyone ever screwed with her, they were going to get this in their eye, and it was a stiletto heel," Carroll said, holding up a hand as if mimicking holding a shoe. "She's a force to be reckoned with."

Yet his account did little to settle the question of why it had happened. Did Ana's words suggest that Stefan was "messing" with her that night, as she claimed? "Houston stiletto-heel stabbing suspect claims self-defense," reported *Good Morning America*. Or was Ana Trujillo primed and waiting, eager to strike out with little or no provocation?

As Christi Suarez watched the news reports, a TV reporter knocked on her door. Soon Suarez, too, granted an interview, one where her face was concealed. Loyal to a woman who'd once been her friend, Suarez recalled a time when Ana once complained that Stefan held her arms and gave her a bruise. Was that true? Suarez didn't know, but she told the reporter that as she saw it, this was a case of two people who shouldn't have been together. In the interview, Suarez never mentioned the changes she'd witnessed in Ana, the troubled and sometimes violent woman her friend had become in recent years, the one with vacant eyes, who believed in witchcraft. "I sided with Ana," said Suarez. After she did, she rarely slept. "My dreams got worse. I guess I had a guilty conscience."

In Suarez's sleep, Stefan appeared, saying that the night he died wasn't as it was being portrayed by Ana, that he would never have hurt her. He wanted Suarez to tell others, to clear his name. "Please leave me alone," she begged him. "I have to go on with my life."

Shaken, the next day Suarez bought holy water and blessed her house, to keep away evil spirits.

Chapter 17

Held on a bond of $100,000, after her court appearance Ana was transported back to the jail, where she asked to see medical personnel. On the scene the night of the killing, she denied having any injuries, but now she complained of pain. On her chart, a nurse noted "generalized bruises all over her body" and scars on Ana's forehead, thumb, knee, chin, and right middle finger. "I was fighting with my fiancée," Ana told the woman.

When she mentioned a knot on the back of her head, however, Ana instead linked the injury to another altercation, one already documented to have resulted in bruises like the ones she showed the nurse, the fight with Chanda Ellison.

On Ana's chart, the nurse wrote: "The patient said she is shocked to hear that she is accused of hurting her boyfriend." When it came to her drinking, Ana said that she only indulged in one or two glasses of wine approximately two times a week.

To the nurse, Ana explained that she stayed away from modern medicine, instead trying more "holistic" methods. On her notes, the nurse said that Ana complained that in prison she suffered from depression and anxiety, and that she'd been unable to properly mourn for Stefan. According to the records, Ana talked excessively during the interview but "did not appear sad."

While the case unfolded in the press, behind the scenes, investigators sought out interviews and information, trying to determine what had happened behind closed doors in apartment 18B that led to Stefan Andersson's death.

Officer Travis Miller stopped in at John Jordan's office four days after the killing and picked up a handful of subpoenas, for surveillance video from The Parklane, Bodegas, and Bar 5015, along with call records from Yellow Cab, all to pull into focus Stefan's final night. "I want to talk to the driver," Miller said. "I'm hoping the cab has video or audio equipment."

From the prosecutor's office, Miller went to Bodegas, where the manager divulged what he knew about Stefan and Ana, describing them as regular customers. The memorial the bar set up in Stefan's honor remained on a table near the window. Later, Miller would hear of the incident in the restaurant, the time months earlier when Ana entered and, unprovoked, bit Stefan.

From Bodegas, Miller drove the short distance to Bar 5015, where credit-card records showed Stefan and Ana spent their final night. Once he arrived, Miller handed the manager a subpoena for video from the bar's security cameras. Miller left with a copy on a DVD.

From 5015, the investigator then drove to The Parklane, where he went through a similar process with Lil Brown, producing a subpoena for all the building's surveillance video for June 8 and the early-morning hours of June 9. While they didn't collect the video that day, Brown agreed to make copies to comply.

Rosemary Gomez and Reagan Cannon saw the press coverage of the killing at The Parklane the day after their tumultuous taxi ride with Stefan and Ana from Bar 5015. They hadn't called police, however, to report what they knew. Gomez was worried. Her company frowned on ride-alongs, bringing others with her when she worked. But then, Officer Miller called Yellow Cab, and Gomez was ordered to deliver her cab to the Houston Police Department crime lab, to be swept for evidence. Disappointing the detectives, the car lacked video and audio equipment.

Afterward, Gomez talked to HPD homicide detectives about the cab ride shortly before Stefan's death. In response to questions from the investigators, Gomez described the argument inside the cab, in which a quiet, apologetic Stefan tried unsuccessfully to mollify a belligerent Ana Trujillo.

When they questioned her, the cabbie, however, didn't tell them everything. They didn't ask if she was alone in the front seat of the cab that night, and she left out mentioning that Reagan Cannon also witnessed those final hours.

"Is this the man you picked up at 5015?" one investigator asked, showing Gomez a photo of Stefan.

"Yes," she verified. "That's Mr. Andersson."

The detective then pulled out a photo of Ana Trujillo, and Gomez identified her as well.

In HPD's homicide department, investigators had already begun compiling the murder books, loose-leaf, three-ring binders in which they organized interviews and evidence. Inside they were building a time line, one they hoped would eventually detail the night of the killing. Once they had the Yellow Cab records, the officers had access to the exact times the cab was called, arrived, and left Bar 5015, and drove up to The Parklane's doors.

After finishing the interview with Rosemary Gomez, Miller returned to The Parklane to interview members of the staff who worked the early hours of June 9. Explaining the scene he saw when the cab pulled up, the valet, Roland Ouedraogo, gave his account, followed by Florence McClean, the concierge, who picked up the story at the point Ana walked into the lobby, visibly angry, shouting at Stefan to come inside. After he finished asking questions, the detective asked McClean if she had anything to add to her statement. "I know people warned Mr. Andersson to stay away from Ana Trujillo, that she was crazy," the concierge said.

When Lil Brown arrived at HPD for her interview, she brought copies of the apartment building's reports on Ana, everything from paperwork on the night she cut the refrigerator hose to the many times Stefan signed forms to allow her into his apartment and to bar her from entering. In addition, Brown brought the subpoenaed footage from the surveillance cameras.

A murder investigation resembles piecing together a complicated puzzle, consisting of physical evidence and interviews. As they work, detectives slowly draw a picture of the dead as they talk to families and friends and learn how and where the deceased spent their time. With Stefan Andersson, perhaps, this was especially true, for in the vast city, his Houston was a small world. And at each place he frequented, there were those with remembrances of the white-haired man with the Swedish accent, the one who enjoyed striking up conversations with strangers, adopting some as friends.

Later that day, at the Hermann Park Grill, an HPD investigator listened to the memories of the staff, who detailed what they saw on the day before the killing, a lazy afternoon like so many others when Ana played on her laptop while Stefan sat outside and sunned. The detectives also asked about the couple's history at the grill, and in response they learned of the many arguments waged over the months in front of the staff and customers. One worker recounted a day Ana appeared angry, and he'd asked Stefan, "What's up with her? She's acting strange today."

"Today?" Stefan answered, as if to imply it was more the rule than the exception.

The days wore on, and the interviews continued, as investigators followed leads, moving through Ana's and Stefan's pasts. "When Ana drank a little, she got kind of silly," Jim Carroll told a detective as an HPD camera recorded the interview. "When she drank a lot, she got mean."

Then the hotel manager repeated what he'd told reporters, the incidents where Ana Trujillo boasted that if any man "fucked with me" she would get him with "this," taking off her stiletto heel and holding it like a hammer.

On June 20, Sergeant Triplett and Officer Miller drove to Park Plaza Hospital. By then, they'd done a records search on Ana Trujillo Fox and found the DWIs and the old theft-by-check charge. They'd also discovered the complaints Ana filed against Brian Goodney, the man she'd hit with the candlestick, and James Wells and Chanda Ellison for the May 26 fight, after Ana bit Wells.

Inside the hospital, the two officers handed a clerk a grand jury subpoena for Ana's records. Days later, they returned to pick up graphic photos showing Ana's bruising after the fight with Chanda Ellison.

Unaware of the progressing investigation, in the jail Ana again complained to the medical staff of what they described as generalized pain. "Patient states both knees are swollen," the nurse wrote on her chart. Yet she also noted that Ana walked without a limp.

On June 21, an article on the case came out in *People*. Describing Ana as a former TV host on public access for her work with Christi Suarez, the magazine stated that "investigators are trying to determine if Trujillo stomped Andersson with the shoe or held it and struck him as she claims."

In the piece, Ana's former employer, Lott Brooks, was quoted as saying that Ana suffered from battered-woman syndrome and that she was nonconfrontational and would not have started the fight.

About that time at HPD's homicide department, the investigators sat down before a computer and slipped in a thumb drive with the surveillance video from Bar 5015. In her interview, Ana had claimed that she tried to leave the bar for hours that night, and that a drunken Stefan refused to call a cab. But as detectives watched the last twenty minutes of the night's video, what they saw was a direct contradiction of her statement. Instead, Ana sat on a barstool partying and talking to others, while Stefan attempted to lure her out the door to the waiting cab.

At the bar, the officer had also picked up a copy of Stefan's credit-card receipt. When they looked it over, they had the time the bill was paid, 1:11 A.M. That gave them another entry to mark on the time line under construction in the growing murder book.

Two weeks after Stefan's death, at 6:30 A.M. on Sunday, June 23, the prosecutor, John Jordan, met the two forensic officers on the case, Duncan and his partner, Aguilera, at the apartment. Once there, they conducted a walk-through, the officers recreating for Jordan what they believed, based on the physical evidence, happened inside 18B on the night of Stefan's death. Jordan listened and digested all he heard, picturing the scene in his mind, how the hair on the couch marked the first point of violence, then following the blood evidence as Stefan attempted to flee toward the hallway, while Ana beat him with her shoe.

"The jury will need to understand the blood evidence," Jordan told Duncan, saying it had to be organized to be presented in the courtroom. "This is of major importance."

Duncan agreed, and the next day HPD's blood man returned and spent four hours drawing a quadrant map to catalog the spatter, steplike boxes forming a grid of squares on the hallway walls. The one-foot-square blocks were then marked numerically, starting at the floor, and alphabetically, left to right. Inside each box, Duncan outlined the blood spatter in marker to make it stand out. When finished, he photographed and documented his work, clearly illustrating that the preponderance of the blood was low, within two feet of the floor.

Once he finished mapping the blood, Duncan used dye to enhance the transfer impressions he'd found on the wall, hoping to raise enough detail to find ridges and be able to identify fingerprints. In the end, he succeeded well enough

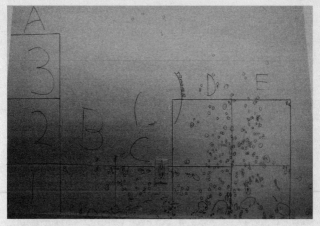

Chris Duncan's wall diagram

to confirm that the stain came from a bloody handprint but not enough to pinpoint the source.

While Duncan worked on the blood evidence, another officer inventoried the contents of Ana's three suitcases, still propped up against a wall in the hallway. When the list was brought to Jordan, he scanned it and thought that it probably represented nearly all of her clothing and shoes. "It looked to me like she was moving to Waco, not just going for a weekend visit, as she claimed in the interview," said the prosecutor. "It seemed like most of what she said in the interview with police wasn't true. She wasn't going for a weekend. And Stefan wasn't expecting her to return."

While the police investigation unfolded in Houston, in Dallas, Annika Lindqvist learned that Stefan had appointed her executor to his estate. After so many years as colleagues and friends, it was a good choice, and Annika soon began pulling together what had to be done. Friends and family called talking about Stefan, needing others close to him with whom to grieve. "We all missed him," she said. "So I started working on the memorial service."

In keeping with his life, mindful that he wouldn't have wanted a religious ceremony, she booked the event at The Wine Therapist, on Skillman, a small Dallas establishment that served food, with dark-wood tables and benches, its walls covered with the type of abstract modern art Stefan loved. Over the years, Stefan had been there a time or two and liked it.

To prepare, Annika drove into Houston to pick up her dead friend's ashes. Once she had, she stopped at The Parklane. The apartment still hadn't been released by HPD, so she couldn't go inside it, but even walking into the building was difficult. On that day, her intention was only to pick up Stefan's mail, but in the lobby, Lil Brown greeted her. "Oh, sweetie," Brown said. "Are you doing okay?"

Behind her sunglasses, Annika began to cry. "I felt the presence of death," she said.

In Houston, four days before Stefan's memorial, John Jordan and Officer Travis Miller drove to The Parklane and again took the elevator up to 18B for a last look at the scene before releasing it. They reviewed where everything happened, Jordan making mental notes for a time in the future when he'd describe it to a jury.

In the jail that same day, Ana was housed in the hospital wing, where she complained of mounting anxiety. "Patient reports some depression. Said she's been having some flashbacks little by little and she said she has trust issues . . . said she internalizes her feelings . . . she has been meditating, praying, and speaking with other inmates for encouragement."

The obituary in the *Dallas Morning News* and the *Houston Chronicle* ran with an accompanying photo, a black and white of a dashing Stefan. The obit said only that Stefan died in his home "due to unforeseen circumstances." It also stated that he would be remembered "for an amazing sense of humor, honesty, a brilliant mind, and above all love and generosity. He will be greatly missed by his family and many friends around the world."

On Saturday June 29, twenty days after his death, approximately 130 friends and family, including his sisters and nieces from Sweden, met at The Wine Therapist to remember Stefan's life. On a table, Annika placed photos of Stefan beside a canister holding his ashes.

A congenial crowd, they mingled quietly. Stefan's old neighbor from his years living at The Village, Mark Bouril gave a eulogy, describing Stefan's impressive accomplishments, yet saying that he was a humble man. "He recognized that we are all flawed in some way, and he did not hold that against us," Bouril said of his friend, whose passing left a void in his life. ". . . He understood intuitively that we are all works in progress."

In his talk, Bouril recounted a few of the many good times they'd shared, the friends he'd made through Stefan, and told endearing and funny stories, including about the day Stefan lost a bullet in the garbage disposal and assumed Americans had a tool specially designed for just such an occurrence. At the end, the crowd raised their wineglasses and toasted their lost friend.

Off and on among the laughing, there was crying, and at times one or another of the friends talked in hushed tones about the end of Stefan's life, wondering how anyone could have brutally murdered such a gentle man. The table holding his ashes seemed to draw them, and many stood and talked to Stefan, saying good-bye.

In Houston one afternoon, Teresa Montoya walked the few blocks from her salon to the jail after work and asked to see Ana. They met in the visitor section behind a Plexiglas wall. Ana's face was lined, and she looked decades older than the last time Montoya had seen her. The story Ana told that day was similar to the one she told police, that Stefan was obsessed with her, so much so that he wanted to move to Waco with her and buy a house for her and her younger daughter, Arin. But that he also had a dark side, wanting to control her. "Tell me you were on drugs or drunk out of your mind when you did this," Montoya said, not wanting to think that her friend could have committed such carnage sober. Yet Ana denied she was at all compromised. In her account, Stefan had a drinking problem, not her.

As she had throughout, despite all the witnesses who watched her drinking escalate and those who saw her intoxicated on that fateful night, Ana claimed she'd had no more than two shots of tequila. "He'd been drinking all day," she said of Stefan. "I was just trying to leave . . . he attacked me."

As Montoya stood to leave, Ana sobbed, and begged, "Pray for me."

In Waco, Margie Sowell, a longtime family friend, talked with Ana's mother, Trina. Later, Sowell would describe the conversation that took place that day. When the subject of Ana came up, Margie said that Trina told her that she worried about her daughter. As Margie would recount the call, Trina said that she wasn't sure what Ana had gotten into, but that in the months before the killing, Trina was uncomfortable being around her oldest child. "Trina said she didn't like having Ana in the house. She said Ana was doing strange things, like rituals," said Sowell. "She said it depressed her to think about what was going on in Ana's life."

About that same time in Houston, the university ran a tribute in memory of Stefan on its Web site. Beside his photo, it read: "A research professor and talented biochemist . . . During the course of his career, Andersson's research influenced several topics, including women's reproductive health, benign prostatic hyperplasia and prostate cancer."

After the memorial service, Annika and one of Stefan's sisters, her husband and daughter, drove to Houston, to meet with the probate attorney. On the way, they stopped at The Parklane. The first thing they did was stand at the bench where Stefan used to feed his squirrel. At the base of the tree, they scattered a handful of his ashes, and Annika pinned a photo of Stefan on the tree. For a few moments, they stood quietly in yet another remembrance.

Then they took an elevator upstairs to 18B. By then, the bloody carpet and wall boards were removed. The furniture remained pushed to the sides of the living room, and the apartment looked very different than it had when Annika was there last, when Stefan rose early to look out the windows over the park and see the sunrise. The cocktail table blocked the fireplace, covered with Ana's art project. The notes were gone, logged into evidence by police, but Annika tried to decipher the meaning of the dyed paper, the lines of salt, and Ana's bangle bracelets arranged in an arch. It all seemed very odd.

Looking through a small leather briefcase they found in the apartment, one they thought might have been Stefan's, Annika and the others discovered more of Ana's notes. On some she'd drawn spiral after spiral. They also looked over her old medical bills and the notes bearing phrases in which Ana documented her feelings. "I want to know who decides my worth," said one. On a sheet of paper dated just weeks before Stefan's murder, Ana talked of body mutation, of melting into the body of another, of shape-changing. "If I decide to melt with me . . . I want your body. If I decide to melt all over your body . . . reshape . . . change," read another.

The oddest perhaps was a note on pink paper dated a month before Ana bit James Wells, in which she mentioned the massive explosion that took fourteen lives and injured 160 in a fertilizer plant in the small town of West, outside of Waco. In her note, Ana wrote of a full-moon eclipse, which astrologers judged to be a highly potent sign, which occurred on April 25, the day President Barack Obama presided over a memorial service for those who lost their lives in the explosion.

Crawling up a crease in the center of the paper was what appeared to be a plea for a spirit or a demon to appear: "I would like Lustre Ante (unreadable word) Mulato to materialize. I will reunite with you Christian Leaver. Your circle of Faith Hope Trust. I light love. Free will. For the Greater Good Wills. (sic) "

Lying on the paper was a single brown feather.

Feeling like a detective, wanting to help the prosecutors and also to understand what had unfolded in the apartment the night her good friend perished, Annika read the notes and photographed each.

Later, in the basement, as if what they'd found upstairs wasn't peculiar enough, Annika opened a wooden box with a note on one side and sticks, leaves, and finger-type bowls on the other. Perhaps the strangest item discovered that day, however, was a small, primitive tower with a broken wheel on the top, made from leaves and sticks, the type of shape sometimes seen in movies as objects used in rituals. Days later, Annika called John Jordan to report what she had found. The prosecutor listened but didn't see any of it as relevant to the case. Still, it was interesting, and undoubtedly a clue into Ana Trujillo's mind.

Annika would later estimate that on that day she and Stefan's family spent perhaps thirty to forty minutes in the apartment and the basement combined. There would be much to do later, to organize and clean out Stefan's possessions, but that would wait for another day. The appointment with the probate lawyer loomed. When they left, Stefan's sister took little by which to remember her lost brother, but it was something that embodied memories, his favorite sweater.

Saddened and still grieving, they drove from The

Parklane's lot. As they did, Annika looked back and noticed that the photo she'd posted of Stefan was gone. In front of the tree stood a homeless man, undoubtedly one of the many Stefan had befriended, clutching the photo to his chest, perhaps also remembering fondly a man he'd thought of as a friend.

Chapter 18

In August, as Houston sweltered from the summer's heat, a daughter of one of the assistant district attorneys in John Jordan's office mentioned that she'd heard that Ana Trujillo had quite a reputation in the bars and restaurants clustered around the Rice Lofts.

Early on, Jordan had started talking to another of the lawyers in the DA's Office about the case, Sarah Mickelson, who worked in the domestic-violence unit. She'd been the one the morning after the murder to recommend that Jordan call in Chris Duncan, the blood expert. Mickelson had worked with Duncan on an earlier case, the stabbing of a sixty-nine-year-old man. Enthused by "the CSI stuff," Mickelson found Duncan's specialty fascinating, and in the courtroom, so had the jury.

Slender, with long straight blond hair falling about her shoulders, Mickelson looked more like an actress than a tough prosecutor, but she'd watched *Law & Order* with her grandmother and grown up wanting to "put bad guys in jail." Her five years in the Harris County District Attorney's Office had lived up to her expectations, as she investigated the cases, pulled the clues together, and heard the life stories of those involved. Among her other talents, Mickelson was a good listener, a thoughtful woman who worked with child abuse, sexual assault, and domestic-violence victims. "I'm there when the worst has happened," she said. "I'm there to give them closure and at least justice. That's a good feeling."

Sarah Mickelson

When Jordan heard about Ana's reputation in downtown Houston, he asked Mickelson to take a scouting trip with him, to go into the restaurants and ask about Trujillo. Early one evening, the two prosecutors circulated from place to place, carrying a photo of Ana with them, showing it to the managers, who put out the word that the prosecutors were there.

In between serving customers, the waiters and bartenders told their stories. Many remembered the woman with the long dark hair, the one they had to watch closely, because when she drank, she had a volatile temper. There were tales of Ana throwing drinks at waiters, shouting at patrons, acting out. Mickelson compared what she heard of Ana's angry outbursts to what she knew of the crime scene, the copious amount of blood spatter and the pool near Stefan's head, the gruesome photos of his head and face. "I thought about hitting him while he lay there, the blood spatter exploding around her and on her, and I couldn't imagine anyone continuing to strike while seeing that. The crime was pitiless."

In August, a grand jury formally indicted Ana Trujillo for the murder of Stefan Andersson.

That same month, Annika returned to Houston to put Stefan's affairs in order and clean out his apartment. The experience would be an emotional one for her. At times, she felt anger toward Stefan, frustration that he didn't seek out help. She knew that he had a big heart, and that he'd never been able to turn away anyone in need, but why, she wondered, did he keep allowing Ana Trujillo back into his life? Why couldn't he just have told her no?

As she cleaned out the kitchen cabinets, Annika disposed of the few objects Stefan kept there, mainly his unused prescription meds accumulated over the years. She smiled, remembering how she'd always thought of him as a hypochondriac, certain one day he had Lyme disease and another that he had some other malady. High on a shelf in one cabinet she discovered the keys to the Mercedes, which she'd been looking for since arriving. For a moment, she wondered why he'd stored them in such an inconvenient place. Then Annika remembered the car, still dented from Ana's accident. "Stefan must have put them there to keep her from taking the car out while he slept," Annika said. "Stefan had been such a trusting man, and I thought about how sad it was that she'd taken even that away from him."

Among Stefan's papers, Annika found the receipt from when Stefan paid to have the car fixed. Such a mess Ana Trujillo had made of his life. The meticulous scientist, so careful with his few possessions, and everything he left behind seemed damaged by their relationship, including the black-leather couch he'd bought when arriving in Houston, pocked with burn marks from Ana's cigarettes.

The days were long and hot since the power had been turned off in the apartment, and the bright sunshine streamed in the floor-to-ceiling windows. At night, Annika walked the apartment with a flashlight, an odd experience, thinking about the violence that had unfolded there.

Saddened, Annika continued to work her way through the apartment. As she did, she cleared the coffee table of Ana's art installation. It seemed such a paltry effort. The notes had been taken, but Annika photographed what was left before she threw away the dying bamboo stalk and cleared away the paper and salt. The bracelets she put into a growing pile. Ana's attorney had asked John Jordan for some of her things, but the list struck Annika as strange, not including anything but a bag of crystals and the small briefcase of her paperwork and drawings that Annika found when she'd been in Stefan's apartment that June. Not limiting the pile to be turned over to the few items on the list, Annika pulled all of Ana's things together, including a small box with twigs, notes, and a bowl inside that she'd found in storage.

Carefully, Annika photographed everything inside the boxes, to document what the woman accused of murdering Stefan had with her that night. In the process, Annika also discovered Stefan's iPhone. When she looked at the photos, she found scores of selfies and videos taken by Ana. Some of the videos were of Ana in exotic poses attempting to look sensual at Stefan's apartment, and another, a half hour long, simply examined her hand. The ones Annika found the most disturbing were taken by Ana on her nights out with Stefan, including a few in Bar 5015. In them, Stefan sat alone, nursing a glass of wine at the bar, while Ana flitted from man to man, flirting.

Ana's art box
(Courtesy of Annika Lindqvist)

When Jordan and one of the detectives arrived to pick up Ana's things and talk with her, Annika felt on edge. She turned everything over to them, and they left. Looking back, she'd assess that she was still in shock from Stefan's death. "I didn't ask any direct questions about the investigation," she said. "If I had, I assumed they wouldn't have answered."

In the murder book on the Trujillo case, accounts of the investigation accumulated. When he noticed the mention of an unidentified man in the cab in an interview with the valet at The Parklane, Sergeant Triplett called Rosemary Gomez and she told him about her common-law husband, Reagan Cannon. Days later in a recorded interview, Cannon confirmed what Gomez had said about the fare that night, talking of Ana Trujillo's anger and her drunkenness as she screamed throughout the drive from Bar 5015.

Among those who were more reluctant to talk to the police was James Wells. "James, stop feeling sorry for Ana," Chanda chided him. "It could have been you!"

Wells's attorney, Allette Williams, backed Chanda up, saying that she, too, believed that Wells as easily as Stefan could have fallen victim to Ana's inner rage. For months, Wells resisted. Then, eventually, he began to understand that the two women were right. Ana bit him without cause that afternoon, an indication of what she was capable of. "I started thinking that she could have murdered us all in our sleep," he said.

When the police asked questions, Chanda and Wells answered as honestly as they could, describing the woman Ana Trujillo had become.

In November, after they'd heard from Stefan's friends about the incident where Ana bit Stefan at Bodegas, investigators sought out Anders Berkenstam and interviewed him at his house. On that day, Stefan's friend and fellow scientist discussed how once Ana began acting strangely, he and his wife pulled back, not wanting to be around her. "She said strange things," he said, describing one day when he held a glass of water and Ana asked if he had a fish in it. Stefan, on the other hand, at least at first, didn't seem concerned by what he saw as her quirkiness.

"Stefan was really nice to her," Berkenstam said.

"See any acts of violence between the two?" Sergeant Triplett asked. "I heard about an incident at a restaurant. Can you explain that?"

Berkenstam did, saying Ana "appeared suddenly, as if out of nowhere . . . She was extremely aggressive. She approaches him and bites his cheek . . . It was quite bad . . . There was a real bite mark on the cheek."

As she so often did to have an excuse to see someone later, Ana left behind something that day, her bag with her laptop. Determined never to see her again, Stefan refused to take it home and left it with the restaurant manager, who'd brought alcohol to clean his wound.

Later that afternoon at another restaurant, frightened and hiding from Ana, Stefan became emotional and cried. "Ana's done a lot of crazy things," he said. Listing a few, he talked of the night she cut the refrigerator hose, the night she took his car and banged it up.

Stefan, Berkenstam said, had told him that on one occasion, "She was trying to strangle him!"

"Did he ever tell you that he loved her?" Triplett asked.

"In the beginning, definitely," he said. "Stefan was a genuinely nice guy. I got the impression that he regarded her as his ex-girlfriend."

"Did you ever see Mr. Andersson physically attack Ana?" Triplett asked.

"Never!" Berkenstam answered.

While law enforcement investigated her case, Ana was moved into Pod 2B, the jail's mental-health unit, after she fought with another inmate. As the weeks passed, she complained of dizziness and anxiety, especially before court dates, and said she sometimes "shook all over."

Talking to one of the mental-health professionals on the staff, she said she had flashbacks to her childhood and instances of abuse.

Attending psychoeducational group sessions at the jail, Ana chose one on building healthy relationships. "Patient reports feeling 'peaceful,' states she thinks relationships are characterized by 'how you're getting along with others.' She also states, 'There are different levels of relationships' . . . Patient discussed her past relationships . . . said her most important relationships are with her children."

In the month since he'd been hired, Jack Carroll had been trying to get Ana's bail lowered, but the judge steadfastly refused. Every time Carroll saw her, Ana begged him to do all he could, but while he wasn't charging her for the case, he wasn't eager to put up her bail, and she had no funds. Ana's mother had testified at one of the hearings that the family would watch over her if she were released, but the judge steadfastly denied Carroll's motions.

Meanwhile, one of Ana's friends continued to struggle with what to do. First Christi Suarez's ex-boyfriend told her that Stefan had contacted him, then, as the months passed, other friends said they received psychic messages from someone who needed her help. Suarez assumed it had to be Stefan. "How can I help him?" Suarez asked her friend Raul Rodriguez.

"You know her. You know he was afraid of her. You have to defend this man," he answered.

On the news, Suarez usually heard the case mentioned in the framework of domestic violence, and that worried her. What if people believed it was true, that Stefan Andersson was the violent one? "I knew he never touched her," said Suarez. "And I felt bad for his family, when he was just trying to help Ana."

Yet the revelations in the media about the amount of alcohol Ana drank that night and her strange past had taken a toll on her image. When he took the case, Jack Carroll expected an outpouring of concern in Ana's favor from the anti–domestic violence community in Houston and across the United States, backers coming forward to help fund her defense, since she described herself as a victim of intimate-partner abuse. But that hadn't happened. In fact, as more came out about Ana Trujillo, the support appeared to be evaporating.

Chapter 19

That fall, Ana filed a grievance at the jail, charging that when she was admitted in June the staff ignored a gash on the back of her head. She complained of light sensitivity and migraines, and demanded an MRI of her skull. When she talked to a nurse, she claimed the head wound could have been responsible for her "confusion" at the time of Stefan's killing. "Client said that she talked to her mom recently and was upset because her mother said something on the phone about not trusting her," the nurse noted. The patient appeared moderately depressed and anxious, "likely due to the seriousness of her case."

In November, Annika Lindqvist walked out of Stefan's apartment for the last time, locking it behind her and dropping the key at the concierge desk.

About that time, Anders Berkenstam and his wife, Pernilla, perhaps shaken by Stefan's death, moved back to Sweden. Months later, when John Jordan offered to fly him in for the trial, the scientist declined, citing health concerns. When Jordan suggested conducting his testimony via Skype, Berkenstam also refused, labeling it as too stressful. Preparing for the trial early the coming year, Jordan felt frustrated. Berkenstam was the only one to actually see Ana bite Stefan in a completely unprovoked attack, something Jordan wanted jurors to hear.

Setting aside his disappointment, Jordan continued to

prepare for trial, enlisting the aid of an expert on domestic violence, Jennifer Varela, a clinical social worker and the Harris County District Attorney's director of family violence services. Still assessing the fairness of Ana Trujillo's prosecution, the prosecutor wanted someone outside his immediate office to review all the records. "We wanted a true believer, someone who worked with domestic-violence victims to look at the case. We thought maybe she would look at the records and call us and say, 'This woman is the victim,'" he said. "It was a lot to overcome, with Trujillo saying it was self-defense, and we felt like the world was watching."

An earthy woman with curly dark hair and a gentle manner, Varela spent hours poring over the records. What she learned was how others saw Stefan, as a kind man who lacked the ability to say no to others, who let people take advantage of him to sidestep any conflict. Looking at his account of his childhood, she came to the conclusion that this weakness was a result of never feeling safe as a child. As an adult, Stefan became the extreme opposite of his father, totally nonaggressive. The alcohol may have served as a way to self-soothe, to help mediate depression with its roots in his childhood.

"I'd never had a victim so meek," Varela said. "While it is often embarrassing and hard for all victims to seek help, it can be doubly so for men, who see themselves as wimpy. They don't want to be seen that way."

That the evidence showed Stefan never fought back took a particular toll on John Jordan. There were but a few strands of Ana's hair in Stefan's dead fist, and no aggressive, only defensive, wounds on his body. Detectives had seen no cuts, no bleeding, and no fresh contusions on Ana. "That bothered John a lot," said Sarah Mickelson. "That Stefan just lay there and took it. That was hard to understand."

In contrast, Jennifer Varela read the reports of Ana Trujillo and her frequent angry episodes that often resulted in acting out violently yet being so charming and apologetic afterward that she suffered no repercussions. In one interview, a restaurant owner explained how Ana hit one of his staff. Yet the next day, he let her back into the restaurant. "That was just Ana," the man said.

Before long, Varela saw Ana Trujillo as someone who was manipulative, who craved attention, and who, when intoxicated, was filled with rage. Trujillo was a risk-taker, one who knew no boundaries, who could be charming and exhilarating, but over time became exhausting to be around. For men, Varela thought early relationships with Ana were probably exciting, before the craziness took over.

One of the deciding factors for Varela, as she weighed the relationship, was that when she compared all the witness accounts of the relationship, she found no indications that Ana had ever displayed any injuries she claimed to have suffered at Stefan's hands. Yet Stefan had a black eye, and he'd confided often in friends about Ana's attacks, the times she came up from behind and jumped him, that she got rough during sex, and that she'd tried to choke him. When she examined the case, Varela thought of how Stefan must have felt, how embarrassed he must have been to have let Ana take control of his life.

In the end, for Varela, there was one overwhelming deciding factor: "Everyone who knew Ana Trujillo told the same story, that at first Stefan loved her, but that ended. She said she was still his girlfriend, but it was obvious that Dr. Andersson wanted nothing to do with her."

When Varela viewed the video of Trujillo's interview with police, she saw an extremely narcissistic woman, one who justified everything she did by blaming others, and one who took things she'd done to others and turned them around, in her accounts claiming to have been the victim.

What set off that final altercation? Varela wondered if Ana, having left her phone in the cab, had used Stefan's and seen his text messages with the new woman he was dating. Or perhaps, after that disastrous cab ride, Stefan had finally announced that he was done with Ana and wanted her forever out of his life. Describing what happened that awful night, Varela said, "Ana flies into a rage, starts hitting him, and doesn't stop."

In Ana Trujillo, Varela saw traits she'd documented in other women who are abusive to their significant others, including a long history of violence toward people other than their partners. While men most often used violence to control and target their spouses, in Varela's experience, women acted more indiscriminately and were motivated by anger. "For these types of women, this is a way of dealing with the world," she said.

Chapter 20

In the Harris County Jail, Ana continued to sit in on group sessions on topics such as: Listening to My Inner Messages; Challenging Harmful Self-talk; Restructuring Cognitive Distortions; and Reacting to the Outside World.

In one session, Ana blamed her current state of affairs on her past, saying that her worldview changed when she was "violently attacked by a coworker," not identifying the person. She talked of Stefan, again calling him a Dr. Jekyll and Mr. Hyde, who suffered mood swings. In her account, although not attracted to him, she tried to heal him using what she called her "special electromagnetic abilities for bringing injuries to the surface, so that he could see how powerful her methods were and help her develop the science for them."

"The client's beliefs have been catastrophically challenged," the social worker wrote. "May be delusional . . ."

In a motion hearing on the case, Jack Carroll again asked for a reduced bail, and Judge Brock Thomas turned him down. That, Carroll said, left him shouting at Ana through the Plexiglas with deputies in the area, feeling unable to prepare for the trial. When he watched the video of her interview with the police, he consistently came away believing that she told the truth. "She did what she had to do to get away from him," Carroll said. "To me, it was a pure case of self-defense."

Around the world, the case continued to attract headlines. London's *Daily Mail* ran an article just before Thanksgiving with a photo of Stefan Andersson in a bar, one with his hands raised above his head, as if surrendering. In the comment section on the Net, one reader typed: "In the feminist America (sic) legal system, women can get away with just about anything."

"You're afraid of a 44-year-old woman?" another poster answered. "You just lost your man card, Dude."

In December, Annika Lindqvist met with John Jordan and Sarah Mickelson at the DA's office. By then, Jordan had asked Mickelson to second-chair the trial, act as his cocounsel, and she'd agreed. Jordan thought they made a good team for the case, balancing well. He was more laid-back, while she was formal in the courtroom. That she had a history prosecuting domestic-violence cases gave her added credibility in a case where that was one of the issues. "Sarah has a good reputation, and she's compassionate," he said.

At the meeting with the two prosecutors, an animated Annika asked a long list of questions, still trying to figure out the case, coming up with ideas and suggestions, wanting them to understand Stefan. Eager to do whatever she could for her lost friend, she'd given them a time line of Stefan's life, from his birth in Sweden, through his schooling and career, concluding with what she knew about his relationship with Ana Trujillo. Rethinking the meeting, on her way home to Dallas, Annika worried that she'd said too much. Stopping to send a text, she typed to Mickelson, "Sorry about any rambling. I have so much I want to tell you about Stefan."

"You have too much on your shoulders," the prosecutor responded. "You need to let us help you."

For the first time since Stefan's death, when Annika read that text, she felt the weight lift.

In December, after months of trying to gain his client's release, Jack Carroll found an ally. Ana's mother had pulled together the $10,000 needed to put down with a bail bonds-man to get Ana out of jail.

That news again made the papers, and when Carroll talked to reporters, he told them that he expected that self-defense would be a major issue in the case and that there would be evidence that Ana Trujillo was being abused by Stefan Andersson. "I'm going to have a limited time to try to get a jury to understand that although Ana has had problems in the past, she is a kind person at heart," he told one reporter.

As John Jordan and Sarah Mickelson considered the remarks of the man who would be their adversary in the courtroom, they felt relieved. Having done their homework, they knew Carroll would have a difficult time portraying Stefan as an abuser. What Jordan had worried about was that Carroll would take another tack, using the eggshell de-fense, claiming that Ana had overreacted and killed Stefan because of a buildup of prior violence and victimization in her life. Using that approach, Carroll could have argued that prior injuries Ana suffered at the hands of others rendered her as fragile as an eggshell. In such an argument, her past would have made her hypersensitive and resulted in mis-interpreting Stefan's actions, leading her to genuinely feel threatened and fear for her life.

Since Carroll chose a self-defense argument, however, that wasn't on the table.

The afternoon Ana was released from jail, articles ran in newspapers announcing that the infamous stiletto killer was free on bond. Hours later, she showed up at James Wells's apartment, knocking on the door. Chanda Ellison answered, thinking that the landlord wanted to pick up the rent.

"Hey, Chanda," Ana said, smiling as if nothing had hap-pened.

"Are you kidding me?" Ellison responded. "The same person you left here still exists. I speak for both of us, James and me, when I tell you that you cannot be here. You are going to walk away from this door and never think about coming here again."

With that, Chanda closed the door.

The phone rang incessantly for days after, Ana calling, presumably looking for a place to stay.

Her daughter out of jail and awaiting trial, Ana's mother rented her a small apartment in Houston, so that Ana could be close to Jack Carroll's office to prepare. Not long after, on a downtown street, Teresa Montoya recognized Ana despite dark glasses and a floppy hat. "You look like hell," the hairdresser said.

"I know," answered Ana, whose hair was growing out, streaked with grey.

That afternoon, Montoya skipped work and the two women went to the Aquarium, a downtown amusement venue with a Ferris wheel and an aquatic carousel, restaurants and games. "We acted like little kids," said Montoya.

They ate sushi, and afterward Montoya took Ana to the salon. There Montoya colored and cut her friend's hair. On her ankle, Ana wore an electronic monitor and had to return to her apartment by nine. Montoya drove her to the apartment, where Ana thanked her.

Early in 2014, at the DA's office, Mickelson and Jordan continued to prepare their case. To get ready for trial, scheduled for April, they met with Dr. Ross, the assistant medical examiner, to discuss the autopsy. During the meeting, Ross told the prosecutors what they expected to hear, that unlike in the movies, she couldn't pinpoint an exact time of death, but the forensic pathologist estimated that it might have taken thirty minutes up to an hour for Stefan to have bled out and had his heart stop. While the death tied to the head trauma, the pathologist also mentioned that she couldn't rule out that Stefan had suffered some type of heart event from a rush of adrenaline pumping through him during the attack. And she still believed it was very possible that his breathing had been restricted, either by strangulation, from Ana sitting on his chest, or both.

Looking at the time line, reconstructing what they knew about the events of that night, the prosecutors judged that the most likely scenario was that the altercation began at 2:13, when Stefan's next-door neighbor heard a man yelling. That continued for only minutes, then the apartment fell quiet. Approximately an hour and twenty minutes lapsed before Ana called 9-1-1, ample time for the first responders to have found the blood coagulating and drying on the carpet.

Finally, in February, DNA reports on the swabs taken from the scene arrived, and they, too, suggested that the clash had been one-sided. All the samples matched blood taken from Stefan's body during the autopsy. None of the blood on the murder scene tied back to Ana Trujillo.

That information in hand, the prosecutors discussed how they saw the upcoming trial, and the stance they would take in the courtroom. One thing Jordan considered interesting was the tarot-card book, along with the stories he heard of Ana's interest in witchcraft and the occult. Was that something they wanted to put in front of the jury? "It was so bizarre," he said. "She had such strange behavior, you just throw it out there and the jury decides what to believe, as long as it is credible evidence."

Mickelson, on the other hand, thought of the book's being open to the death card as a strange coincidence, something they could mention at the trial but not explore further, not something that was important. She worried that bringing up the witchcraft stories could muddy the case. After thinking over the situation, Jordan agreed.

Lining up their witnesses, one they decided not to put on the stand was Jim Carroll—the hotel manager who said Ana told him she'd hit anyone who tried to "mess with" her with her stiletto heel. That call was Jordan's decision. Carroll had given multiple interviews on the case, and Jordan was uncomfortable with the situation. "I tend to be skeptical of people who court the press," he said. "I felt unsure about it and decided the comment could cut both ways."

As they prepared, they, too, considered how they would present the man at the center of the case, Stefan. As kind as he was, as gentle, Stefan was flawed; he drank heavily and could be considered an alcoholic. Yet neither prosecutor thought that was something the jury would focus on. "Clearly, it was an addiction," said Jordan. "But people adored him, and I started to see him as Norm on *Cheers*, shy but friendly."

"Stefan Andersson had his own demons," said Mickelson. "He was lonely. He had friends across the world, but he lived alone. He suffered from depression, and he drank too much. In the end, I thought he just felt sorry for Ana, and perhaps she was companionship. I thought the jury would understand that."

In the weeks before the trial, the prosecutors held final interviews with witnesses; two were the cab driver and her common-law husband, Rosemary Gomez and Reagan Cannon. During that meeting, something surprising happened, when Cannon told the prosecutor two facts he had forgotten earlier: that Ana had left her phone in the cab, and that in the middle of the night, Cannon called Stefan's phone, and Ana answered. When Jordan asked where Ana's phone was, Cannon said he still had it at home.

The next day, Jordan sent an officer to pick up Ana's phone from Cannon, and the prosecutor subpoenaed both sets of cell-phone records. Once they arrived, Jordan found the call Cannon mentioned listed at 3:37 A.M. That piece of evidence was a missing link. For the first time, Jordan understood why Ana called 9-1-1 when she had. Wherever her mind had gone after the killing, whatever she was doing in that apartment while Stefan Andersson lay dying, the call broke the trance and brought her back to reality. She'd suddenly realized what she had done, that she couldn't cover it up, and that she needed to call and report the killing.

Finally, just a week before opening statements, Jordan

and Mickelson went to the HPD property room with the two
CSU officers who'd worked the case, Duncan and Aguilera,
to view the physical evidence one more time. Out of a box,
they pulled Ana Trujillo's high-heel shoe, still covered in
Stefan's hair and blood. Jordan looked at it, put it back in the
box, and felt ready to proceed.

Still, there was much to consider.

In the days leading up to the trial, the tension built, as
Jordan and Mickelson wondered if Carroll would put Ana's
medical records from the jail into evidence, the ones in
which she showed bruises to the nursing staff and claimed
to have suffered injuries during the fight with Stefan. If
Carroll did, the prosecutors thought it could help their case.
"That would open the door for us to bring in James Wells
and the medical records from the fight with Chanda Ellison," said Jordan. "That would help us show who Ana Trujillo truly is."

To prepare in case that happened, Jordan asked Wells and
Ellison to his office, and they brought their attorney, Allette
Williams. That day they discussed the physical evidence,
and Williams, who knew how Ana had bitten Wells, would
later say she told the prosecutors she, too, believed that Ana
was indeed capable of striking without warning. Yet her
client equivocated when he discussed the woman he'd once
tried to help. "James Wells still cared about Ana Trujillo,"
said Jordan. "Despite everything, he still made every excuse
for her."

To the prosecutors, however, that didn't matter. What
they wanted to hear and did hear was that his story was consistent: that Ana had attacked him without reason. As much
as Wells cared about Ana, he wasn't willing to lie for her,
and his story hadn't changed.

At the same time, just a block from the DA's headquarters,
in his own second-floor office in a building next to a bail
bondsman, Jack Carroll, too, worked on the Trujillo case.

His hopes that domestic-violence-victims organizations would come to his client's aid had evaporated, and Carroll, along with the formidable cost of clearing his calendar for the preparation and the trial, was in the difficult position of personally paying for expert witnesses. "It cost me some money," he said. "But I figured it was a high-profile case, so it was worth it. And I thought the court would reimburse me after the trial."

One of those experts was Dr. Lee Ann Grossberg, a forensic pathologist who worked briefly for the Harris County Medical Examiner's Office before setting up a consulting service. Carroll hired her to review the autopsy and crime-scene photos.

After she did, Grossberg told Carroll something he found interesting, that in her opinion, while admittedly garish, Stefan's wounds were superficial, none fracturing his skull or facial bones. In fact, Grossberg wondered if Stefan might have died of a heart attack. Similar to one of the medical examiner's theories, Grossberg thought it was possible that, terrorized by the altercation, Stefan's body flooded with adrenaline, driving up his blood pressure and leading to his death. If Stefan hadn't died of a heart attack but loss of blood from his dozens of wounds, Grossberg agreed that Stefan might have lingered. Either way, Carroll was left wondering if there was the possibility that medical personnel might have been able to save Stefan's life.

On the 9-1-1 tape, Ana claimed Stefan was alive when she called, and, after talking to Grossberg, Carroll decided that might have been true. Yet there was no evidence that the first responders made any effort to restart Stefan's heart or to give him CPR. Plus, in Carroll's view, the dispatcher took too long on the phone before sending EMTs to the scene.

Thinking through the possibilities, Carroll developed a theory in direct contrast to the prosecutors'. In his view, it wasn't Ana's fault that Stefan died. Instead, she struck in self-defense, then the medical personnel hadn't rendered proper aid. "If 9-1-1 had done their job and the EMTs had performed CPR, Stefan Andersson might still be alive."

Along with forming his argument for the trial, Carroll prepared his witnesses. As they worked on the case, Ana told her story many times, and he continued to believe she was justified the night she killed Stefan. As he saw it, the jury would believe her as well, and he had a chance at a not-guilty verdict. "I thought I had a good case," he said.

During their meetings, what the defense attorney saw in his client wasn't the troubled woman others described but a strong woman with a history of being abused. "She got around these alcoholic weaklings. She's kind of macho," he said. "They'd get a belly full of booze and push her a few times, and you're going to get it, that's when storm clouds would gather."

In his own dealings with Trujillo, Carroll saw those clouds gathering. When he disagreed with Ana, although completely sober, her eyes flashed, and her mood changed. "You just don't do that with her. I saw that. Tried to boss her around a couple of times, and it didn't work with her . . . put her heels in . . . she's a little aggressive."

Carroll, who'd been raised by a working mom, a strong woman who'd moved him to a rough part of Miami, where he constantly had to defend himself, saw Ana as like women he'd known as a boy. "She was a woman who liked to drink with the boys, got drunk, and acted out," he said. "Maybe she could have walked away, but she didn't. I didn't when I was a kid in Miami."

Yet the defense attorney worried how a jury would see his client. Carroll found that Ana had a difficult time focusing. As she had during her police interview, in their discussions Ana segued from one relationship to another, unable to concentrate on Carroll's questions, her train of thought habitually running off track.

Understanding her limitations, Carroll worried about Ana testifying. Yet in a self-defense case, that seemed mandatory. To find her not guilty, jurors would want to hear Ana describe why she took Stefan's life. His saving grace, Carroll thought, would be if the prosecutors played his client's police interview for the jury. If that happened, the jurors would hear Ana tell her story without having to put her on the stand.

"I was hoping," said Carroll. "But I didn't know what they would do."

Chapter 21

Stefan Andersson would have enjoyed the bright spring sunshine on the morning of March 31, 2014. After rising early and gazing out over the golf course through his apartment's vast windows, showered and shaved, he might have walked in the door at the Hermann Park Grill and ordered his favorite veggie omelet. His laptop open on the table before him, the morning would have dissolved away as he researched pertinent studies for an upcoming court case, one where he'd been hired to testify as an expert witness. As afternoon approached, however, the laptop powered down, Stefan, a glass of wine in hand, could have claimed a black wrought-iron chair on the grill's patio. For the remainder of that day like so many others, he could have happily basked in the bright Texas sun.

Instead, at 9 A.M. on that date, Stefan's cremated remains were encased in a canister beside his photo on Annika Lindqvist's Dallas living-room table, and Ana Trujillo, her thick black hair pulled back and anchored by no-nonsense clips, sans makeup, wearing a business suit with a red blouse, sat nervously next to Jack Carroll, waiting to begin the first day of her trial. On the fifteenth floor of the Harris County Criminal Courthouse at 1201 Franklin Street, in the 338th District Court, on what was undoubtedly one of the most important days of her life, Trujillo bore scant resemblance to the ebullient Latina in flashy tight clothes and sexy stiletto heels Stefan had known and once loved. "Ana's mother told her to look as plain as possible," said a family member. "I thought it was a mistake, not to be herself. But Trina thought Ana shouldn't look like what the prosecutor said she was, a woman who lived off of men."

Ana Trujillo in the courtroom next to her lawyers
*(Pool photo, Brett Coomer/*Houston Chronicle)

At about nine twenty that morning, Judge Brock Thomas, a matter-of-fact former prosecutor and criminal-defense attorney who'd first been appointed to the bench, then elected in 2012, called the trial to order, instructing Trujillo to rise to hear the indictment. Representing the state of Texas, John Jordan solemnly read the charges: "Ana Trujillo, aka Ana Fox, hereinafter styled the defendant . . . on or about June 9, 2013, did then and there unlawfully intend to cause serious bodily injury to Stefan Andersson . . . and did cause the death of the complainant by intentionally and knowingly committing an act clearly dangerous to human life, namely, by striking the complainant with a high-heel shoe." Because of the bruising discovered during the autopsy,

Jordan continued on, reading the alternative possibilities for cause of death, first that Ana had suffocated Stefan by impeding his breathing by "applying pressure to the torso of the complainant." Secondly: that she'd murdered Andersson by strangulation, tightening her grasp around his neck.

As the courtroom fell silent, the crowd in the gallery stirred. In the second row on the right sat Annika with Stefan's two sisters, Anneli and Marie, and one of his nieces. Nervous, Annika hadn't slept particularly well in the nights leading up to the trial, the stress wearing on her. Meanwhile, Ana's family watched from the benches on the left, Gene and Trina Tharp, and one of Trina's sisters, who'd traveled from Mexico to support her niece. The Ana she'd known had been a kind young girl, one much removed from the woman on trial.

Around the families bunched a crowd of spectators sandwiched into every available seat. Some were simply curious about the sensational case and wanted to see it play out in the courtroom. The trial had also attracted a mob of media, making up three rows of reporters from local, national, and international outlets, print and broadcast, including a *Good Morning America* producer.

The reading of the indictment concluded, Sarah Mickelson stood to address the jury.

As they'd prepared for trial, Jordan and Mickelson had discussed whether or not to do an opening statement. Jordan was ambivalent, while Mickelson believed jurors needed a road map of their case. Because she'd argued so passionately in favor of an opening, Jordan decided Mickelson was the best one to initially address the jurors. Now that moment had come, and Mickelson quietly began: "On June 9, 2013, a 9-1-1 call went out for an assault in progress. That's unusual for this part of town, Hermann Park, the Museum District."

From the 9-1-1 call, Mickelson painted the picture of that morning in The Parklane's 18B, describing the first glimpse of Stefan's bloodied body in the hallway. "It looked like something out of a horror movie," she said. But the story

Sarah Mickelson addressing the jury
*(Pool photo, Brett Coomer/*Houston Chronicle)

had begun months before, when Trujillo and Andersson
first met. From the beginning, the couple "was not a good
match." Stefan was habitually mild-mannered, while Ana
had an explosive temper. And early on there were reports of
her odd behavior. "You're going to learn that as their relationship progressed, it also deteriorated."

Always, Mickelson was mindful of the hurdle before the
prosecution, the presumption that when violence enters a romantic relationship, the woman is the victim. That night,
as Stefan walked through the lobby, after the squabble in
the cab, Mickelson contended that he had finally lost all patience with Ana, realizing that "she was more trouble than
she was worth."

Not even fifteen minutes later, the sound of an argument
and a shaking wall signaled a quarrel, then more than an
hour of silence in 18B before Ana Trujillo called for help.
What did she do all that time, with Stefan bleeding on the
hallway floor?

Mickelson suggested that in this case forensics told the

story, most importantly the blood evidence on the floor, the walls, on Trujillo. Then there were the defendant's strange practices, evidenced in writings she left behind, ones that talked "about forgiveness and higher forces, along with her purse and a tarot-card book. Coincidentally, it's opened to the death card."

Such an odd case, with so much strange evidence. Would Mickelson and Jordan be able to draw jurors a convincing map?

Jack Carroll had a lot riding on the trial; he'd invested time and money. And now, after months of preparation, it began. The lanky lawyer with the slight swagger in his walk unfolded from the chair and sauntered toward the jury box. In contrast to Mickelson's depiction of the evidence, Carroll proposed his theory: "You're going to learn, and the evidence is going to show, a sordid and tragic tale of two very lonely people who were progressively going downhill. You're going to learn that there's alcoholism involved with this, that there's spousal abuse."

In the gallery, Annika bristled, as Carroll branded Stefan an out-of-control alcoholic. "You're going to hear a normal day for Mr. Andersson was a full-tilt boogie, drinking," the attorney said. Stefan's addiction, Carroll maintained, set the stage for his death by leading him to be domineering and abusive toward the woman in his life, a woman Carroll described as Stefan's fiancée, Ana Trujillo.

From drinking in the early-morning hours to getting the shakes if he didn't have a beer or glass of wine by noon, in Carroll's opening statement Stefan's life revolved around his thirst for alcohol. "He would drink, and he'd drink, and he'd drink." And when he drank, Carroll insisted, Stefan Andersson became abusive.

When jurors listened to the 9-1-1 call, Carroll contended, they would hear a woman desperate to save the life of the man she loved. For at that point, Stefan wasn't yet dead. In fact in Carroll's view, Stefan's death wasn't caused by his injuries but by emergency personnel who took too long to arrive and didn't begin lifesaving measures. "I submit to you that they didn't even check him," said Carroll. "There was a lot of blood, and they declared him dead."

Once Andersson was declared deceased, Carroll said, all eyes turned on Ana Trujillo. "They decided like that, that she was guilty of murder," he said, snapping his fingers.

There was evidence, he said, to back up his theories. Where Mickelson said Trujillo had no injuries, the defense attorney insisted that wasn't true. "I want you to look. I want you to see her face, where you can see a black eye forming. When they take her clothes off, there's a photographer there . . . he wants to get her hands, because she said she was bitten. They want to do their investigation to back up their theory of murder."

Would the jurors agree?

Time and again, Carroll returned to the subject of domestic violence. All Ana Trujillo wanted to do that fateful night was leave, to go to Waco to see her family, but a drunk and angry Stefan Andersson attacked her. It followed a pattern familiar to domestic-violence experts, he said, and that further proved his view of the case. "You're going to hear that when the woman decides to leave, that's the most dangerous time."

Before the jury, Carroll alluded to the eggshell theory John Jordan worried the defense would concentrate on, that damaged by prior abuse from others, Trujillo misjudged and overreacted. Carroll, however, didn't dwell on this aspect of the case, sure that self-defense made his best argument, concluding: "The evidence is going to show that Ana Trujillo did the only thing that she could do to get away from Mr. Andersson."

Opening arguments ended, and on the stand was the prosecution's first witness, Annika Lindqvist, whose usual broad smile appeared tight and tired. Stefan had been one of her great friends for many years, and she now understood where the defense was going, that his character would be assailed.

"Who is this?" John Jordan asked as he showed her a photo of Stefan in his laboratory at the University of Houston.

"It's Stefan," Annika replied. The photo was then shown to the jurors, who saw for the first time the face of the man at the center of the trial. In response to questions, Annika explained Stefan's education and his specialization in reproductive science. They'd worked closely, and for a brief time their relationship became romantic. Recounting why it ended, she cited her love of nature and his fascination with the bustle of a busy city. "We just didn't have that much in common."

In his opening, Carroll had focused on Andersson's drinking. Now Jordan asked Lindqvist: "Was Stefan someone who liked to drink?"

Yes, he did, she said, but she added not to the extent that it had become a problem for him at work or socially. She also said that Stefan had never been a mean drunk, and, in fact, would become even more polite and mild-mannered.

The Stefan she knew was once an athletic man, but in his advancing years, never used the gym membership she teased him about owning. Although single, he was far from a solitary figure, constantly in touch with friends and family in Texas and around the world. Annika's Stefan was a man who surrounded himself with friends, one who enjoyed life.

"Was his drinking one of the reasons you broke up?" Carroll prodded, as his opportunity to question Lindqvist began. She denied that it was or that Stefan's drinking affected his job. That was something Carroll had prepared for. He had a motion pending before the judge, one to introduce Stefan's personnel files from UH into evidence. In it was information regarding the dead man's stint in rehab. The judge had ruled that the defense attorney couldn't bring the information in unless a witness personally knew about Stefan's stay at the PaRC rehab hospital. "Did you know if the University of Houston ever sent him to a drug rehabilitation program?" Carroll asked.

"Yes, they did," she answered. With that, Jack Carroll had what he needed to ask more questions about Stefan's stay in the twelve-step program. At the time, Stefan had been off center, Annika explained, under stress in a new city. He'd been drinking more than usual, throwing his electrolytes out of balance, and he'd collapsed.

Running with the opportunity, Carroll asked what effects alcohol can have, and Annika, from her expertise in biology, listed the possibilities from physical illnesses such as liver disease to emotional and psychological effects, resulting in irrational behavior. But that wasn't the Stefan she knew. "He wasn't drunk drunk. He drank, but he wasn't a drunk," she explained.

"So you're telling the jury he wasn't an alcoholic?" he countered.

Annika shrugged slightly. "No. Of course, he was an alcoholic." He hadn't stopped drinking, she maintained, but after rehab, he drank less. Yet Carroll insinuated the many friends she described Stefan as having were bartenders and waitresses, and that his life revolved around alcohol. Frustrated, Lindqvist countered, "Stefan knew a lot of people. He didn't judge if they were waitresses or if they were professors at the university."

"Isn't it true that Dr. Andersson was basically a loner, and he spent most of his time alone in bars and restaurants drinking?" Carroll asked.

Stefan did frequent restaurants and bars, but not alone, she said, instead running with a group of friends. But how much did Annika know about Stefan's life once he moved to Houston? Carroll queried. For instance, what did she know about the final day of her friend's life? Stefan, she answered, was on a sabbatical, redirecting his career, and she imagined he'd stuck to his usual routine, going "from one of his

258   Kathryn Casey

places to another, talking, socializing, being friendly, drinking, and eating."

From the very beginning, it seemed, the trial's battle lines were drawn, and the territory fought over was Stefan's character.

Through his questions, Carroll attempted to whittle away at the image of Stefan as a distinguished man of science. For a professor, Carroll suggested Stefan's eighty-thousand-dollar salary seemed low, although Annika countered that it wasn't unusual for a PhD working in research. When Carroll implied that Stefan had been fired from the University of Houston, Annika explained that, in the world of research, grant money often dried up, and scientists were forced to look for new funding.

"You didn't talk to him; you don't know what he did?" Carroll charged, returning to Stefan's final day. "So you don't know what happened?"

"No," she answered.

Both sides had organized their cases based on their trial strategies, and with his second witness, John Jordan intended to counter the scenario the defense attorney painted in opening arguments of Stefan as a lover who became violent when Ana threatened to leave. In fact, the prosecutor planned to show that Stefan had moved on and wanted her out of his life. To prove his point, John Jordan brought to the stand a woman who shared his last name—although they weren't related—the woman Stefan dated during the final months of his life.

In a business suit, her dark hair pulled back, Janette Jordan's English accent filled the courtroom as she described the Stefan she knew: "Very charming . . . very pleasant, very soothing to be around, very comforting, very intelligent." As she portrayed it, at the time of his death, the relationship was blossoming. When the prosecutor asked if the connection was turning romantic, she said, "Absolutely."

Throughout Annika's testimony, Ana displayed little reaction. But with Stefan's girlfriend on the stand, Ana stared intently. If she'd known about Stefan's love interest, this was the first time Ana saw her, and the woman on trial appeared to be miffed and sizing up her rival. Trujillo's look of disdain remained as Janette Jordan talked about the brunch date she and Stefan had planned for the day he died.

As always, some things weren't allowed in the courtroom, including hearsay; Stefan had talked about Trujillo with the new woman in his life, describing his ex-girlfriend as "crazy." But the jury wouldn't hear that. Instead, all that the judge permitted was a milder phrase, that Janette Jordan's impression was that Stefan was "frustrated" over his relationship with his ex-girlfriend.

In contrast, Carroll's first question made Stefan sound lecherous, an older man who lived with Ana and planned to marry her while dating Janette on the side. "Was he trying to have a relationship with you after he proposed to her?" he asked.

"I have no idea," Janette Jordan answered.

The day ground on in the courtroom, and the testimony continued, including from a handful of the Hermann Park Golf Course Grill staff who described Stefan for the jury, from his arrivals for breakfast, to his first glass of merlot around noon. They all agreed he was a polite man, and none said they'd ever witnessed any anger, not even at Ana Trujillo although she'd taunted him, shouted, and made scenes.

"Did you ever see Dr. Andersson yell at Ms. Trujillo?" Sarah Mickelson asked Erika Elizondo. She answered that she hadn't ever heard him raise his voice. "If you were to describe one of the parties as being aggressive, who would that be?"

"Ms. Trujillo," Elizondo answered.

On the afternoon that Ana shouted at Stefan, then

walked out with another man, the aging professor sat head bowed, appearing sad, and embarrassed. And when Elizondo noticed Stefan's black eye, he refused to say how it happened.

With the same employees, Jack Carroll inquired more about Stefan's habits. Yes, he came early and stayed late, and all agreed there were times when he seemed intoxicated and a few where they told him they could no longer serve him. Yet what they didn't say was that at some point Andersson reacted with anger.

On the stand, Rosemary Gomez appeared nervous, and she grimaced at times, as if she preferred being anywhere but testifying at a murder trial. Yes, she was the cabbie who picked Stefan and Ana up at Bar 5015 shortly before 2 A.M. on June 9 of the previous year. On that night, Ana Trujillo first lashed out at Gomez, then Stefan and Cannon. "From the moment they got in my cab, it was a problem. . . . She was angry because I wasn't doing what she said. . . . She was mad at Mr. Andersson for not saying nothing to me. . . . He was just sitting in the back of the cab as quiet as can be and just calm."

At The Parklane, Trujillo's tirade continued when she discovered the locked cab door. By the time Gomez was alone with Stefan, the driver feared for him so much that she held his hands and prayed. "Let me take you to a motel," she suggested.

"I'll be okay," he said. The next day, she saw the news reports, the video of The Parklane and Trujillo in an orange jailhouse jumpsuit, wearing handcuffs. Identifying the disruptive woman who'd been in her cab, Gomez pointed at Ana Trujillo.

"Did Mr. Andersson appear completely sober to you?" Jack Carroll asked Gomez.

"Yes," she answered.

"So, in your opinion, he wasn't drinking?"

"In my opinion, he was just quiet," she explained.

"You lied to the police about having your common-law husband with you?" During his direct examination, John Jordan had already introduced the fact that Gomez hadn't mentioned Reagan Cannon because having him in the cab violated company rules, but Carroll took it a step further, questioning Gomez's truthfulness.

"Did you happen to know that Ana was at that bar with Mr. Andersson for six hours begging to leave the entire time?" Carroll asked. Gomez didn't answer after Jordan objected, and the judge sustained it.

"How much did he give you?"

"Twenty dollars on the credit card," Gomez said.

"For a seven-dollar fare?"

There's a practice some attorneys call "kissing the ugly baby." It's the need to address problems with one's own witnesses, embracing what could be disturbing if heard from the other side. John Jordan did this with Reagan Cannon on the stand. "You have, to put it modestly, some prior convictions?"

"Multiple," Cannon admitted. With that, Jordan listed them for jurors, including forgery, credit-card abuse, burglary, theft, and possession of a controlled substance. Yet why Cannon rode with Gomez at night was understandable, a matter of safety. She was a woman in a big city, picking up strangers and driving them to their destinations. "You don't know who you're putting in your cab."

Of the two people who entered the cab that night, it was Ana Trujillo whom Cannon described as drunk. "She was pretty lit," he said. In addition, he made no secret of his disdain for her, describing the woman on trial as "cussing, belligerent, outrageous, disrespectful, and controlling. . . . She wanted to be in control of everything and just be the boss."

One of the final things Cannon said to Stefan was, "Get her out of your life."

When Cannon called Stefan's phone at 3:37 that morning, Ana wailed so hard he told her to stop. She did, and talked plainly, "like turning a light switch on and off."

When Carroll took over the questioning, he chastised Cannon, asking if he ever considered that the defense could be looking for Ana's phone. The ex-con screwed his face into a frown. "Never thought about that stupid phone, to be honest with you."

"Did you call Ana a fucking cunt?" Carroll charged, his voice rising in the courtroom.

"No, I didn't use that word," Cannon said. "I called her a slut."

Lil Brown was on the witness stand when Sarah Mickelson put a photo of The Parklane in front of the jurors. Explaining the condo records, the general manager described the yo-yo pattern that began in September 2012, when Stefan first signed a form allowing Ana into his apartment, then revoked it. Back and forth, it had gone, until Stefan became so worried about Trujillo that he changed his lock not once but twice.

Seated at the defense table beside his client, Carroll didn't protest when the business records were entered, until Mickelson referred to those documenting the night Ana cut the refrigerator hose, saying she thought she heard it talking to her. After a bench conference with the judge, Mickelson agreed not to delve into it. Rather than what was in that report, what she wanted the jurors to hear was Lil Brown's conversation with Stefan a few days later, when she cautioned him that Ana Trujillo was troubled. "Get away from that young woman," she'd said.

Gradually, Mickelson worked forward, to the evening before the killing, putting into evidence surveillance tape from the building's loading dock, on which Stefan and Ana moved her boxes into a storage unit. Then jurors watched the lobby video of them walking out as they left for the evening. After the tumultuous cab ride, the cameras again caught

Trujillo as she stormed through the lobby. Finally, a weary Stefan, shoulders slumped, ambled toward the elevator, in the last images of him alive.

"Did you know if Dr. Andersson had a drug or alcohol problem?" Carroll asked the witness.

"I'm not aware," Brown answered.

". . . You felt you needed to talk to him because of his decision-making processes?"

"Absolutely not," she said, but rather she felt the need to discuss the incidents involving Ana Trujillo.

"He would ask that Ms. Trujillo not be admitted, and then he would change his mind?"

Brown answered, "Obviously, yes, sir."

On redirect, Mickelson asked pointedly about Carroll's question regarding whether Stefan used alcohol or drugs. The conversations Brown had with her resident, she said, didn't involve *his* behavior. "Who were they about?" Mickelson asked.

"Ana Trujillo," Brown replied.

The Parklane's night concierge, Florence McClean, agreed with her boss's recollection of the relationship. It was tumultuous. That final night, when Ana walked in, she seemed agitated, and she shouted out to the cab where the driver held Stefan's hands and prayed. "Stefan! Come inside!" After he told her to go upstairs, Trujillo did. Minutes later, Andersson followed, dejected, uncharacteristically not responding to McClean's greeting.

"When is the next time you're made aware something has happened in 18B?" Mickelson asked.

"When the police pulled up outside," McClean answered.

After the apartment staff's testimony, John Jordan's efforts toward nailing down the time line of June 9, 2013 continued with Stefan's next-door neighbor. "I looked at the clock, and it was 2:13 A.M.," Karlye Jones said. "I heard a banging noise, like someone was moving furniture or hitting the wall . . . muffled shouts." The voice was male, Jones said, "masculine."

Jordan looked pointedly at the jurors as he asked, "Did you ever hear the sound of a female voice asking for help?"

"I did not," Jones said. "I heard no woman's voice at all."

Yet moments later, when Jack Carroll asked, Jones backed off slightly, saying the voice was loud, a ten on a scale from one to ten, but then adding, "I'm pretty sure it was a man. I'm not definitely sure . . . It was very, very angry."

"Did it sound like a man shrieking in pain?" Carroll asked.

"No," Jones responded. "It was just an angry man."

"If a man was talking to you in that tone, would you be afraid?" Carroll asked. Jordan objected, and that was a question Jones never answered.

For more than a day, John Jordan and Sarah Mickelson centered on the time line of Stefan Andersson and Ana Trujillo's relationship and the all-important final hours before his death. Throughout, Ana acted unconcerned. She rarely appeared as if truly listening. More often than not, she gazed about the courtroom and at the jury box, as if excited by the notion that she was the center of such great attention. Neither had she cried. Then Jordan played the 9-1-1 call.

"I need help," she keened, in a garbled voice.

"Where are you located?" the 9-1-1 dispatcher asked. Ana repeated the address, her shrieking quieted when the woman told her to calm down so she could understand.

"What did your boyfriend do?"

"He started beating me up . . ."

"Is he there now? . . . Are there weapons there?"

"No ma'am," she cried. "He just drank a lot . . . He's not breathing. . . . I need help now."

"So what do you mean he's about to die? What's going on with him?"

The sounds of breathing, heavy and labored, and Ana ordering, "Breathe. Breathe, Stefan! . . . He's bleeding. He's about to die."

Only then in the crowded courtroom did Ana Trujillo sob, her entire body shaking, perhaps pulled back to that moment in time.

Chapter 22

At the playing of the 9-1-1 call, the focus of Ana Trujillo's trial for the murder of Stefan Andersson transitioned from their relationship to the investigation into his death. The first law-enforcement officer on the stand was also the first to respond that night, Ashton Bowie. "It was a pretty horrible scene," he said. Stefan's "face looked swollen, and there was a large pool of blood around him. . . . I believed that his head had probably been blown out with a gun."

What did the woman covered in blood say unfolded in 18B that night? "She said, 'I don't know what happened. We were arguing.'"

Although Trujillo's sobs drew him to the apartment, once inside, Bowie said he judged her demeanor disingenuous. Her wails reminded him of a child's crocodile tears, put on for an audience. No tears trailed her cheeks or welled in her eyes. When she asked him to perform CPR, Bowie felt stunned. To him, the man appeared dead far too long to be resuscitated.

Instead, he called his supervisor, requesting homicide and a representative from the medical examiner's office. This wasn't a medical emergency, Bowie judged, but a potential crime scene.

"Do you recognize these?" Mickelson asked, handing Bowie a stack of photos. He did. They were taken that night of Ana in her bloody T-shirt and jeans, her face and arms smeared with blood. When the prosecutor asked where

Bowie saw the majority of blood, he pointed to the legs of Ana's jeans. "Did she require any medical attention at the apartment that night?"

"No," Bowie said. "She did not."

"Did Ms. Trujillo tell you that she suffered any injuries?"

"No, she did not."

To Jack Carroll, it seemed obvious that his client was being unfairly treated. The case wasn't a murder but self-defense. To win, he had to convince the jury that in apartment 18B on that horrible night, any woman would have felt compelled to fight for her life. "Before you got there, you don't know what transpired, do you?" Carroll prodded.

"No, sir," Bowie agreed.

"And you don't know who the aggressor is, do you?"

"No, sir."

Repeating what his client told him, Carroll charged, "Wasn't it true that you drew your service weapon and pointed it at Ms. Trujillo?" The officer denied he'd removed the gun from its holster, only covering it with his hand. Carroll also wanted to make another point based on Ana's description of the events, her contention that Stefan was alive when Bowie arrived. "Did Ms. Trujillo ask you to give Mr. Andersson CPR?"

"Yes, she did."

"Did you check for a heartbeat?" Carroll inquired.

"No, I did not."

"**D**o you recognize this?" John Jordan asked Ernie Aguilera, the first CSU officer on the scene. The "this" Jordan referred to was a diagram of Parklane 18B. With that, the witness used the black-and-white drawing to walk the jurors through Stefan's apartment, entering through the hallway, into the living room, kitchen, and bedroom. "We see here in the hallway you have a figure. What does that represent?"

"The dead person inside the apartment," said Aguilera.

Explaining how he worked a crime scene, Aguilera then described marking the evidence with numbered placards, including Ana's backpack on the black-leather couch. Once numbered, he'd taken a picture of the backpack, then removed and photographed its contents. One item found inside was the tarot book. "Was the book open to that page?" John Jordan asked, indicating a page inside the book.

"The same page," Aguilera answered.

Although Mickelson had mentioned the death card in her opening, Jordan let the suspense build, waiting to show it to the jury. Instead, he turned his attention to Ana Trujillo's stiletto shoes, asking how many were found. "There were two?"

"Yes," Aguilera said, as he opened a cardboard box. From it, the CSU officer pulled the alleged murder weapon.

At that point, Jordan held up to display for the jurors the cobalt-blue suede stiletto high-heeled shoe, the brand Qupid and the size a nine. A slight intake of breath ran through the courtroom, accompanied by a mild murmur as the audience reacted to the sight of the shoe's heel and sole stained with dried blood and bearing strands of Stefan Andersson's white hair.

Carrying that image with them, the jurors broke for lunch on what was the second day of the trial.

Once they cleared out of the room, the attorneys approached the bench to confer with Judge Brooks. Something was on all their minds. "We haven't decided whether we're introducing the statement or not," said Jordan. He and Mickelson were still tossing back and forth thoughts on what might happen if they did. They wanted Ana to testify, and they worried that playing the interrogation video could convince Carroll that he didn't need her. At the same time, they saw the video as important evidence, offering insight into Trujillo's character.

Not reacting, Carroll nodded, careful not to indicate he had a preference. The defense attorney had already decided how he'd proceed based on their actions, but worried that if prosecutors suspected, they'd opt not to play the video, and that was something he dearly wanted.

"**W**ere there three suitcases next to the door?" Jordan asked Officer Aguilera that afternoon. Aguilera said there were and that they were in the crime-scene photos. Along with photographing the suitcases, he'd done the same with the contents.

The morning's session had ended in high drama, the introduction of the shoe, the weapon used to kill Andersson. Now Jordan returned to a subject he'd mentioned earlier, the black backpack with the book inside, a book he described to the jury as a tarot-card book. "Who opened it to the death page?" Jordan asked.

"That's the way we found it," Aguilera responded.

Once Jordan allowed the jury to digest that shocking fact, he asked Aguilera to read that page, including: "This card can mean that someone around you is coming to an end of their life. . . ."

The peculiarity of the book in the backpack was readily apparent to those in the courtroom. Trujillo was on trial for murder, and she carried with her a book open to a page that talked of death. At that, Jordan passed the witness.

"I have no questions, Your Honor," Jack Carroll said, and Officer Aguilera left the courtroom.

On the stand, Chris Duncan described his specialty, blood-spatter analysis, for the jurors, saying, "It uses natural science to see how stains develop, their mechanisms of creation. . . . How it originated. Where did it come from? How did it get there?"

Using his findings, Duncan explained what each piece of evidence meant about the killing, starting with the tufts of Stefan Andersson's white hair on the black-leather sofa. The hair was found there, Duncan said, because the couch was where the fight began, when Ana grabbed Stefan by the hair.

The words from Trujillo's writings, found in the coffee-table installation, filled the courtroom, as Duncan read the odd phrases. Trujillo was "calling on a higher power," "asking for justice."

"I ask for you and your Spirit & Soul To be at Peace, Your Mind calm . . . your heart pure . . . Strength." Dripping from a heart drawn in a corner of one note was the phrase, "Tears of blood."

Regarding the blood evidence, Duncan pointed out areas of interest, starting with a single, round drop of blood in the living room, suggesting the dead man still stood at the time. That image was followed by state's exhibit 67, a photo of the transfer, a place where something bloody brushed against the hallway wall. The image Duncan gave the jury was of Stefan reaching out a hand, struggling to stay upright, before he fell to the carpeted floor.

In the crime-scene photos, blood sprayed all three walls surrounding the body. The brutality of the attack became even clearer when Duncan explained that he found blood on walls more than four feet from the body. Yet what struck Duncan was that the majority of the blood was less than two feet high on the wall. What did that mean? "The preponderance of blows were . . . conducted with Mr. Andersson on the floor."

When it came to cuts and bruises on Stefan's arms and hands, Duncan assessed those as "defensive wounds. . . . He's blocking something from hitting his head. . . . He was trying to defend himself with his hands up to his face."

As Duncan's description of the event developed in jurors' minds, Jordan unboxed Ana's jeans and held them up in front of the jury box. The dead man's blood, dried dark brown, saturated the thighs and knees. More blood seeped high up between the legs. The largest stains, Duncan said, came from direct contact with a substantial blood source, perhaps from Trujillo kneeling in the pool of blood next to Stefan's head.

Laying out a mannequin on a table to demonstrate, Duncan lined up a diagram of the blood on the wall, illustrating how the preponderance of the spatter clustered close to the body on the floor. When Jordan asked Duncan what the bloodstains on the jeans revealed about the position of Trujillo's body, the two men began a demonstration.

Ana Trujillo's bloody jeans

Climbing onto the table, Jordan asked Duncan to position him as Ana must have been that night. In response, Duncan had Jordan kneel on the table, straddling the mannequin's chest. In his hand, the prosecutor held the clean shoe, the partner to the bloody stiletto. At her station to the right of the judge, the court reporter, Jill Hamby, typed the verbal testimony, while in the courtroom a crowd of spectators stared silent and tense as the reenactment unfolded before them. Playing the killer, Jordan wielded the long, thin stiletto heel over and over again, pounding it onto the dummy's face and head.

Before releasing the witness to the defense attorney, Jordan had a housekeeping matter. On the 9-1-1 call, Trujillo said that she performed CPR on Stefan. What the prosecutor asked was if Duncan noted any evidence that Trujillo kneeled next to Stefan's body, on his side, where she most likely would have been if she'd tried to resuscitate him. "No," Duncan said, explaining that he saw no transfers from her bloody jeans on that section of carpeting.

John Jordan's courtroom demonstration
*(Pool photo, Brett Coomer/*Houston Chronicle)

"You don't see any evidence of that, do you?" Jordan asked.

"That is accurate," Duncan verified.

"Are you testifying that this surface was causing all the blood spatter?" Jack Carroll asked, indicating the slender tip of the heel of the shoe Jordan used in his demonstration. Duncan responded that it was not only the heel but other parts of the shoe that that hit the body, based on blood found on the shoe's sole and the heel stem.

Couldn't Ana have straddled Stefan's head on her knees, leaning over him while attempting to give him CPR? While possible, Duncan shrugged and said that wasn't a position he'd ever been taught in a CPR class. Yet the officer did agree that such an arrangement would have put Trujillo's right knee in the blood pool, explaining stains that soaked that leg of the jeans.

As the blood testimony continued, the defense attorney worked at laying the groundwork for his own theories. "If I were wrestling and put my hand on the wall, would that be a transfer?" he asked. The CSI officer said it was. Like Jordan, Carroll had a picture he wanted implanted in jurors' minds: "If I were to grab your leg, and I was holding you, let's say I was about to tear ligaments in your leg . . . would you do *anything* to get out of it, if I was causing you extreme pain?"

Jordan quickly objected, and Duncan wasn't allowed to answer, but Carroll had made the suggestion in front of the jurors. The blood-spatter expert did agree with Carroll's next question, however, an alternate theory for the wounds on the dead man's wrists and arms. Instead of defensive wounds, Duncan said they could have been caused by Trujillo's attempting to force Stefan's hands away if he attempted to strangle her. As to what position Trujillo and Andersson were in at different moments, Duncan said there were probably many: "I believe both parties were moving."

". . . Did you see any bruising from a hand, strangulation on Dr. Andersson's neck?"

"I did not, but . . ." Duncan responded. Carroll cut off the answer, saying he wanted a yes or no answer. "Okay," the crime-scene officer said, "I did not."

The testimony important for both sides, the heated exchange continued, Carroll asking what the forensic officer reviewed to make his assessment of the case, particularly had he watched Ana's recorded interview with the police. Duncan said he hadn't until after he'd written his report because his role was diagnosing the forensic evidence. "I didn't put the whole story package together. That really is a task of the homicide investigator."

Earlier that day, a decision had been made, and after Duncan left the stand, prosecutors played Ana Trujillo's recorded interview for the jurors. It was a gamble. Jordan and Mickelson wanted Trujillo to take the stand, and they knew playing the interview might convince Carroll he didn't need to take that step. Still, they were hopeful. "We believed that Ana Trujillo wanted to talk, that she was so narcissistic she'd insist on talking to the jury," said Mickelson. "We wanted her on the stand, but we also wanted the jury to see that interview."

For the rest of that day and the next morning, Mickelson manned the recording equipment, displaying on courtroom monitors Ana's interview with detectives on the morning of Stefan's death. On the screen, Ana flip-flopped from one relationship to another, claiming man after man had fallen deeply in love with her, then hurt her. What was so startling was that she didn't inquire into Stefan's condition until more than an hour into the interview tape.

While it played, Carroll sat back satisfied at the defense table. "I felt like I'd won," he'd say later. "It was a victory. I couldn't have asked for more."

After the tape ended, Carroll told reporters how pleased he was with the turn of events, saying he no longer intended to put his client on the stand. When Jordan and Mickelson heard, the prosecutors winced at the consequence of their decision. "Yet we felt that we'd made the right call," said Jordan. "That tape was damning, and we wanted the jurors to see the Ana Trujillo the investigators saw that night, a woman who always claimed to be a victim and one who showed no remorse and no concern about the death of a man she claimed to love."

Captain Juan Riojas, a paramedic, had been on the first ambulance to respond, and along with a squad of other medical personnel, assessed Stefan Andersson. What they saw was a man who suffered incredible head trauma, who wasn't breathing and had no pulse. When Jordan asked if there was protocol for such situations, Riojas reviewed the agency's patient-care guidelines, "We arrive on scene and there is a person or a—doesn't have a pulse, is not breathing, and is not responding due to trauma-related incidents such as exhibited that day . . . multiple trauma to the head—yes, we can pronounce him dead on the scene."

"And did you do that?"

"Yes. We did." What had Riojas written about Trujillo in his report: "One female detained. No injuries noted on her."

"Is it customary to take ten minutes in a life-or-death situation to dispatch EMS?" Carroll asked. When Riojas reviewed his report, he said the initial 9-1-1 call had come in at 3:41, and he'd been dispatched seven minutes later. The defense attorney also wanted to know why an EKG wasn't used to check Stefan for cardiac rhythms. "Isn't that protocol?"

"No, sir," Riojas answered.

This was an area Carroll saw as important, and he pushed Riojas, asking if cuts to the head bleed profusely and if alcohol thins blood, accelerating bleeding. "I couldn't tell you that, sir," Riojas answered.

Handing Riojas photos, the two discussed the pool of blood on the carpet next to Stefan's head. While Carroll suggested it wasn't dry, Riojas insisted EMTs on the scene saw not only drying but coagulation, which he said indicated Stefan had been dead for half an hour or more.

A photo of Ana Trujillo showed smudges of blood on her face, including around her lips, and the defense attorney asked if that could have resulted from attempting CPR. Riojas said that was possible. "Is it possible that Dr. Andersson bled to death while the EMS personnel were there?" Carroll asked pointedly.

"No, sir," Riojas said. When Carroll asked him to read the narrative from his report, Riojas did, but instead of helping the defense attorney, the report seemed to confirm that Stefan had been dead for some time, when Riojas read: "skin is cold and pale."

The back-and-forth intense, an angry-appearing Carroll charged that the EMTs were also too eager to accept Ana's assurance that she wasn't hurt. "Could she have been in a state of shock?" he asked. "Did you check her eyes? Did you check her pulse?"

Riojas said he hadn't.

If Ana Trujillo was injured on the scene, however, the next witness found no evidence she bled. None of her DNA was found in any of the samples taken from the walls, the carpeting, or the blue-suede stiletto shoe. All the blood tested from the scene came from a single source, a male, Stefan Andersson.

The courtroom bristled with energy, tense, as the trial continued, both sides fighting hard. Next, Sarah Mickelson called a physician to the stand to discuss lab reports from Stefan's autopsy. In his opening statement, Jack Carroll had implied that the dead scientist had multiple addictions, not only to alcohol but drugs.

"Did you see Dr. Andersson from these results abusing any prescription medication?" Mickelson asked. The doctor said he saw no such indications of abuse. Stefan had a type of antidepressant in his system, but within the prescribed dosage. The tests found no traces of other drugs he had prescriptions for, including Vicodin.

On the other hand, Stefan's alcohol level was high at .13, above the .08 limit for driving. Yet someone like Stefan who drank daily, and fairly large amounts, while somewhat impaired, would most likely not appear intoxicated, the physician ventured. "He wouldn't be falling-down drunk."

One of the drugs Jack Carroll mentioned in his opening was ecstasy, so Mickelson asked: "Was there any ecstasy in Dr. Andersson's blood?"

"No," the witness replied. ". . . We ruled that out."

Sitting at the defense table, Tim Donahue, a young attorney Carroll brought on to help with the case, took over, asking the doctor why Stefan's heart and blood-pressure medications weren't on the results. Those weren't tested for, the physician responded, since they weren't important to the case. Quickly, much of Donahue's questioning turned to a prescription the dead man had for Abilify, which the doctor on the stand described as a drug most commonly prescribed to bolster antidepressants. Donahue asked if there was another use for the drug, to treat schizophrenia.

"Yes," the doctor responded, and the drug also had a role in treating bipolar disorder.

"What would happen if the person is bipolar, and they don't take the medicine?" Donahue asked.

"They would not be getting therapy," the doctor answered.

When Donahue suggested that Andersson, a PhD in pharmacology, could have taken something to mask the appearance of ecstasy, the witness disagreed, saying, "Ecstasy is something we specifically test for. So we did the test, and we did not see it."

To make sure the jurors understood that Stefan had a reason to have the drug the defense attorneys had asked about, Mickelson inquired, "Is it fair to say that Abilify is commonly used for . . . depression?"

"Yes," the witness answered.

"**W**hat time did you arrive on the scene?" John Jordan asked Officer Travis Miller, who'd just transferred into HPD's homicide division shortly before Andersson's brutal death.

"At 4:45," he answered. From there, the officer recounted his role in the investigation, seeking out witnesses, video surveillance, and documents pertaining to the killing. The day before, the jurors had watched the long, torturous interview detectives conducted of Ana Trujillo. Now Jordan entered another video into evidence, surveillance footage from Bar 5015, taken the final night of Stefan's life.

The courtroom quiet, on the screen the ghostly figures populated the interior of the bar. Seated on a barstool, Ana danced, flirty and free. In the former video, she said she'd tried to leave Bar 5015 for hours that night, but a drunken Stefan refused. Instead, what jurors saw was a tired-appearing Stefan repeatedly approaching Trujillo. "Now, what we're seeing there," Jordan asked, "does it appear that the defendant is trying to get Dr. Andersson to leave, and he's refusing to leave?"

"No," Miller answered. "It appears like he's trying to get her to leave. She continues talking to other people, as he walks outside and is walking back and forth."

As the video played, most eyes in the courtroom focused on the screen, but a few observed something odd at the defense table. Jack Carroll appeared not to notice, but beside him his client, a woman on trial for murder, nearly danced in her seat. The moments recorded were within hours of what she described as a brutal fight in which she killed the man she said she loved. But at the defense table, Ana never shed a tear. Instead, her eyes lit with excitement. Ana Trujillo relished being the center of attention, and she acted thrilled to have everyone in the courtroom watching her image on the screen.

The following morning, Officer Miller again took the stand to detail the drinking spree at Bar 5015, when Stefan and Ana consumed a bottle of wine, four Absolute vodkas, and six shots of Don Julio Silver tequila. And as a final piece of business, the prosecutor entered into evidence Ana's booking photo, showing jurors that on the night she was arrested, she looked little like the modestly dressed woman at the defense table.

On cross-examination, Carroll returned to many of the questions he'd asked before, about whether or not Stefan was given sufficient medical care by the first responders, or if he was too quickly written off as dead. When it came to the wounds on the dead man's hands and arms, the defense attorney again posited that those could have occurred even if Stefan had been the initial aggressor who was later forced to try to shield himself from Ana. Miller agreed that was true.

When Carroll asked if Miller attempted to find sources to back up Ana's description of Stefan as violent, Miller said that he had. "We looked extensively for someone who would take Ms. Trujillo's side in the story. Our questions were unanimously the same questions with every single person. We're not leading. We did everything that we could in order to find someone who would stand by your defendant."

At the defense table, Carroll frowned, as if doubtful.

If earlier the prosecutors had served up a victory to Carroll by playing the interrogation tape, a situation then unfolded that worked to the advantage of the prosecutors; Carroll put into evidence a record from the Harris County Jail clinic dated June 11, two days after the killing, when Ana complained of bruises and a healing bite on her right middle finger. When the defense attorney asked if Miller knew about the fight the night Stefan died, the homicide detective said, "I knew about the fight two weeks prior."

Carroll persisted, asking if Miller had seen any bruises, would that have made a difference in the decision to charge Ana with murder. The homicide detective denied that it would have impacted the investigation, saying the bruises in the jail report didn't match how Ana described the physical altercation she claimed to have had with Stefan, not that he beat her, but that he held her and wouldn't let go.

What about the "shiner under her eye?" Carroll asked.

"I didn't see it," Miller said. "Neither did the other two detectives."

Over and again, Carroll attempted to ask what Miller would have done in the situation the defense attorney said Ana was in, one in which she was being attacked. Wouldn't Miller defend himself any way he could? Each time John Jordan objected, and the judge ruled the defense attorney's question wasn't relevant, so Miller never answered.

Throughout Miller's testimony, Jordan waited. Bringing in the jail medical records had opened the trial up for the prosecutors, allowing them to put before the jury evidence about the bruises Ana suffered in her fight with Chanda Ellison. On redirect, Jordan asked if Officer Miller was aware of the violent altercation Ana had two weeks before Stefan's murder. "Did that incident involve Stefan Andersson at all?"

"No," Miller said.

At that point, Jordan displayed on the courthouse monitors photos of Ana's injuries from the Ellison fight. Angry contusions scattered over her body including those locations she'd complained about at the jail, under her eye, on her side, her thigh, her chin, and her lip. Did the fight with Chanda explain bruising the jailhouse nurse saw on Ana?

If Ana had those injuries prior to the killing, however, shouldn't the investigators have noticed them on the night she was booked? "You didn't see any bruises when you arrested her for murder?" Carroll prodded.

"It's undetermined," Miller said, explaining why they might have been missed. "At the time of her arrest, she was covered in blood."

Back and forth the testimony went, the prosecutors making their points and Carroll doing his best to refute each. Who was winning? Who was losing? What would jurors remember?

The questioning of the detective had been heated, Carroll appearing angry at times.

As Officer Miller left the courtroom, John Jordan pulled his notes together for his next witness, one of the most important of the trial, Dr. Jennifer Ross, the medical examiner who autopsied the body. At that point, Stefan's sisters and niece left the courtroom, a not-unusual thing for families to do when grisly photos of a loved one will be shown.

First, Jordan asked Ross about Stefan's overall health. She detailed her findings, saying his arteries and heart—although slightly enlarged—were in fairly good shape for a man of fifty-nine. His liver, however, showed some disease, the infiltration of fat not uncommon with heavy drinkers, a condition that could have caused his blood to be thinner and ooze more when the body was injured, but otherwise would have had little effect.

Displaying an initial photo of Stefan on the autopsy table, Ross described what she saw, severe blunt-force trauma to the face and head. "Anything created with an object," Ross explained, defining blunt force. "It could be of small or large surface."

"Would you consider the bottom of a heel to be a blunt object?" Jordan asked.

"Yes," Ross answered, saying that the term "sharp object" was reserved for stab wounds from such items as knives or a shard of glass. The shoe's stiletto heel, she explained, had a small but a flat surface. A long list of the injuries Stefan suffered were then put before the jury, lacerations and contusions to the face, the head, the ears, the arms, the hands, and the back.

At multiple times, Carroll had characterized Stefan's injuries as superficial. Now Jordan asked the assistant M.E. if she agreed. "No," Ross said. "They've penetrated the skin." She'd counted twenty-five injuries, but there were undoubtedly more, because it was obvious that strikes fell on top of each other, masking the true number. In at least one region, the injuries were "all clustered," making it impossible to count.

The photos were shocking and sad, Stefan's life ended, his remarkable intellect silenced, by a barrage of blows that left him swollen, bruised, and bleeding. L-shaped, U-shaped, and square puncture marks and lacerations resembling the shape of the stiletto heel pocking his head and face. "Some of them penetrate through the full thickness of the scalp," Ross said. "Others aren't as deep, but they do penetrate the skin."

A close-up of one wound on the courtroom monitors, Ross testified that these were the types of injuries she would expect from being hit with the heel of the size 9 stiletto. During the attack, the physician described the effects on Stefan's body. As his blood pressure rose, adrenaline flooded his system, and his heart raced. While one injury would have caused some bleeding, such extensive injuries caused significant blood loss. Some blows were so powerful, the lacerations exposed sections of skull.

"The most damaging injuries were to the head," Ross

said, after Jordan asked about the wounds on Andersson's arms and hands, which she, too, characterized as defensive.

On the interior muscles of the neck, Ross found hemorrhaging. "Can you rule out with medical certainty that there was some strangulation in this case?" Jordan asked.

"No, I cannot."

Could the abrasions on Stefan's back have been inflicted while he was attempting to flee? Yes, said the physician. And they, too, appeared to have been the result of being beaten with the stiletto heel. In addition, bruising around his right shoulder blades could have been caused by hitting the wall, perhaps as he fell.

Finally, Jordan asked what the effect might have been if Ana, as he'd portrayed, straddled Stefan, sitting on his chest. "That could make it difficult to breathe," Ross said. Stefan could have tried to get up, while Trujillo forced him down, causing even more stress, raising his blood pressure and releasing more adrenaline. One finding seemed to corroborate that, internal bruising around Stefan's ribs. The effect could have been, according to the physician, "an arrhythmia or abnormal heart rate that could lead to sudden death."

In the end, it appeared Jack Carroll could have been right; perhaps the wounds to the head, at least initially before Stefan bled out, while horrifying were somewhat superficial. But did that matter if the injuries pushed Stefan into some kind of catastrophic event, either massive blood loss or a heart attack, or a combination of both that ultimately caused his demise?

The horror of what Stefan Andersson endured was demonstrated by the physician as she assumed the position she believed, based on the location of his injuries, he was in during the attack, on his back, his face turned to the right, his hands in front of him in a desperate bid to fend off the blows.

Using a PowerPoint, Ross illustrated for jurors that the measurement and shape of the heel matched the wounds on Stefan's face and head. To fully explain why the injuries were deadly, she also displayed an X-ray of the shoe, revealing the metal support that began in the arch and extended into the heel, ending in a thin five-and-a-half-inch rod.

There seemed no doubt that the shoe's heel matched the medical examiner's gruesome photos of the wounds, and from the defense table, Jack Carroll rose, and said, "Your Honor, I'll stipulate to the heel causing the wounds."

Since Ross had a medical degree, Jordan also asked her to address issues the defense raised with Officer Miller. Showing Ross Ana's booking photo, he asked specifically about one injury Carroll said she suffered in the altercation, a black eye. "Would you expect to see some kind of visualization in this photo?"

Ross said she would expect to see swelling or discoloration of the skin, and that she saw neither. Another injury Carroll mentioned was to Trujillo's wrist. When shown a photo of that area, Ross, again, said she saw nothing more than what could have been a shadow. "But we'll agree it's not significant?" Jordan asked.

"It's a small contusion, if it's real," the doctor answered.

Other photos produced similar responses from Ross, who said she couldn't tell from the photos if there were slight discolorations or if what the defense claimed were injuries were merely shadows. If she could have seen what Carroll talked about, Ross also said she wouldn't have been able to tell the age of the wound without examining it in person.

Certainly there were no bruises or injuries on Ana similar to the defensive wounds on Stefan's arms. At that juncture, Jordan brought home one more point, that Stefan's death wasn't mercifully quick. Based on the injuries, Dr. Ross said, "Dr. Andersson was alive for a significant portion of the incident to receive those injuries in those defensive positions."

Showing the physician photos from Ana's hospital examination on the day after her fight with Chanda Ellison, the prosecutor displayed one of a severe bruise at the base of the chin and asked if such an injury would disappear in two weeks. The doctor replied that discoloration could have remained. The same could have been true, Ross said, of other bruises documented in the photos from the Ellison fight, suggesting that perhaps those injuries were the ones the jail nurse saw and recorded.

Finally, Jordan turned to another matter introduced earlier, testimony about the toxicology screen on Stefan's body, asking why Ross requested more than the usual tests. She explained it was because she found it odd that there was no evidence that Stefan fought back. When she checked for the date-rape drug and others, she wanted to see if Stefan had been drugged and incapacitated. She found no such indication.

In the end, although she couldn't rule out a heart event or suffocation, what Dr. Ross said she believed was that the most likely cause of Stefan Andersson's death was blood loss from the maze of puncture wounds, abrasions, and cuts caused by blunt-force trauma to the head.

"Is the heel a blunt object capable of causing serious bodily injury or death?" Jordan asked.

"It is," Ross answered.

Before Jack Carroll took over questioning the assistant ME, Jordan called for a bench conference to discuss the defense attorney's questioning of witnesses about Stefan's medications in which he suggested the drugs were treatments for bipolar disease and schizophrenia. "It's irrelevant," the prosecutor told the judge. "Stefan Andersson wasn't schizophrenic. He had a mood disorder. He was depressed, and that's why he had the medication."

Carroll objected, and the judge issued a ruling, that the defense attorney, while not being able to delve further, could ask what diseases the drugs could be used to treat.

All didn't start out well for Carroll with his questioning, however. First, he asked Dr. Ross if EMS had used an EKG on Stefan, and she said she'd seen no evidence they had. But when he inquired about the most effective way to determine if a heart was beating, Ross didn't say an EKG but rather what the paramedics on the scene had said they'd done, checking for a pulse.

Things only got worse when Carroll asked if the wounds to Stefan's scalp could be described as superficial. "The majority of the wounds to the scalp were fatal," the pathologist answered. "They contributed to his death."

Renewing his self-defense argument, Carroll then asked repeatedly if the clumps of Stefan's white hair found on the couch and the floor could have been evidence of a fight in which Ana grabbed his hair to fend him off when he attacked her. "That is possible," the doctor said, as Carroll brought home one of his primary points.

"Based on your autopsy, do you know who the first aggressor was back on June 9, 2013?" Carroll asked.

"No, I don't," the physician answered.

"Would it be possible that Ana Trujillo was striking Dr. Andersson's arms and his head defending herself?"

"It's possible," Ross said.

Yet when Carroll asked if it couldn't take days for a bruise to develop—suggesting that perhaps that was why his client's injuries weren't visible on the photos taken at the time of her arrest—the physician contradicted him, saying that signs of the contusion would become visible if not in minutes within hours.

The rapid-fire questioning continued, with Carroll repeating arguments he'd used on prior witnesses, including asking about ecstasy in the dead scientist's body. No, Ross said, they hadn't found any indication of the drug. The only drug had been an antidepressant, one Andersson had a prescription for, and it was within the prescribed levels.

"Was it possible Stefan Andersson was alive eighteen minutes after Ana Trujillo called 9-1-1?" Carroll asked, quoting the length of time between her initial call and EMS's arrival on the scene.

"It's possible," she said. But then she also testified that

according to the EMS records, "When they arrived on the scene, he was pulseless, and they don't [attempt to] resuscitate a person that is pulseless."

It had been a tense cross-examination, and when it ended, John Jordan said: "The state rests."

Later that day, Jordan and Carroll talked for a few minutes. "I think I've got you, John," Carroll said, smiling. "I think it's going really well for us."

As he walked away, Jordan wondered if they were watching the same trial. He'd felt that the prosecution case was strong, and that the jury would see through the defense arguments. Could he be missing something? Something that Jack Carroll saw in the jury?

Chapter 23

As he began the defense portion of the trial, Jack Carroll felt good about the way he'd handled the prosecution's witnesses. As Carroll saw it, he was putting on a multipronged attack. The first goal was to draw an opposing picture of the deceased. Instead of a respected scientist, Carroll depicted Stefan the way his client described her dead lover, as a lonely, abusive drunk.

The tall, lean Texan with the bushy mustache and the carefully cut suit introduced his first witness, Yolanda Ruiz, another of the staff at the Hermann Park Grill. "He was in there all the time," said Ruiz, who'd worked at the golf course for more than a decade. Arriving around eleven most days, Stefan often stayed until six or so in the evening. While others said he had a glass of wine every hour or two, which totaled up to something more than a bottle a day, Ruiz estimated that he drank up to three bottles. Yet she said she'd never seen Stefan drunk.

On cross-exam, Jordan went for the core of his own case. Yes, he suggested, perhaps Stefan had a problem with alcohol, but that didn't mean that he was violent. "Was he always nice to you?" the prosecutor asked. Ruiz said the dead man was a gentleman, never a sloppy drunk or belligerent, as were some of her other customers.

Another aspect of Carroll's strategy was his theory that Stefan was too quickly declared dead. Toward that end, in quick succession, he called four EMTs who had been on the scene. To a man, they said Stefan was dead when they entered the apartment. One, David Davila, repeated what the prosecution witness had said, that lifesaving measures weren't initiated because the first EMTs on the scene checked Stefan's carotid and femoral arteries and found no pulse. Carroll had questioned whether body temperature could be assessed by touch while wearing gloves, but Davila volunteered that it could, and that Andersson's body was already cooling, indicating he'd been dead for some time.

While those first witnesses might have been disappointing, Carroll appeared resolute, as he attempted to chip away at the prosecutors' depiction of the events surrounding Stefan's death. High on the list were assertions that he never fought back. As evidence, Jordan had presented testimony that first responders saw no wounds on Ana from the altercation.

To counter those claims, Carroll called Chidi Iwueke, a registered nurse who worked in the jail's mental health unit, where Ana was housed. When asked how Ana appeared two days after her arrest, Iwueke said she had a knot on the back of her head and bruises on her upper and lower torso, thighs, knuckles, cheeks, eyelids, chin, buttocks, hands, and legs, and a healing bite mark on her right middle finger. "I was in a fight with my fiancé," Trujillo told her.

"Would the bruises you made note of be from a horrific fight?" Carroll asked.

"I don't know, sir," the RN answered.

The prosecutors had been expecting this testimony, and as they had when Carroll raised the subject with prior witnesses, they were eager to offer another explanation. On cross-exam, John Jordan mentioned that Iwueke had noted in her report that Ana, who claimed an injured knee, walked with a steady gait, not limping. As to the bruises, he suggested they predated the night Stefan died. "Are you aware that Ana Trujillo was treated at Park Plaza Hospital two weeks before the killing?" he asked.

The witness said she wasn't, and Jordan handed her a

copy of Ana's hospital records, asking Iwueke to read out loud the list of injuries Ana sustained in her fight with Chanda Ellison. As Iwueke did, it quickly became clear that the locations of the contusions from that fight were similar to those seen by Iwueke in the jail. As an example, Jordan

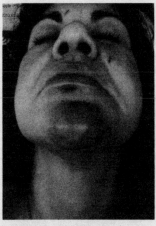

The bruise on Trujillo's chin

displayed a photo taken after the Ellison fight of Trujillo's horribly bruised and swollen chin. "That's pretty significant, right?" he asked.

"I see a bruise there," said the RN.

"Would you agree with me that two weeks later, when in the jail, she could still have some signs of that bruise under her chin?"

Iwueke nodded. "It's possible."

The same was plausible for the other injuries Iwueke saw on Ana, Jordan suggested. That

argument seemed bolstered when it came to the contusion on the back of Trujillo's head, since a jail doctor had noted on his report that Ana told him not that it occurred in the fight with Stefan, but two weeks earlier, during the fight with Chanda Ellison and James Wells. From one point to the next, Jordan noted discrepancies in Ana's accounts. In October, three months after she'd entered the jail, for instance, she complained she had a wound in her scalp the night she was booked, and that it had been ignored. "Did you see a gash in her head?" Jordan asked

"I don't recall," the nurse answered.

Methodically, Jordan worked his way through Ana's jail medical records, putting before the jury tidbits they might not have known had Carroll not entered them into evidence. One piece was particularly interesting; while in jail, Ana complained that her own mother didn't trust her. Yet there were passages damaging to the prosecution, as well, including one where Trujillo described Stefan as a "Dr. Jekyll and Mr. Hyde."

The trial continued, and throughout that day a debate ensued in conferences with the judge regarding a demonstration the defense had planned. At times, John Jordan threatened to object, based on its relevancy and the expertise of the witness involved, but in the end, he entered no opposition, and on the afternoon of the defense's first full day, Jack Carroll called to the stand a dark-haired, muscular, thirty-nine-year-old martial arts expert named Chris Martinez, a man Carroll knew from a downtown Houston gym.

"Are you here to demonstrate in order to assist the jury in understanding what happened to Ana Trujillo on June 9, 2013?" the defense attorney asked his witness.

"Yes," Martinez answered.

With that, a man Carroll brought in as a stand-in for Ana, a retired HPD homicide investigator named Allen Northcutt, walked to the front. In a start-and-stop demonstration, during which Jordan entered objection after objection, Martinez and Northcutt acted out how Carroll speculated the fight unfolded. What he particularly wanted jurors to see was a wrestling hold Martinez put on Northcutt's leg, which put Martinez's body weight against Northcutt's knee.

"Is that painful?" Carroll asked Northcutt, standing in for Trujillo.

"Yes," he answered.

The judge struck the testimony after Jordan objected, because Northcutt wasn't sworn in as a witness. But the jurors had heard it. Would they believe Stefan had Ana in such a hold, inflicting pain and giving her no option other than to fight back?

On cross-exam, Jordan had Martinez detail his credentials, practicing in martial arts for three decades, since the age of nine. "You're not a fifty-nine-year-old college professor, are you?" Jordan asked pointedly. ". . . Would you agree with me that Stefan Andersson was not in the same physical condition as you?"

"Correct," he said. In fact, Stefan had never taken any martial arts training. On further questioning, Martinez agreed with Jordan that the moves he'd demonstrated were complicated, and it was unlikely that most people knew them.

When Martinez said he'd only been asked to show what was possible, Jordan responded by asking, "Just because something is possible doesn't make it reasonable, right?" The martial arts expert agreed.

Then, to dissect how the demonstration differed from Ana's account of how Stefan died, Jordan played a portion of her police interrogation, stopping after Trujillo mimicked what she said Stefan told her that final evening, that he would never beat her. Jordan asked if that was a strange thing to say if Andersson did intend to be physically violent with Trujillo. "No," Martinez said. "It doesn't seem logical, but it could be deceptive."

Yet as they continued through Trujillo's interrogation, and she talked not of any wrestling hold but said Stefan held her in a bear hug, Martinez admitted that the description Ana gave of the fight didn't match what he demonstrated to the jury. "Very different than what y'all showed . . . ?" Jordan asked.

"Right," Martinez confirmed.

Effectively using the defense witness as his own, Jordan turned the testimony to what Trujillo described in the interview, that she got on top of the aging professor and pounded him with her shoe. When she said Andersson growled, Martinez agreed that what Trujillo heard could have been a death rattle, stressed breathing as Stefan's body shut down and saliva accumulated in his throat and lungs. Then Jordan pointedly asked what the biggest problem was with Martinez's demonstration, and after some prodding, he said, "The toehold."

In her long, circuitous interview with police, Trujillo had never claimed Stefan cinched her legs into a painful hold. "That was the whole demonstration about where she possibly was in fear of serious bodily injury or death, because of having this complex leg hold on her, right?" Jordan asked. Martinez agreed, then the lead prosecutor on the case continued, "And she never mentioned anything about that on the video, right?"

"Correct," Martinez answered.

After showing the witness photos of the clumps of Stefan Andersson's hair on the couch and floor, Jordan asked if that would have been painful, and Martinez agreed that it would. "We have where possibly the encounter begins, and the only evidence of anybody's having any pain whatsoever in this case is Stefan Andersson, right?" Jordan asked.

Martinez concurred: "By the hair-pulling. Yes."

On point after point, Martinez agreed with Jordan. Yes, it was true that many men might find it difficult to hit a woman and rather try to contain them. And if they attempted to hold them, a woman could have access to one thing, a man's hair.

In front of the jury, Jordan homed in on Carroll's depiction of what had happened the night of the killing, principally that Stefan held Ana in a leglock. Pointing out that in the crime-scene photos, Stefan's legs are extended straight, he asked Martinez, "Wouldn't you expect that if in the moments before all this happened, like you just showed, he's in some sort of a jujitsu-championship wrestling crazy way hold . . . his legs would be somewhat to the side, or off to the side?"

Looking perplexed by the possibilities, Martinez answered, "Man, if you're getting hit in the head with something, there is no telling what could happen. How you land. How you fall. I don't know."

Point by point, Jordan took Martinez through the prosecution's scenario of the events, based on Duncan's assessment of the blood evidence. And more often than not, the defense witness agreed.

Perhaps the most damaging information Jordan put before the jury with Martinez on the stand was that the shoe she'd used probably wasn't an arm's length from the body, as she'd said, but on the other side of the hallway, with its partner shoe and Stefan's loafers. Why, after all, would she remove one five-and-a-half-inch heel while continuing to wear the other to walk around the apartment?

On redirect, it seemed that Jack Carroll was in the prickly position of having to repair the damage by pointing out that his witness was neither a blood nor a crime-scene expert, and that he'd spent no more than minutes preparing the demonstration. This time, rather than use Northcutt to represent Ana, Carroll stepped in to play her part, as he again put Martinez through a demonstration of his theory of how Ana, fighting back, had been forced to strike out at Stefan. The jurors were attentive, some standing up to watch. While seated at the defense table, Ana sat up pin straight and smiled, as if entertained by the spectacle in the courtroom.

As he had when he'd first taken the stand, Martinez agreed again with Carroll's points, but then sounded less certain when John Jordan questioned him. In the end, both sides pulled at the witness, suggesting scenarios, and caught in the middle on the witness stand, at times Martinez agreed with both.

An attractive, bright-eyed woman with long, highlighted, dark blond hair and a pleasant smile, Lee Ann Grossberg was a former Harris County assistant medical examiner who ran her own Houston consulting firm. Since 2001, she'd been a forensic pathologist for hire, one who assessed cases and delivered her opinions in court. With Martinez, Carroll had attempted to bring home his self-defense theory, although perhaps to mixed results. With Grossberg, the defense attorney had another aspect of his case to explore: the cause of Stefan Andersson's death.

While the assistant ME who'd performed the autopsy ruled the cause of death as blunt-force trauma and said that since Stefan was pulseless he couldn't be resuscitated, Carroll consistently presented a differing argument, that Andersson might have met his demise because of insufficient medical care. Dr. Grossberg agreed, saying what stood out when she read the EMS report was that, "I found it surprising that a defibrillator patch was not applied to Mr. Andersson's body to look for any electrical activity in the heart."

Under Carroll's questioning, Grossberg explained how patients who'd received EKGs and other medical interventions arrived at the morgue with defibrillator patches attached. None of that had been on Stefan's body, and there was no mention of lifesaving measures included in what she described as a skeletal EMS report.

"Do you happen to know if Dr. Andersson was dead when EMS arrived?" Carroll asked.

"I don't know," Grossberg responded. Contending that it was possible the scientist was still alive, she then agreed with Carroll's description of the injuries on the body as superficial. "There were no fractures to any of his bones. There was no internal bleeding. No damage to any of his vital organs."

As she explained, Grossberg said that while she agreed the cause of death was the injuries to the head and face, the true mechanism might have been an underlying medical condition, such as a heart attack. Yet that was something Dr. Ross, who'd done the autopsy, had also mentioned, so it wasn't anything the jury hadn't heard before. Where Grossberg's analysis differed was that she theorized Stefan could have been alive on the scene when first responders arrived. And if he was, and the cause was a heart attack, there was the possibility that he could have been treated and lived.

There'd also been a mention of the possibility of strangulation in the autopsy. When it came to the bruising and scraping around Stefan's neck and the contusions on his chest, Grossberg argued that those could have occurred in a physical fight.

Despite these points brought up during her direct testimony, when Sarah Mickelson cross-examined Grossberg, the physician said she had no problem with Dr. Ross's autopsy of Stefan and also agreed on the manner of death, homicide. While Grossberg said other factors might have entered in, such as a heart attack, "It cannot be called a natural death."

Without the blunt-force trauma to the head the heart attack—if Stefan had suffered one—would not have occurred. So in the end, Grossberg conceded that it didn't matter what actually killed Andersson. Whether it had been a heart attack or blood loss, he'd died as a result of the beating.

From that point on, Mickelson brought Grossberg back to the autopsy photos, showing the injuries, the contusions, the blood, and the scrapes on Andersson's body, asking her how they could have occurred. The depiction the prosecutor put before the jury was of Stefan on his back on the floor—as the blood expert, Duncan, had described—while Ana brought the heel of the shoe in her hand down over and again. Stefan turned his head to the right, and put up his arms, explaining why he suffered the majority of wounds to the left side of his face and head and the defensive wounds to his arms. So much blood and gore.

For the most part, Grossberg agreed that theory was possible, but at times she pointedly said the wounds could have happened in other ways. She didn't fully endorse the prosecutors' theories; nor did she dismiss them. "This is a dynamic occurrence. . . . There are just so many different scenarios," Grossberg demurred.

In yet another demonstration, in the front of the courtroom, Jordan assumed the position Ana said Stefan was in that night, holding his cocounsel, Mickelson, in a bear hug. What the two prosecutors then demonstrated was how difficult it would have been for Ana, her arms restricted, to inflict the injuries found on Stefan. In fact, when Mickelson described the injuries to Stefan's hands, the pathologist granted that they could have happened as the prosecution suggested.

As for the wounds on Stefan's back, Grossberg acknowledged that they didn't match Ana's description of what transpired that night, of flailing at Stefan with the shoe as he held her and refused to let her go. "Can't it be consistent if someone was running away or walking away, and I were to strike them with the shoe, and it were to travel down?"

"It could be," Grossberg said.

Although the defense attorney repeatedly suggested that Stefan had taken ecstasy, Grossberg agreed with the previous physicians, saying there was none found in the body and that the drugs that were present were prescription drugs, all within a therapeutic range.

Yet again, the testimony moved in another direction—the back-and-forth of a hotly contested trial—when Jack Carroll asked the "but for" question: "But for the lack of medical care, is it possible that Dr. Andersson could have survived?"

"We will never know," Grossberg responded.

Finally, Mickelson relayed the EMS testimony to Grossberg, repeating how all the officers on the scene said Stefan had been checked for a pulse, breathing, any signs of life, and none were found. In fact, the first officer on the scene said that the blood pool next to the body was already drying, and the blood was coagulating. The body felt cool to the touch. Grossberg agreed that if Stefan was pulseless and hadn't been breathing for ten minutes or more, he could not have been resuscitated, but she also held firm, saying that without an EKG she couldn't know if he was still alive when EMS arrived.

With that, Jack Carroll announced that the defense rested. The question hanging in the air: What would the jurors believe?

Although the defense had finished putting on its case, the guilt-or-innocence phase of the trial didn't end. Instead, another impassioned argument unfolded at the judge's bench, Mickelson and Jordan contending that Carroll, by claiming Ana's injuries were from a fight with Stefan, had opened the door to put on rebuttal witnesses. Usually, testimony of extraneous offenses, other actions by an accused that puts him or her in a bad light, isn't permitted unless there's a conviction and a trial moves into the punishment phase, during sentencing. But after arguments from both sides, Judge Thomas ruled that prosecutors would be allowed to put on James Wells and Chanda Ellison, to testify about where Ana's bruises might have come from and her propensity to violence.

On the stand, James Wells spoke quietly, appearing ill at ease. Under Jordan's questioning, Ana's friend told jurors about his relationships with both women, that he considered Chanda and Ana good friends, that they lived together, and that he had sexual relationships with both.

"I guess the young people call it friends with benefits?" Jordan asked. Wells confirmed that, and said that Chanda didn't object to his being with other women, including Ana.

At the witness table, Ana watched Wells intently. She nodded at times, as if agreeing, smiled, or scowled when he said something damaging to her, shaking her head as if it were too much to believe. What she didn't know was that Wells didn't want to be there, either. He'd had a long struggle, trying to decide whether or not to take the stand. "I still cared about Ana," he said. "I didn't want to see her in prison."

To the jury, Wells laid out the events of Memorial Day weekend 2013, the day he met Ana at the Hermann Park Grill. He brought her home to the apartment. "She looked normal," Wells said. "She actually had her lips puckered up like she was going to kiss me." Instead, she leaned toward him and bit him on the head.

"Ow!" he screamed. He pushed her back and said she looked at him angrily, and warned, "Oh, ho, ho, ho! You're a dead man!"

James Wells on the stand
*(Pool photo, Brett Coomer/*Houston Chronicle)

From there, Wells detailed the rest of the day, leaving
to take a call and returning to find Ana bruised from her
fight with Chanda, the drive around during which Ana cried,
eventually saying she planned to return to her family in
Waco, and the next day, when she filed a report, and police
showed up at his apartment. "I could hear the officer close
his book. I heard him say, 'You know what? I believe y'all.
I kind of knew there was more to the story than she was
telling me.'"

After that, nothing happened. "You were never charged
with anything?" Jordan asked.

"No," Wells answered.

Jack Carroll wanted to know if it wasn't a rather impossible situation to live with two women and have sexual
relations with both. "Not if you're honest about it," Wells
answered.

"Is Chanda a jealous person?" Carroll asked.

"No," Wells answered.

The next witness Jordan called was Chanda Ellison, to fill in the blanks in Wells's account of the Memorial-Day-weekend biting incident.

Yet first, Jordan set the stage, asking what his witness observed on the occasions she spent time with Stefan and Ana. In response, the woman on the stand said she saw no hint of anger in the dead man. To the contrary, she described Andersson as loving toward Ana. "Whatever Ana asked for, Stefan gave her."

From there, Jordan asked questions to elicit her account of the bite incident. What she said closely matched Wells's testimony. But there'd been that gap when he wasn't there, when he left the two women alone that Jordan needed Ellison to fill in, and she detailed the all-out fight that erupted, Chanda wielding the stick, and Ana repeatedly attacking her, screaming "no one tells me what to do!"

Chanda Ellison testifying
*(Pool photo, Brett Coomer/*Houston Chronicle*)*

They fought and wrestled, Ellison inflicting bruises with the stick, and Ana not backing off, not giving up, until Wells returned to the apartment and told Ana that she was going to have to leave.

"You hit Ana with a stick?" Carroll prodded, sounding aghast.

"I sure did," Ellison answered, staring him down as he sat at the defense table. ". . . To defend myself against her, yes I did."

"Did she break the skin?" Carroll asked about the bite to Wells's head. When Chanda said that it left indentations, Carroll bit his own finger, and asked, "Do you think if I bit myself, it would cause indentations?"

Carroll continued to push, asking if she and Wells faced any charges for assaulting Ana, especially Chanda, since she used the stick, which he labeled a potentially deadly weapon. Recounting how the officer came to the door and questioned her, Chanda said she wasn't worried, that she and Wells had been cleared.

"Is that what you did to her?" Carroll asked, holding up a picture of Ana's horribly bruised chin.

"Yes." When he held up a photo of Ana's black-and-blue back, Chanda said, "I did whatever I could to get her off me."

Moments later, Carroll passed the witness, and both sides rested. All that remained were closing arguments, then the jurors would have to decide who told the truth.

"For the last week, all we've heard the defense sell is self-defense. Self-defense sounds sexy. Self-defense sells news-papers. But we've met Ana Trujillo. We've seen her talk on this video, and we have now seen all the evidence in this case. We know what happened on June 9, 2013, was not self-defense," Sarah Mickelson said, standing before the jury to begin closing arguments. "The defense is going to ask you to sign off on the way in which Ana Trujillo ended the life of Stefan Andersson. They're going to ask you to sign on that dotted line and put your stamp of approval on twenty-five blows with the heel of a shoe to a man's forehead that was less than two feet off the ground."

To believe that Ana acted in self-defense, Mickelson said, jurors had to judge that the woman on trial feared losing her life. "What evidence did we see of that?" From the moment of the 9-1-1 call, in which Ana seemed uncertain what type of event she wanted to report, to the arrival of Officer Bowie on the scene, through the interview with the detectives in homicide, Ana never uttered an explanation for why she felt in fear of her life.

Over and again, the prosecutor brought up examples of how unconcerned Ana was for the man she said she loved, the one she described as her fiancé, including during the interview, when she didn't mention him for more than an hour. In the interview tape, when detectives asked Ana if Stefan was ever physically abusive to her, at first she paused, as if trying to think of an instance, then she instead described the abuse as mental. "Doesn't say he hit her," Mickelson said. "Doesn't say he pushed her. Didn't punch her. Didn't throw her."

There were things the jurors would never know, like precisely what was said in that apartment that night. But there were other things they did know: that Stefan walked to the elevator that evening appearing dejected, mortified after seeing Ana act out yet again; less than fifteen minutes later, the next-door neighbor heard banging and angry voices, then Karlye Jones heard a man's voice shouting in 18B. "She never heard the defendant cry out for help," said Mickelson. "At 2:13 A.M., Stefan Andersson is yelling. Then it's quiet. We heard from Captain Riojas of the Houston Fire Department that he believed Stefan had been dead for at least thirty to forty-five minutes when he arrived."

Stefan's body was cold and pulseless, Mickelson said, and there was nothing the first responders could have done—despite Carroll's suggestions otherwise—to revive the scientist. Whether jurors believed Stefan had died of strangulation, a heart attack, or blood loss from the wounds to his face and scalp, all that blood pooling on the carpet and splattered against the wall, all were products of Ana's attack, and all were murder.

One of the most important parts of the interview video, Mickelson said, was when Ana finally brought the discussion around to Stefan Andersson, a man she said she loved, and was told that he died. "She doesn't shed a tear," the prosecutor pointed out. "Doesn't really flinch . . . The only person Ana Trujillo cries for is herself. I would submit to you that when you find her guilty of murder, you're not telling her anything she doesn't already know."

"Decide for yourself what the evidence is!" Jack Carroll ordered as he took the floor. The jurors hadn't heard Ana on the stand because he'd advised her not to testify, but they had the 9-1-1 tape and the exhaustive interrogation video. "I want you to ask yourself, is that woman acting? I want you to think: Well, if she's acting, would she qualify for a nomination for an Academy Award?"

Bristling at Mickelson's characterization of his pathologist's testimony, Carroll insisted it was indeed possible that Stefan was alive when EMS arrived, and if he was, "It's not murder!"

Walking back and forth in front of the jury, Carroll picked up evidence photos, throwing them back down. "Somebody screwed up here! That's without question," he charged. "To me, it sounds like she's desperate, like she's trying to perform CPR, not trying to murder somebody."

Contending that prosecutors didn't produce a reason for the killing, Carroll then said, "How can you prove someone murdered someone if they don't have a motive?

"This was a domestic-violence call . . . The most dangerous time in domestic violence is when the woman is leaving," he said. "So, I'm not saying that Dr. Andersson was murdered by EMS or Officer Bowie, but I'm saying he might have still been alive when they arrived. They didn't do anything. They just said, 'He's dead.'"

To those in the audience, it appeared that Carroll felt confident of his case and his client: "How many times did you hear me object? What evidence did I try to keep out? I wanted all of it to come in. When I first got this case, it took me a little while, but I realized that I've got an innocent woman!"

At times, Carroll pointed at Trujillo, uttering the word Reagan Cannon said he'd used when he talked to her, "slut." It was as if he wanted the jurors to see her as he saw her, a tough but a good woman who was being unfairly branded. In the interview, he said, detectives weren't listening to Ana's account but building their case because they prejudged her and ignored the evidence.

His hoarse voice booming in the courtroom, Carroll described his version of the events of that night, as his client tried to flee. How she grabbed her shoe, the only weapon available, to fend Stefan off, and how she later fought to save his life, giving him CPR. "That's where all the blood came from on her mouth."

The wounds on Stefan's arms, Carroll stressed, might be defensive wounds, but that didn't exclude him as the one who struck first, who went after Trujillo, who then responded by hitting him with the shoe.

As his allotted forty-five minutes drew to a close, Jack Carroll said: "Defensive wounds? Strikes? What would you do if someone gets you in a hold and was grabbing your foot, and they're going to tear the ligaments and tendons in your knee, causing you pain? What would you do if you know that the threat of serious bodily injury was there, and you thought you could die?"

Carroll paused before answering his own question. "You would defend yourself."

As to the bloody killing, the twenty-five or more strikes to Stefan's head and face, Carroll said the number wasn't to be considered because if Ana was in fear of her life and justified to strike him once, then she was justified to strike him twenty-five times.

One strike or twenty-five, it was still self-defense.

Where Carroll had appeared flushed with emotion, John Jordan coolly walked before the jury and smiled slightly. "Defense counsel said, 'I'm going to leave it up to your imagination.' You heard him say that several times right? Which is exactly what the defense is. But don't blame Mr. Carroll for what he just said to you . . . It's not his fault . . . The problem is that he's stuck with the words and acts of Ana Trujillo."

Then Jordan frowned, his voice quiet: "Welcome to Ana's world," he said. "Whatever the scenario, she's the victim."

Again the focus returned to Ana's day-of-the-killing interview with homicide detectives, when they inquired about Stefan, and she instead rehashed every failed relationship she'd ever had with a man, how they'd all loved her, then turned against her and misused her.

The truth, Jordan said, was very different, epitomized by the Bar 5015 surveillance tape: Ana said she'd been trying to convince Stefan to leave for hours, but what was seen on the tape was the opposite: a tired Stefan trying to coax a still-partying Ana out the door and into the cab. "In Ana's world, Officer Bowie, responding to the accident, pulled a gun on her . . . Again a victim. In Ana's world, it's not her fault. It's EMS's fault . . . that's what they want you to believe."

Grabbing on to the threads of what little remained of the unraveled Ana Trujillo, Jordan wove a picture of a woman divorced from reality, one so narcissistic that she had to constantly be the center of attention, who described herself as the most desirable of all women, sought after by man after man. "In Ana's world, it has nothing to do with the fact that you hit somebody twenty-five times about the face that caused the death," he said, talking quietly to the jurors. "Because in her world, it's always someone else's fault."

That world, however, didn't exist. "We're not in Ana's world. We're in the state of Texas. We hold murderers accountable, and that's what we're asking you to do today."

What could be more fitting than for Stefan, a scientist, to speak through the scientific evidence left at the scene? Retracing the prosecution's theory of how the attack unfolded, Jordan detailed the forensic findings, principally the hair and blood evidence. Then he took a seat in the witness chair and addressed the jurors from the place where the testimony first came, while he narrated what so many, from the staff at The Parklane and Hermann Park, to Stefan's friend Annika Lindqvist, and Rosemary Gomez, the cab driver, had testified to, explaining how it all fit together to paint a portrait of a gruesome murder.

John Jordan during closing arguments
(Pool photo, Brett Coomer/ Houston Chronicle)

In Ana's world, she wanted jurors to believe that when Cannon called at 3:37, her fight with Stefan had just ended. But in the real world, Jordan said, the fight took place nearly an hour and a half earlier, at 2:13, when Stefan's neighbor heard the altercation. The captain had testified that Stefan was dead at least half an hour when police arrived. "That fits the time line, doesn't it?" Jordan said. "Argument happens at 2:13. He's dead by three o'clock."

What did Ana Trujillo do for that hour and a half, as

Stefan Andersson lay dying then dead on the hallway floor? What she didn't do was call for help. Bringing the jurors to those moments while Stefan was being attacked, the prosecutor asked them to imagine the horrible pain of the assault. "To suggest that this is anything close to self-defense is offensive, and we all know that," he concluded. "As you know from the testimony, this defendant has been called 'the stiletto stabber.' It won't be until your just verdict that she ceases to be the stiletto stabber. And she will then forever be Ana Trujillo, murderer."

At that, the jury left the room to deliberate the case. The gallery had been full throughout closing arguments, but now the spectators filed out as well. In the hallway, Ana Trujillo could be seen walking with her family, smiling slightly, appearing confident. Perhaps she believed Jack Carroll, who told her that he felt confident that they would triumph, and that this day would mark her return to the outside world, acquitted of murder.

Ana surrounded by supporters
*(Pool photo, Brett Coomer/*Houston Chronicle)

That remained Carroll's opinion, as he nervously waited for the jury to return. During the trial, Carroll told John Jordan that he believed the jury would weigh the evidence and come in with a verdict in Ana's favor, and he'd seen nothing to change his mind. All the money and time he invested in the case seemed worth it to free a woman he believed unjustly accused. In addition, a win would bring him the attention he'd taken the sensational case to garner.

Meanwhile, Sarah Mickelson and John Jordan felt just as confident. They judged they had the science behind them, evidence that they trusted jurors wouldn't ignore, showing that Stefan wasn't the aggressor but a victim.

It's not uncommon for many to judge how a jury is swaying by the length of time they remain in deliberation. All of the attorneys involved circulated back to their offices to wait it out. No one expected the decision to come down so quickly, but just under two hours later, the jury-room buzzer sounded twice.

Minutes later, the attorneys and spectators filed back into the courtroom, and Ana took her place beside Jack Carroll. Judge Thomas cautioned the gallery to remain silent as the verdict was read. The tension in the room made it all feel as if it were unwinding in slow motion, as the jurors walked in and took their chairs.

In the otherwise silent courtroom, the judge read the words that Annika, Stefan's family and friends had been hoping to hear: "We the jury find the defendant, Ana Trujillo, also known as Ana Fox, guilty of murder."

Chapter 24

The jury had made its decision, rebuffing self-defense as justification and branding Ana Trujillo's killing of Stefan Andersson a murder. That question was answered. In the courtroom the following morning, as he prepared for the punishment phase of the trial, Jack Carroll reeled from what he saw as his failure. Not only had jurors come back with a guilty, but they'd done it in a remarkably short period of time.

Meanwhile, despite the exhaustive testimony, few understood the real Ana Trujillo, who she had been and who she became as her life took a spiral that brought her from working suburban wife and mother to a homeless woman who used her body to convince men to take care of her and in return hated them for doing it. The jurors didn't yet know that Ana sought out and embraced a troubling underworld, a dark, mysterious place that many found terrifying.

Yet even then, with the guilty verdict in, the defense had hope.

In Texas, unless a defendant chooses otherwise and entrusts her fate to a judge, juries first decide guilt or innocence. Then they have a second task: sentencing. For the newly convicted, the punishment phase of a trial offers a second opportunity to use everything at their disposal to raise questions in jurors' minds, hoping doubts might fight their way to the surface and result in lesser sentences.

In the Ana Trujillo case, as is often the circumstance,

the jury had a wide range of possible sentences to consider, from probation to life. And word around the courthouse was that many of the lawyers—prosecutors and defense attorneys alike—thought that here Jack Carroll held a firm upper hand. In their views, Jordan and Mickelson overreached by going for a life sentence. "Few thought that jurors would come down hard on a woman," said Jordan, who understood that the consensus was based on a long history of women getting lighter sentences than men. But considering the brutality of the murder, the prosecutors felt justified in pushing for the maximum. "We hoped that in this case, we had an exception."

While they opted to do opening statements for the trial, both sides agreed to forgo exercising that right in the punishment phase and proceed directly to presenting witnesses. At this point, now that Ana had been found guilty, prosecutors had greater latitude in the evidence they put before the jury, its goal to convince the jurors that Ana was a habitually violent woman, one who needed to spend her life behind bars.

Toward that end, the initial witnesses Jordan called to the stand were the police officers who arrested Ana in 2008 and 2010 on DWIs. The first officer described the dangerous episode when Ana drove the wrong way on one of Houston's largest freeways. Both emphasized how contentious she became with them, cursing while flagrantly drunk.

On the stand, James Jimenez cut an impressive figure, at six-foot-two and 280 pounds, as he described how the much-smaller Trujillo jumped him, pulled his hair, and took him down to the sidewalk outside Teresa Montoya's office building in 2011, her eyes burning angrily at him, after he ordered Ana from the beauty salon where she'd been entertaining a man. "What did it feel like when she pulled your hair?" Jordan asked him.

"It hurt real bad," Jimenez said. Only by sitting on her did he hold her until police arrived. Under questioning by Jack

Carroll, the former security guard said that he'd initially thought of Ana as a friend. "She was . . . charming."

Anuj Goel, the software engineer who lived in the Rice Lofts, saw Ana from the beginning as someone he wanted to keep out of his life. She was loud, drank too much, and he heard stories of her acting out. Like Stefan, Goel lived in a building with tight security, but Ana managed to get in, and one evening he came home and found her inside his apartment. "I felt violated," he said. "It was a really scary situation."

Through the testimony, Mickelson and Jordon developed a profile of Ana's violent and unpredictable mood swings. Examples lined up, accounts of her bad acts, especially when drinking. The Waco restaurant manager offered to call her a cab, and an intoxicated Trujillo shouted to take his hands off her. Moments earlier, she'd been petting a young boy on the head in a high chair, to the dismay of his concerned parents.

At that point in the trial, Brian Goodney took the stand and recounted the evening Ana Trujillo hit him with the candlestick. "Did you see this coming?" Jordan asked.

Brian Goodney acting out the night Ana Trujillo hit him
(*Pool photo, Brett Coomer*/Houston Chronicle)

"Absolutely not," Goodney answered.

"Now, had y'all been in an argument at all that evening?" Jordan asked.

"We never argued," Goodney said. "I don't ever remember us ever having any real disagreement. We were not lovers . . . We were just friends."

That night, Ana hadn't appeared angry at Goodney, but when he turned his back to open the door, she clubbed him. The chilling image jurors were left with was of Goodney waking up and seeing Ana sitting on the hallway floor staring at him. She simply stood, calmly stepped over him, opened the door, and walked out.

Throughout the trial, Jack Carroll painted Stefan Andersson as an out-of-control drunk, but in the punishment phase it became ever clearer that the one with the more dangerous addiction was actually Carroll's client. On the stand, the manager from Sambuca described Ana as one of the top three customers in his fifteen-year career he watched out for, because they acted out when intoxicated. Then one of his employees, a bar-back who took out garbage, washed dishes, and helped stock the bar, described how an agitated Trujillo slapped him twice after he'd picked up a bracelet left on a table and asked if it was hers.

Despite all the testimony about Ana's bizarre behavior, the depth of her foray into darkness, however, didn't enter the courtroom until Officer Brian Shepherd described the night he had her handcuffed in the backseat of his squad car after arresting her for public intoxication. Ana fumed at him, and he heard her curse him and his family. "*La familia*" and "*muerto*," she muttered, sounding as if she talked to an invisible entity. Shaken, Shepherd turned up the radio so he wouldn't have to listen while he drove her to jail.

"I called you," said Christi Suarez, when asked how she'd gotten in touch with prosecutors. For nearly a year, Suarez was haunted by her last talk with the dead man. She'd stayed in the background, not wanting to get involved. It wasn't until three days into the trial that she picked up the telephone, called the DA's Office, and told Sarah Mickelson what she knew about Ana Trujillo and Stefan Andersson. But then, Suarez refused to return phone calls from Jordan, and he'd sent an investigator to track her down. "I was afraid to do it," Suarez admitted. "I was subpoenaed to be here."

On the stand, Suarez wasn't allowed to tell jurors everything Stefan said to her just two weeks before his murder, that Ana once tried to choke him. But the TV producer did testify that Stefan feared Ana and that he'd asked her to leave his apartment. "I think although she seemed to be a very nice, humble person who liked to help people, I think she did have another side to her. I think that she was very manipulative as far as, she always felt that she had a lot of power, and I think when she didn't get what she wanted or the person didn't agree with her, then she turned to be violent."

"When you say she felt like she had a lot of power, what do you mean by that?" Jordan asked.

Suarez took a deep breath and looked steadily at Jordan, keeping her eyes far from the woman who'd once been her friend. "Ana claimed to be very spiritual; but she actually practiced, like, Wicca. I don't know what you would call it. So, she actually at some point thought she had some sort of powers."

At the defense table, Jack Carroll shouted out an objection. The result was that when the testimony started again, moments later, the judge had ruled that he wanted no more talk about Ana Trujillo's spirituality. But John Jordan did get in why he'd had to subpoena Suarez to get her on the witness stand. "Why didn't you come forward before last week?" he asked.

"It's a little strange to hear, but I think that I had been getting spiritually attacked. I was having nightmares. I couldn't sleep. My fiancé would stay up with me all night, praying," she said, quietly, as if straining to be understood. "After the incident happened, you know, because I knew what Stefan had told me . . . it was very troubling to me. Like I said, I was having a lot of issues with that, and I was very fearful of that."

"And you were reluctant to come forward," Jordan said.

"Yes, I was scared," Suarez answered. "You don't want to be against someone that could possibly cause you harm, even without being around you as a person."

Jack Carroll had objected to Suarez's testimony about his client's spiritual beliefs, but then asked about them himself, prompting Suarez to explain what she meant when she said Ana spiritually attacked her. By then, Suarez's hands shook on the witness stand as she felt Ana's eyes on her.

"What would happen is that Ana would come into my dreams and then all of a sudden, she would appear somewhere randomly in Houston, and she would find me again. After this incident occurred, I continued to see her in my dreams, and Stefan. It sounds crazy, but I had two mediums come forward and tell me they had a message from him, that he needed my help. Of course, I met him a couple of times. I was not a very good friend. I didn't know him that long . . . It's hard to be going through that when you can't sleep at night and you stay up for hours upon hours having people . . . pray for you and bless your house."

Suarez had been talking fast, trying to get it all out, hoping those in the courtroom would understand. She took a breath, and continued, "That's what I mean by being spiritually attacked. It's almost like you're being haunted by a ghost. That's why I'm here shaking today because . . ." At that, she stopped talking, looking around the courtroom, as if needing help to go on.

"You think that you're doing the right thing against a person that was a friend of yours . . . ?" Carroll prodded. "You just out of the blue contacted the assistant district attorney assigned with this case?"

"Yes, sir," Suarez answered. "She brutally murders a

man that did nothing but help her, and I know of her violent-drunk history. Yes."

". . . Do you think that after you get through testifying the spiritual attacks will stop?" Carroll asked.

Jordan objected, and the judge sustained, so Suarez wasn't supposed to have answered, but she did, "These are people that I knew, and it's going to be there forever."

The first part of Jordan and Mickelson's punishment strategy was to show the jurors who Ana Trujillo had become, a violent, dangerous woman. That accomplished, they began demonstrating to the jury that this was not a victimless crime, that Stefan Andersson mattered. Not the lonely drunk depicted by the defense, the dead man had family and friends. He was loved. On the stand, Stefan's ex-wife, Jackie, wept softly as she talked about the kind and generous man she had once loved, one who'd been so close to her father that their relationship survived the divorce. Although she hadn't kept in touch with Stefan, she said, "I knew if I

Jackie Swift on the stand
*(Pool photo, Brett Coomer/*Houston Chronicle)

ever needed him, I could call him . . . I never had that opportunity."

A college student, one of Stefan's nieces, Ylva Olofsson, told the jurors that Stefan had always been close to her, helping when she'd moved to California two years earlier, to study psychology. Good news or bad, Stefan was the first one she called. "He was more like my brother," she said in her lyrical Swedish accent. "Even if he didn't know how to help me, he found out how to help me . . . I think of him every day. I've lost my best friend . . . It's just so unfair . . . No one is ever going to forgive what happened."

Stefan's sister Marie cried, too, talking of her lost brother. When it came to Stefan's death and the horrific way he died, the investigation going on in the U.S. while the family yearned for information in Sweden, Marie said, it was "a nightmare." As for Ana Trujillo, when it came to Stefan's family, "She destroyed our life."

Others took the stand, including friends. One had given her baby girl the middle name Stefani in Stefan's honor. They all missed the funny, kind, gentle man, who took their concerns to heart, eager to listen to their troubles and to try to find ways to help them. Not disconnected, even after the move to Houston, many heard from him multiple times each week, eager for his phone calls, assuming he would always be there.

When it was her turn, Annika talked of Stefan's wake, to which more than a hundred people traveled from many parts of the U.S. and the world, meeting in a wine bar to toast the man they all loved. "I had friends telling me it was like an Irish wake," Annika said. "People went up and talked about Stefan, and what a loss it was for them."

That day, Annika recounted the pain of hearing the untrue accusations that the good man she'd known had a violent nature, and what the loss of her friend had done to her own life. "I took care of him in many ways, but he also took care of me," she said. "Stefan was a listener . . . He was a constant in my life . . . and he's gone."

Each day of the trial, Jennifer Varela, the domestic-violence expert who'd consulted with the prosecutors, sat in the second row, listening to the testimony, taking notes, and trying to make an unbearable situation as comfortable as possible for Stefan's family. She arrived with pads to soften the seats, blankets to keep them warm, and a stash of chocolates to share midafternoon, when their energy dwindled.

While she'd found many of the witnesses interesting, the one she'd most anticipated was Julia Babcock, a psychology professor at the University of Houston. Varela had read Babcock's work on domestic violence and wondered what the psychologist made of the relationship of Stefan and Ana. To Jennifer, it was obvious who the aggressor was, where the truth lay, but perhaps Babcock, hired as a defense expert, would see it differently?

"I've spent about seven, eight hours with Ana Trujillo in face-to-face contact," Babcock told the jury. She began by answering Carroll's questions about domestic violence, including that victims are often embarrassed and unwilling to disclose their situations. When she mentioned victims, she used feminine pronouns, like "she"; for the abusers, her language assumed the identity was male, as in "he." But then, the vast majority of victims were women and abusers men, so that wasn't inaccurate or unfair.

Much of what Babcock said fit the description Ana Trujillo had given. Yes, it was true that violence often escalated at the time a woman attempted to leave. Such assaults could include psychological abuse, which Ana claimed during her interview with police, and holding, grabbing, containing, and preventing movement was included in such assaults. Often to the outside world, abusers appeared normal. "Some people are like that, charming in public but behind closed doors can be terrors."

The side effects of such violence could include depression and self-medicating with drugs and alcohol.

From the witness stand, Babcock repeated the litany of charges Ana made against the men in her life, beginning with her ex-husband, who she charged had sexually assaulted her. In Ana's version, Brian Goodney hit her, knocking her unconscious. Another man, Trujillo said, stalked her. That man tried to control her mind, body and soul. "In being a spiritual, religious person, she was particularly frightened by him wanting to control her soul."

From there, Carroll concentrated on what he characterized as Stefan's abusive behavior, from choosing the restaurants and bars he and Ana went to, to wanting her to wear stiletto heels. From the characterizations Babcock gave, it appeared Ana told the therapist that Stefan didn't want Ana to work or to have a car at her disposal.

"Have you seen abusers who are pleasant to the woman ninety, ninety-five percent of the time?" Carroll asked.

"Absolutely," Babcock said. "Especially when alcohol is involved."

Based on what Ana said, the psychologist testified that Stefan hadn't kicked Ana out but the opposite, that Ana left him, moving in with James Wells to escape Stefan.

Tracing Ana's history, Babcock had determined that up until 2009, her subject led a normal life, but then things changed. After the incident with Brian Goodney, Ana became depressed and anxious, she drank more. "Drinking gave her this courage," the psychologist said. "I think it also gave her this aggressive stance: I'm not going to be a victim anymore."

Babcock said Ana didn't look for older men to foot her bills but rather those were the men she met. And the violence in her, the anger that fueled that terrible rage that erupted in the attack that took Stefan's life, that the psychologist said built up over years of abuse at the hands of other men, who'd used and controlled Trujillo. What Julia Babcock described was the fragile-eggshell defense John Jordan had worried about, the one that said that Ana was so damaged by prior abuse at the hands of other men that she overreacted in the moments she murdered Stefan.

"I see a woman who was formerly high-functioning, who

had many bad things happen to her," said Babcock. "She thought she could heal herself with spirituality and religion and new-age kind of healing that didn't work. She tried to self-medicate with alcohol, and that made things worse, not better."

Restating what the psychologist had said, in cross-examination, Mickelson asked Babcock if she was saying that Ana Trujillo had been the victim in multiple abusive relationships "the last one being an abusive relationship with Dr. Andersson."

The psychologist agreed, qualifying the statement by saying the only time Stefan had been physically abusive was on that final night.

Going over what the therapist drew on to form her opinion, Mickelson then asked what records Babcock reviewed, and the jurors learned that Babcock hadn't interviewed Ana's family or friends, or done any investigation to determine Stefan Andersson's character, instead relying on Ana's interviews.

"So would you agree with me, Doctor, that the majority of your opinion comes from information that was provided to you from Ms. Trujillo?"

"Absolutely, yes," Babcock answered.

"Would you agree with me then that if the information that Ms. Trujillo provided you was inaccurate, that your opinion in this case could be inaccurate, right?"

Again Babcock answered, "Yes."

"Because you agree with me that the opinion you give in this courtroom can only be as good as the information that you rely on, right?"

"That's correct," she said.

As Mickelson asked questions, it became obvious that there were many things that Babcock didn't know. First, that rather than try to keep Ana confined to his apartment, Stefan repeatedly attempted to ban her from entering it, by giving orders that she not be allowed in the building. The psychologist didn't know that Stefan had twice gone so far as to have his locks changed to keep Ana away.

"You would agree with me that both males and females can be the perpetrators of domestic violence?" Mickelson asked.

"Yes," Babcock answered, acknowledging that it could be as embarrassing for a male victim as a female victim to admit being abused.

As she gave her opinion, the therapist reiterated that she believed Ana overreacted on the night of Stefan's killing, based on her description of prior abuse. "I think there was a physical altercation between the two of them. I think they were both physically aggressive. I think she used excessive force defending herself. She was defending herself, using the only object she could . . . She just wanted to get him off of her. She just wanted to leave."

"You know this jury has actually already found Ms. Trujillo guilty of murder, right?" Mickelson asked.

"Yes," Babcock answered.

Chapter 25

The next morning on the witness stand, Ana Trujillo appeared troubled and nervous. She smiled anxiously at times, wearing a black pin-striped suit with a white blouse, perhaps left over from her time as a part-time translator for her former attorney. She wore little makeup, and her long hair fell haphazardly past her shoulders, just a bit of grey in the part; for much of her testimony, dark-rimmed glasses perched on her nose.

Finally, the woman at the center of the brutal killing told her story
*(Pool photo, Brett Coomer/*Houston Chronicle)

This was what John Jordan and Sarah Mickelson were waiting for, the opportunity for the jury to personally listen to Ana Trujillo. Each of the prosecutors had pens perched over legal pads, taking notes, at times heads together conferring quietly, planning what would happen when it was Jordan's turn to ask the questions.

First, however, the witness was in Jack Carroll's hands, as he guided Ana through her history and her life. At times gripping one hand in the other, Ana glanced at the jurors, who for the most part sat back in their chairs and frowned, as if thoughtfully attempting to size up the woman they'd judged guilty of a shocking murder.

Detailing her history, Ana described growing up Mexican American in Arizona, California, and Texas. "I came from a religious family," she said, and Carroll pointed out Ana's family in the gallery. From there, she talked of her education, her time at the Waco junior college, and her work history, starting as a teenager, babysitting, the years spent as an aide with disabled children, then her job with Coca-Cola.

In the bars she frequented in downtown Houston, Ana had described her success in the workplace in glowing terms. She did the same from the stand, claiming not to be an interpreter for Brooks Lott, but suggesting that she was a legal assistant and that she ran his law office, and that she'd set up businesses for others. At Coke, she was not only a merchandiser and sales rep, but in charge of six counties and two thousand accounts.

In surprisingly endearing terms, since she'd accused him of raping her, she talked of her marriage to Marcus Leos, the father of her two daughters. Leos wasn't in the courtroom. By then, he had his own legal troubles and was serving a long sentence for molesting a child. This brought up a touchy subject for the defense. Carroll needed to show Ana in a sympathetic light, and he knew prosecutors would ask why when she moved to Houston, she left her younger daughter in the care of such a man. "Did you think that Marcus Leos was a danger to your daughters?" Carroll asked.

"No," she said, after Carroll pointed out that the accusations against Leos hadn't surfaced until later.

Slowly, Carroll and his client worked their way through Ana's failed relationships with men. When Brian Goodney's name was mentioned, Trujillo recounted in a long narrative her version of the events, much like she'd told the detectives in the interview. On the stand, Ana's voice grew shrill, rising and falling.

At times she sidestepped into other areas of her life, but Carroll brought her back to his original question, what had happened that night when she hit Goodney with the candlestick. Before long, it became easily apparent that her description of that altercation also fit much of what she said happened on that final night with Stefan. In her account, Goodney held her and wouldn't let her go, and like her stiletto shoe in the later attack, the candlestick was just there, handy. "When I started to move, I felt it," she said, reaching wildly around in the witness stand, as if demonstrating how it had taken place that night.

Even the scene of the attack was eerily similar, in the entrance hall of an upscale apartment. In contrast to Goodney's account of being knocked unconscious, Trujillo said she was, and that when she awoke, she kept her eyes closed, fearing what he might do if he saw she'd awakened. "I thought he's going to come back and hurt me. He wants to kill me."

In fact, the account of the altercation with Goodney recalled Stefan's death in such detail that Carroll asked, "Isn't this remarkably similar to what happened with Dr. Andersson?"

Trujillo nodded knowingly, and said, "Unfortunately, it is."

As to the other incidents, including slapping bartenders and throwing drinks at waitresses, Ana simply said that all those charges were false. "Were you surprised at all these witnesses testifying against you? Many of them were saying that you were once friends and once a nice person?"

"Yes," Ana said. "I am."

When her attorney asked if she felt empowered when she drank, something Julia Babcock, the psychologist, had said, Ana objected to the word, instead saying she felt confident. "I am friendly to everyone. And I feel sometimes that gets misinterpreted . . . I am bubbly and social."

When Carroll asked if she had a problem with alcohol, Ana denied that it was true. "No, I don't! I don't!" Yet on further questioning, she admitted that she drank too much, and that she became a different person when intoxicated.

The day had already been a long one with Trujillo's fractured and dramatic testimony, when Carroll finally turned the questioning to the fall of 2012, when Ana moved in with the first man who lived in The Parklane, then met Stefan Andersson. In the beginning, she said the research scientist was charming, charismatic, sweet, and respectful. "A wonderful man." And like so many of the others, he initially seemed interested not in her, but in her theories and plans. When she talked of her work, it was in lavish terms, jumping from one philosophy to another, from her hydrotherapy and oils to music and art therapies, and healing through meditation.

On the stand, just as in her interview with police, Ana claimed that the men in her life initially displayed an interest in collaborating with her, helping her market her art and holistic-healing methods. She made the same claims about Stefan, saying she felt proud to be working with a scientist, a doctor. "We can combine our knowledge together," she said.

Listening from the second row of the gallery, Annika Lindqvist wasn't surprised that her old friend treated his girlfriend's vague concepts with respect. She'd seen Stefan listen to people who were clearly troubled and talk to them as if they made complete sense, simply because he didn't want to hurt their feelings. That part seemed plausible.

Yet Ana said that in the final months before his death, Stefan changed, his health "physically and mentally declining rapidly." At night, she said he fidgeted in bed, and at times she woke up to find him staring at her. She even claimed that he awoke and rolled in a ball and acted "like a baby, calling, 'Momma.'" She didn't initially leave him, she said, because she loved and wanted to help him. In her clipped manner and slight Latin accent, she used words she might have first heard in massage school: alternative methods of holistic healing, modalities, to explain the tack she tried to take to heal Stefan, giving him baths, taking him on walks, listening to music, and teaching him to meditate.

As they went back and forth, Carroll and his client discussed how she spent her days at the golf course with Stefan. Others had testified that Ana drank and used her laptop, sometimes sitting outside chanting in the sun. When asked what she was doing on the laptop, Ana said she researched her tarot cards. In response, Carroll pointedly asked if she was doing research on healing golfers. She said she was and that her theories involved bringing them to "peak performance through using art."

Everything she did, she did for Stefan, she claimed.

It was true that Stefan, like many men, felt particularly drawn to women in high heels. She wore the cobalt-blue stilettos that night to please him, she said. Witnesses had described how she flirted with others in front of him, but when she danced in her chair at Bar 5015, while other men watched, she said that, too, was misunderstood. "I danced for Stefan," she said.

As might be expected, much couldn't be proved, since only Stefan and Ana were present when the scenes unfolded, but at times Ana's testimony contradicted documents in evidence and the accounts others had given on the stand. One was Ana's explanation for why she left Stefan's apartment in January and moved in with Wells and Chanda Ellison. Ana said the decision was hers because she was unhappy with Stefan's behavior, but The Parklane documents and the accounts of the building's staff clearly proved Stefan moved Ana out and banned her from returning. That spring, he'd even boxed her belongings and left them at the concierge desk.

When it came to what Ana described as Stefan's other side,

in the gallery Annika judged those assertions impossible. Stefan had always been supportive of women in the workplace, but Ana claimed he didn't want her to work, so that she would be dependent on him. In Ana's world, as Jordan had called it, Stefan was controlling, forcing sex on her, and abusive. The trouble in the cab, Ana said, began not with her but the driver and her husband, who were irritated because they had to wait, then refused to listen to her directions.

Yet at times, it seemed as if Ana Trujillo veered closer to the truth. For instance, describing Stefan's demeanor that night as quiet and meek, Ana said it was a response to knowing that she was angry at him.

"But was he in fear for his life?" an alarmed Carroll asked.

"No," she answered.

The cab driver's husband, she said, bullied Stefan, and she stood up for him. "I'm the one who defends Stefan all the time," she said, talking about the man she'd killed as if he were still alive. "I want to make sure he gets home and that he doesn't overspend."

When she got out of the cab, Stefan stayed behind talking to the driver, giving her a tip, and Ana said she was irritated with him. Yet she said that upstairs in his apartment, her mood improved, and she told him that she'd had a good evening and that she was excited about leaving for Waco in the morning. "I'm carrying on being all happy. And all of a sudden, he just turns around and changes completely."

Everyone in the courtroom had heard Janette Jordan's testimony, when she said she and Stefan had a brunch date the following day. Others had talked about how excited he was about the new woman in his life. But on the stand, Ana claimed Stefan railed at her, upset because she was leaving for Waco, accusing her of not coming back. She threatened to leave until he calmed down. Looking for her phone, she turned her back on him. Unable to find it, she walked toward the door to leave.

The evidence suggested the fight began in the living

room, with the pulling of Stefan's hair and the first blood found near the kitchen counter, but, in an emotional voice that fluctuated from pleading to anger, Ana said Stefan waited for her in the hallway and grabbed her as she walked toward the door.

The silent courtroom listened, as Ana Trujillo's testimony built. On the stand, she acted out what she said happened, dramatically whipping her arms around, grimacing, raging as she described that night. The fight that ensued, she said, was a series of attacks by Stefan, while she tried to flee. He pushed her against walls and grabbed her from behind. He pulled her around, in what she described as "tussling," and she grabbed him by the hair. She promised to let go if he stopped, and he agreed, but then she said he came at her again.

To illustrate, Jack Carroll walked to the center of the courtroom, in front of the jury, and had Ana join him. As everyone watched, the defense attorney and his notorious client staged a battle, seizing each other by the wrists and arms, pushing and tugging. In her depiction, Ana fell over the couch and described how Stefan threw her repeatedly against walls. She fell down and was unconscious for some unknown period of time, and said when she woke up, she couldn't breathe. Stefan sat on her chest.

There was a time problem, however.

Throughout, Ana described the heated battle as occurring as soon as they returned to the apartment, about the time Karlye Jones heard something hit the wall in 18B. A question loomed: What had Ana done for an hour or more before she called police? When Carroll asked, Ana maintained that the battle unfolded in starts and stops. At times, she said, Stefan became calm, and they talked. When Stefan finally released her, Ana said she crawled on hands and knees toward the hallway. From behind, he grabbed her hair with one hand and her neck with the other. If that were true, however, why weren't clumps of her hair found in the hallway? Anywhere in the apartment? Only a few strands were

Ana Trujillo on the stand
*(Pool photos, Brett Coomer/*Houston Chronicle)

found in Stefan's hand at the morgue. And why wasn't her neck encircled with bruises?

Earlier in her testimony, Ana said their habit was to both take off their shoes as soon as they entered the apartment, putting them near the kitchen counter. Stefan's were found precisely where she described, as was one of her stilettos, suggesting they'd followed that routine on that night. She'd also complained that her ankle hurt, and she hadn't wanted to wear heels, begging the question why on this night, she would have left them on? Yet in her breathless description, she said she had done just that and still wore the high heels as they fought.

The battle, she said, unfolded in segments, and at one point Stefan tried to undress her, implying that he intended to rape her. It was then, she said, that *he* grabbed one of her shoes and hit her in the back of the head. Those in the courtroom who'd heard the evidence were presumably confused by the account, little of which fit the crime-scene photos or prior testimony. Ana did have a bruise on the back of her head in the jail two days later, but James Wells testified that he'd pushed her to get her off of him, and she'd hit her head on the doorjamb. And in the jail, Ana told a doctor the bump was from the fight with Wells.

So much appeared to be Ana repackaging what she'd done to Stefan and claiming he had taken those same actions against her. First, she said he'd hit her with the shoe. Then, moments later, she testified that he sat on her chest, suffocating her, exactly what the assistant medical examiner surmised had happened to Stefan, based on bruising found in his back tissue.

As Ana Trujillo's much-anticipated testimony progressed, little made sense. She'd said Stefan had one of her shoes and hit her with it, then she tried to escape. Yet in her confusing version of the battle, she then described pulling a stiletto off and hitting him with it. Was she saying she tried to run with one five-and-a-half-inch stiletto on and one off?

Perhaps the most troubling aspect was the issue of the

gaping time discrepancy. That approximately hour and a half loomed large, the span between 2:13, when a neighbor heard a man shout, and Ana's 9-1-1 call at 3:41. Her explanation was that at times Stefan grew calm and talked. After a while, she also said that some of that time lapsed when she'd passed out during the fight although she felt uncertain for how long.

Finally, she said Stefan grasped her ankles and put her in the hold Carroll's martial arts expert had demonstrated. Trapped and in pain, she said she had no option other than to strike with the only weapon she had, her remaining shoe. Yet although all the evidence placed Stefan close to the floor, where the blood spatter was found, she testified that he was on top of her.

As they fought, their bodies twisting and moving, she said she managed to ultimately climb on top of him. "How many times did you hit him with the shoe?" Carroll asked. Ana said she wasn't sure.

As blood sprayed from the wounds on his head and face, pouring into a pool on the carpet near his head, Ana said Stefan growled at her. On the witness stand, she made a guttural sound, demonstrating. "I had no idea I was hurting him that badly. I became afraid, almost panicked. I reached over, and I'm like, 'Oh, God, what's going on? What happened?'" She slapped him, she said, to keep him awake, and began CPR. Why didn't she get help when she realized how badly Stefan was hurt? The lobby, she said, seemed miles away, and she couldn't find her phone. She feared that if she stopped CPR, Stefan would die.

The phone rang—Reagan Cannon's 3:37 A.M. call to Stefan from Ana's cell phone—she then made her call to 9-1-1, and before long, Officer Bowie arrived on the scene.

Ana Trujillo sobbed as she described begging Bowie to give Stefan CPR or to let her continue. He said no. In contrast to his testimony, Ana claimed he drew his weapon and pointed it at her, screaming to get down. There seemed so many contradictions. If he had, wouldn't Karlye Jones have heard? She'd testified that while the walls were thick, she could hear talking in the hallways.

"I said, 'Please, can't you give him CPR?'" Ana Trujillo sobbed. "And he didn't touch him. He just left him there. And he wouldn't let me go to him."

Later that morning, at HPD headquarters, why didn't she ask about Stefan, about his fate, until so far into her interview with detectives? Carroll asked.

"I thought they were taking Stefan to the hospital and helping him," she said. "I did not. I did not. He wasn't dead. He did not pass away."

Six hours after Ana Trujillo's testimony began, the defense attorney passed the witness.

"You just conveyed to us the series of events where you beat a man to death . . . I noticed you didn't really start crying and bawling until you got to the point where you told us about the 9-1-1 call. Right?" John Jordan asked when he took over.

"Yes," she agreed.

"You're telling us in slow motion how you beat him to death, and you didn't shed a tear?" Jordan went on to say that Ana's tears began when she recounted Reagan Cannon's phone call, in which he'd called her a liar, and became sobs when she talked of the 9-1-1 call. "Did you notice that?"

"You noticed it," she said, somewhat indignantly.

"Yeah," Jordan said. "I think we all did."

Reminding Ana that the jurors watched her reactions, he asked if she realized that the only time she appeared visibly angry throughout the six days of the trial was when Janette Jordan, Stefan's new love interest, was on the stand, talking about their relationship and how they'd had lunch planned for the Sunday he was murdered. "That angered you to hear that, didn't it?"

"No," she said.

"Because, you see, you had to make sure that we thought y'all were engaged and that he was your fiancé, to buy this whole domestic-violence stuff. Right?"

"No," she said, frowning.

The defense attorney said during his questioning that the first time Ana saw the gruesome photos of Stefan's body was during the trial, and Jordan took the witness back to that statement, asking, "So, the first time that you see Stefan Andersson with his face bashed in because of your conduct was in this courtroom . . . and you didn't cry. Correct?"

"Yes," she acknowledged.

Jordan paused for just a moment, looking as if he were about to sigh. It all seemed just too much, too horrible, that anyone could be that unfeeling, to look at the photos, to see the damage she had done, and not shed a tear.

"I have been crying ever since June 9, every day," she answered.

With that, Jordan turned his attention to Ana's history, asking if was true that when she divorced, she'd sent her ten-year-old daughter to Waco to live with Marcus, her daughters' father. When Ana agreed that she had, Jordan asked, "Her father who you described as bipolar, clinically depressed, suicidal, and a rapist, correct?"

"Yes," she answered.

"Would you agree with me that during this trial, no one has said anything negative about Stefan Andersson other than that he drank too much?" Jordan asked. Ana nodded and indicated she did agree. Yet when it came to her, the prosecutor pointed out, one witness after another had talked about her drunkenness, aggressiveness, and violence. And then there was James Jimenez's testimony, in which he described Ana as suddenly attacking him by grabbing him by the hair. "When you're mad at somebody and you go to attack them, the first thing you do is pull their hair. That would be a logical deduction from the evidence, correct?"

"I don't believe so," Trujillo said, shaking her head slightly.

"The difference is that Mr. Jimenez is six-foot-two, 280 pounds, correct?"

"Yes," she said.

One after another, Jordan repeated the accusations that had been made against Ana Trujillo, her bizarre behavior in restaurants, on Houston's downtown streets and freeways, the charges of public intoxication and driving under the influence. "Will you agree with me that in every situation involving a man, what you basically say is that you're not interested in them . . . and somehow you end up getting charged with something?"

When it came to James Wells, Ana claimed that she hadn't bit him, but as she'd moved in to kiss him on the head, he'd jolted up, and her teeth hit his scalp. With that, Jordan drew the lines connecting the dots that revealed Ana's patterns, including that in many of the cases of violence—Brian Goodney with the candlestick and James Wells with the bite—she attacked the men and then turned around and filed police reports, saying that they had assaulted her.

"I don't see the pattern," she said, appearing peeved. "But they're the ones that are saying I assaulted them."

Jordan then described the incident at Bodegas, where Ana walked into the restaurant and bit Stefan on the cheek, while his friend Anders watched in astonishment. Carroll objected, and the judge asked the jurors to disregard. But then Jordan pointed out that while no one talked of Stefan's becoming violent or angry after drinking, there'd been ample testimony that Ana was a mean drunk.

On the stand, Janette Jordan had described Stefan as "doddery," an English expression meaning older and slightly frail. The jurors had heard about the condition of his body in the autopsy, a slightly enlarged heart and other age-related maladies. They'd also seen his somewhat pudgy, out-of-shape corpse in the crime-scene photos. But the Stefan Ana described was a former wrestler and weight lifter, and she said, "He was very strong."

So much made no sense. She portrayed a man very interested in sex, one who enjoyed seeing her walk nude in the apartment wearing only her stilettos. As she rambled, however, she said that she only had consensual sex with him once. Instead, she claimed that she believed he drugged her at times, and that she'd woken up feeling like she'd had intercourse. "I know I couldn't have drunk enough to pass out," she said, claiming he must have dosed her with a sleeping pill or the like. She said in the mornings, when asked, he said they'd had sex the night before.

Listening, John Jordan listed all the men Ana Trujillo said raped or attempted to rape her, including her first husband and former boyfriends, suggesting yet another pattern in her testimony and her behavior.

"Did Stefan lend you $7000?" Jordan asked, displaying the handwritten IOU. Carroll objected, but the judge allowed it, and Ana said Stefan had given her a loan, money she put into her business. The loan was due on July 7, 2013, not quite a month after she killed him. In her interview with police, Ana claimed money meant nothing to her, that she didn't like to touch it, but Jordan pointed out that obviously wasn't true since she'd taken the money from Stefan.

"Was that a coincidence that the tarot-card book in your purse was open to the death card?" Jordan questioned. "I just have to ask . . . You're the one who's into that stuff. I'm not."

"Yes, that is a tarot book," Ana answered, looking annoyed by the question. "I need to interpret what the cards mean . . . So, I'm not practicing . . . the reading of the cards. I'm studying the subject. If you say you brought it out that way, then, yes, it was a coincidence."

"All right. Fair enough," he answered. "That's all I'm asking."

When it came to the timetable, the lost hour and a half left unaccounted for, Jordan suggested that Ana Trujillo had struggled to fill the gap in her testimony, hoping to explain it away, or it would look bad for her, proving that she'd waited before calling for help.

"I loved Stefan!" she blurted. "I did not kill him."

As during her interview with police, it seemed that Stefan's killing was a mere footnote. Jordan pointed out that on the stand Ana spent four-and-a-half hours talking about her prior relationships, and a full forty-seven minutes on the Brian Goodney altercation, when what they were all there to hear from her was an explanation of why Stefan had to die. His fervor building, the prosecutor asked why Jack Carroll fast-forwarded through much of the fight with Stefan, skipping twenty minutes at a time. Jordan's suggestion was that the defense attorney had to stretch out the assault to fill the time gap.

Posing a question, Jordan listed the assaults Ana claimed to have suffered in her prior relationships, then asked, "We've heard about these people, and you don't think it was important to tell us that Stefan ever physically abused you? . . . The reality is that he never did, did he? He's never laid a hand on you, has he?"

"Yes, he has," she said.

There were housekeeping matters, Jordan wanted to clean up. The first was to ask Ana if she suffered from any mental illness. She said she did not. "You are as sane as they come. Correct?"

"Yes," she answered.

"We've heard so much evidence about Stefan Andersson dominating you. Hiding your phone," Jordan said. "Help me out. What was the other stuff that he did?"

At this, Ana sat silent, unwilling or unable to offer a single example of any physical abuse she'd suffered at Stefan's hands.

In response, Jordan laid out the range of punishment jurors had to choose from, five years to life, then talked about the different ways a murder can happen, including the killing of a bad or violent person, or the quick death of shooting someone through the head. "Can you think of a worse type of murder, when you are thinking about the nature of crime, than being beaten to death?"

"I wouldn't know," Trujillo answered, glaring at the prosecutor.

"And as a result of that beating, bleeding to death?"

This time, Jordan's question was met with only silence. "Do you think it aggravates it if the person being beaten didn't even fight back? That the person who was beaten didn't put marks on you? Didn't grab at you? He lay there. He would rather die than fight back. Do you think, as far as the nature of the crime, it gets any worse than that?"

"That's not what happened," Ana objected. "He did attack me, and all I was doing was trying to get away."

". . . If this jury believes you're lying to them, a life sentence very well may be warranted. You would agree to that, wouldn't you?"

"I'm not lying, but I understand what you're saying," she said.

"Because you killed a human being, didn't you?"

Again, Ana didn't answer. "Pass the witness, Judge," Jordan said.

On redirect, Jack Carroll asked Ana if she intended to kill Stefan, and she said that she didn't. "I never wanted to hurt him. I loved him, and protected him. And took care of him . . ."

"But you smacked him twenty-five times with that shoe."

"Yes, I did. But it didn't seem that I was hitting him that hard or that many times," she said. "I kept begging him to please, just let me go."

At that, Ana Trujillo walked from the witness stand.

Earlier, Stefan's family and friends had talked about their loss. Closing up this final phase of the trial, Ana's then took the stand. Her aunt described the kind, obedient young girl Ana had once been, and how she'd seen her try to help the homeless and poor. "Is she the kind of person that would give a person in need the shirt off her back?" Carroll asked, and the woman said Ana was. "Were you surprised that Ana was charged with murder?"

"A lot," she said. "Her behavior before wasn't like this."

Ana's children had been absent throughout the trial, but during the sentencing, they sat in the audience. And her older daughter, Siana, by then a twenty-two-year-old bank teller, testified on her mother's behalf. She'd also noticed changes in Ana, a transformation from the hardworking mother and suburban wife to a more "spiritual" woman but also a more withdrawn one. At times, "She would just disappear . . . not have contact with anyone."

"Did you see your mother drink more?"

"Yes," Siana answered. With her dark hair, a beautiful young woman, she looked much like her mother had before the wear of the years of alcohol and life on the street took their toll. The mother she knew, Siana said, was so nonviolent, she never spanked them as children. "I've never seen her aggressive towards anyone."

"I'm sorry that she had to become the caretaker for the other three children at eight or nine," Trina Tharp said on the stand, tracing her own history from picking cotton in Arizona to working in hotels and factories, with Ana as the oldest taking care of the younger children.

Suggesting that Ana would not be a problem again in the U.S., should the jury decide to probate her sentence, Jack Carroll asked if Ana had family to live with in Mexico if she was deported after the trial. Trina said that Ana's father's family remained there, and that they would take her in. "Are you all generally nice people?" Carroll asked about the Tharp brood.

"I'd like to think so," Ana's mother answered.

The following morning was the ninth day of the trial, and all that remained were closing arguments from both sides for sentencing. The jurors sat quietly in their chairs, watching as Sarah Mickelson stood before them for the final time.

"We now know that's not just what Ana Trujillo did on June 9, 2013. We now know that's who Ana Trujillo is because for the last two weeks, we've gotten a brief glimpse into the world of Ana Trujillo," she said. "We brought you witnesses from all walks of life. They all came down here, and they all showed us the same thing: that Ana Trujillo

cannot control her drinking. And worse, when Ana Trujillo drinks, she becomes violent. For Stefan Andersson, he
had the tragic misfortune of being the last in a long line of
Ms. Trujillo's victims . . . We are going to ask you for a life
sentence."

Based on the violence of the murder, all of the circumstances surrounding it, including that Stefan never fought
back, any other decision on the part of the jury, Mickelson
branded as unacceptable. What made Ana so lethal was that
she beat Stefan to death for no reason. Even the defense
expert placed that high on a list of indicators that an offender
could strike out yet again.

Ana Trujillo was a contradiction in so many ways. Mickelson admitted as much when she talked about how the
defense expert was right in using male pronouns when she
spoke of abusive partners. So rarely were women the aggres-
sors, that in her years as a prosecutor, Mickelson had seen
few such cases. Was it fair to judge Ana differently because
she was a woman? The prosecutor argued that it wasn't.

"If a man was charged with murder in this case . . . no one
would bat an eyelash at sending him to prison for the rest of
his life if he brutally forced his partner down on the ground
and beat her to death with his hand by punching her in the
face twenty-five times while she lay on the floor helpless.
Juries in Harris County do that every day. And, yet, they
want to ask you for sympathy because she is a woman.

". . . the way that we take equality back in this courtroom
is that you give her the exact same sentence, the exact same
verdict that would be just for a man is just for her. And that
is life in prison."

". . . There is no question that in Ana's world, she thinks
everyone loves her. And there is no question that in Ana's
world, she thinks that she's the queen holding court. Today
is the day that we take the power back from Ana Trujillo
and that we take the sting out of the way that she finds, even
in death, to humiliate a very private, quiet man who led a
simple life with people who loved him."

Still struggling with the jury's guilty verdict, Jack Carroll stood before them, deciding what to say. He began by responding to Mickelson's suggestion that during the trial, Stefan's character had been impugned. "The prosecutor tells you that we tried to tear down Dr. Andersson's character about this. There was no way I could put this whole thing into context without the alcoholism. I don't take any great joy in tearing down someone in front of their family, but we did what we had to do to show that she was in an abusive relationship. Although he was a pretty nice guy, we don't know what happened when they got back home."

Rather than wanting to attack Stefan's character, Carroll said he had no choice if he was to illustrate the position Ana was in that last night. As he continued, Carroll seemed unable to get past the first part of the trial, guilt or innocence, repeatedly asking what he had done wrong that caused them to find his client guilty. "I was walking around so damn cocksure that we had won this case," he said. "When you came back with a guilty after two hours . . . I was a little bit speechless."

As he sauntered back and forth, he held his notes, his arms reaching out to his sides as if pleading, his body language confirming that he felt off base, as if still trying to adapt to a reality he'd thought impossible. Instead of immediately turning his attention to the sentencing, Carroll again argued the case, beginning with Officer Bowie's arrival at The Parklane, replaying the first part of the trial. "What made the difference?" he asked. But the jurors simply watched and stared.

As he paced, the defense attorney talked of the cab driver and her husband, and so many others, asking questions, searching for answers, looking for a breakthrough that would explain how, in his opinion, the verdict had gone so terribly wrong. "It's hard for me to look at y'all the last couple of days because I was walking around here like I had the thing in the bag. I thought I did. It's kind of embarrassing to have to sit across from you and look at you and think: Hey, we've got this thing done. I believe something—because you were out less than two hours.

"So, what was it that I missed? Was it the twenty-five times that she struck him in the head? Was it the demonstration to try to show you all how it started and how it ended? Trying to show you all why she hit him, the testimony about striking him in the arms first. 'Stefan, let me go.' Striking him in the head when he's about to rip her leg in half. What would you all do?"

As he continued, Carroll wound back to parts of the case, what the blood-spatter expert had said, what his own experts testified to, recalling the demonstration he'd done with his martial arts expert.

So many decisions go into trial strategy, and Carroll recalled his internal debate when trying to decide whether or not to put Ana on the stand, then when to do it, in what part of the trial. Early on when the prosecutors played the interview tape, he'd decided that he didn't need her, but now he wondered about that decision in the wake of the guilty verdict. If nothing else, the jury had a man before them who clearly believed in his client and what she told him. He'd worked hard for Ana Trujillo, done his best, and he appeared to be battling the guilt of not succeeding in keeping a woman he viewed as innocent out of prison.

Be that as it may, the only important thing was what the jurors thought not about Carroll but Ana Trujillo. Had seeing her defense attorney's determination changed their minds?

The woman the jurors knew, unemployed and flitting from man to man, who drank too much then struck out in violence, wasn't the only Ana Trujillo, Carroll argued. There was the other Ana, the hardworking wife and mother with the suburban home. "When you go back to deliberate, don't feel guilty about the conviction because you did what you had to do," Carroll said in his final moments. ". . . I don't fault you for that. Who knows? If I was sitting right where you were, maybe I would have done the same thing."

Yet Carroll asked them to look past their verdict and to

focus on the circumstances as he saw them, that Ana had acted believing she had to, because Stefan Andersson was hurting her and threatening her life.

At the defense table, Ana Trujillo cried.

"Show mercy on Ms. Trujillo," he pleaded. "Come back with a minimum sentence . . . so she can get back to Mexico after they deport her."

Finally, John Jordan talked to the jurors, again in a calm quiet voice, at times sitting on a table across from the jury

Ana Trujillo seated next to her attorney, Jack Carroll
(*Pool photo, Brett Coomer/*Houston Chronicle)

box, as if he were in their living rooms. He didn't fault Jack Carroll for his fervor but described the defense attorney as important to the system. "We're supposed to have a defense attorney who's aggressive and passionate, who believes in his client," he said.

"You know, finally, finally after two weeks of trial and ten months, we finally see real tears on Ana Trujillo," he said, gesturing toward her. "For the first time in ten months, she's actually crying, and she's crying because she's crying for herself. She's crying because she understands that this is judgment day. She's crying because she knows twelve citizens of Harris County are finally, finally going to hold her accountable."

Throughout, there'd been no clear motive for the killing, and Jordan addressed that, wondering out loud if it could have been because of the debt, the tarot card in her purse, discovering that Stefan was interested in another woman and had brunch plans for the next day, anger because he hadn't stood up for her in the cab, or perhaps that was the night, after the confrontation in the cab, that Stefan raised his voice to her for the first time and said he'd simply had enough. It was over. He was done with Ana and all the pain, worry, and drama she brought into his life. Maybe he finally realized she wasn't the victim, and he couldn't save her. "The one thing we know about Ana Trujillo is she's not mentally unstable," said Jordan. "She's crazy, but scary crazy."

As evidence, he pointed back at all the testimony from those she'd attacked without reason or warning.

To show that it wasn't a case of a woman without advantages, Jordan gestured toward Ana's parents and relatives in the gallery and said that she grew up in a good family with people who loved her, parents who worked hard to support her. The defense attorney had talked at length about Ana's family, as if suggesting she should be spared to spare them. "This isn't about them," Jordan said. "It makes it worse that she had that kind of background and support of these beautiful people. They try to use family for mercy, but we know that she basically abandoned her ten-year-old child to come to a party lifestyle here in Houston."

In many ways, the case had international overtones. Stefan Andersson had become a U.S. citizen, but was born Swedish. Ana Trujillo's life began in Mexico, but she'd lived in Arizona, California, and Texas. Newspapers and television outlets across the world had followed the case. The jury had members of every socioeconomic background. They were white, black, Latin- and Asian-American, from their twenties to their sixties, a wide cross section of a multicultural city. They represented Houston well, one of the most diverse cities in the world. And now, Jordan said, they were charged with speaking for their community.

Stefan Andersson wasn't a perfect person. He drank too much. But "we're all flawed," Jordan said. "I was always told by my mom, 'We're all human.'"

Yet, Stefan was a good person, the kind of man who took Ana in when she needed help, even though he feared her, even though he said repeatedly that he wanted her out of his life. She reached out to him, and he was there for her, a tragic mistake that cost him his life. "If you want to know everything that there is to know about Stefan Andersson, we know from the last moments of his life. We know that he was a secular man and a scientist and not religious, but when a woman said, 'I would like to say a prayer for you,' he was gracious, and said, 'Sure.'" Jordan continued, "We know even at that moment, his last moments on earth, as he lay there getting beaten to death, he refused to hit a woman. Refused to defend himself. Refused to strike back. This secular man, even before his death, turned the other cheek."

At that, Jordan looked at Ana Trujillo. "That is who you killed."

Concluding, Jordan pleaded, "Send the message that here in Texas we hold murderers, even female murderers, accountable."

The jury filed from the courtroom to deliberate, and a hush stayed over the courtroom. In a matter of minutes, many in the audience silently filed out, fanning across the hallways. How long would it take? What would the jurors decide?

When the jurors came back in that same afternoon, all the questions were answered. Ana Trujillo stood beside her attorney and heard their verdict. For the murder of Stefan Andersson, she was sentenced to life in a Texas prison. Ana wouldn't be eligible for parole until the year 2043, when she would be seventy-four years old.

As the sentence was read, Ana turned her face to the side and sobbed.

Minutes later, outside the courtroom, something truly remarkable happened. Stefan's family stood to the side, quiet, with Annika and a few of his closest friends, when Ana's mother and stepfather approached them. "Saying we're sorry isn't enough. Sorry is for bumping into someone, not something like this," Gene Tharp said. "But we are truly sorry for your loss."

At that, the two families hugged and cried together.

Epilogue

A month after the trial, I had interviews scheduled with the attorneys in the case. My first was John Jordan at the district attorney's office, in the Harris County Courthouse, where the trial had been held. Rather than jubilant over what many saw as a big win—a life sentence for a woman convicted of murder—he seemed satisfied with the verdict yet introspective. "At the end, no one wins," he said that day. "Everyone in a case like this loses. Stefan's family, Ana Trujillo's family. Everyone loses. Especially Stefan Andersson."

Sarah Mickelson, who would soon be married and become Sarah Mickelson Seely, too, felt a sense of sadness along with relief that justice had been done. "This case made me believe that people get it right," she said. "For so long, people wanted to believe that Ana Trujillo was the victim. Much of the news coverage assumed that as the woman, she killed in self-defense. But when twelve people came into a courtroom and heard the facts, they ultimately saw the truth of who Ana Trujillo had become."

Later that afternoon, I sat in Jack Carroll's office. While the prosecutors had put the case behind them and gone on, he appeared morose, and I had the sense that Ana's fate continued to haunt him. One of the first things he mentioned was that in courtrooms, out on the street, other attorneys stopped him to say they didn't understand how a woman who'd claimed self-defense had ended up with the maximum sentence. "People know that I lost it, and that she got life, and that's all that matters," he said. In hindsight, he had come to the conclusion that perhaps he hadn't seen his client clearly, as a jury would, and that he should never have put her on the stand.

Along with the attorneys, following the trial, I, too, considered the case, thinking about all I'd heard in the courtroom and judging what I didn't yet know, what I needed to investigate as I went ahead with this book.

I'd first heard about Ana Trujillo the day after Stefan's murder. I was in London at the time, on vacation with my husband, when it hit the international news in full force. The BBC, CNN, and other networks included it for days in their newscasts, anchors in front of images of exaggerated stiletto shoes. At the time, I hadn't planned to write about the case. It seemed perhaps too sensational. When I returned home to Houston, however, I read more about those involved, and I changed my mind.

What drew me to this case wasn't how Stefan died, but why. For a long time, I had a hard time reconciling his murder with who Stefan Andersson had been, a talented scientist. I couldn't imagine what brought him and Ana together, and when I saw references to indications in the press that he might have been abused by her—a reversal of the roles the sexes played in other cases I'd covered in my thirty years as a crime reporter—I thought that perhaps this case was worth exploring.

Since none of the coverage centered on Ana's spiritual beliefs, her conversion to witchcraft, I didn't know about that angle until I sat in on the trial and the tarot book was shown to jurors. Like others in that courtroom, I was stunned. In the year that followed, while I worked on the research, I found ever-increasing evidence of how entrenched Ana had become in her beliefs, and how they'd twisted her mind.

Was Ana truly possessed? I don't know.

Members of Ana's family told me that they believed that Ana had developed some type of mental illness. They cited this undiagnosed disorder as a reason for her actions, excusing what she had done because she was sick. I found that hard to believe. By all accounts, she'd functioned well until she moved to Houston, and by then she was thirty-eight years old. No one told me they had ever seen any signs of a psychiatric condition before that time. The changes occurred only after she became interested in the occult, abused alcohol, and smoked her chemical-laced herbal cigarettes.

In the years following Stefan's death, an increasing amount of information was reported in studies about the synthetic marijuana Ana smoked, some concluding that it could cause delusions and aggression. Perhaps that was what plagued her. It might have been as simple as that these substances altered her mind. Yet some of those I interviewed said Ana's strange actions started before she smoked the drugs, while she lived in her suburban home with her second husband, Jim Fox. Remember how the neighbors noticed odd things happening around the house? Including the evening Jon Paul Espinoza thought he saw a demon-like animal perched on her roof?

"Did Ana have powers?" Teresa Montoya rhetorically asked one afternoon. "No. People don't have power unless we give them power. Unless we believe. I chose not to believe, so she never had any power over me."

Perhaps that's true. In contrast, Christi Suarez believed, and that allowed Ana Trujillo to enter her dreams. Early on, Suarez talked to me at length for this book, but near the end, she had second thoughts, fighting fears that Ana would again invade her life. Suarez even worried that Ana, housed in a high-security prison hundreds of miles away, would somehow be able to take revenge.

As for me, there were days when I wondered.

Those of you who read my books know that I always attempt to personally interview the convicted killers. I did that in this case as well, within months of the trial. I filed a request with the Texas Department of Criminal Justice, and Ana agreed and signed the necessary forms to allow the interview. The following week, I drove to the prison, a four-hour trip. Along the way, some rather odd things happened.

First, on a deserted highway outside Waco, a large snake shot out at my car off the shoulder. I stepped on my brakes. Perhaps it felt the draft from my car, for as I passed, it instantly whipped back to the grassy edge. In my rearview mirror, I saw it slither off as I slowly drove away.

Later, precisely as I pulled into the prison parking lot, a forgotten tune came on my radio, one I hadn't heard in many years: the Charlie Daniels Band's rendition of "The Devil Went Down to Georgia." In the song, the devil is in search of a soul to steal and challenges a brash young fiddle player to a contest.

The truth is, however, maybe, after hearing so much about devils, demons, and black magic, I was looking for signs. Especially after I arrived at the prison security gate and was turned away. The warden came out to personally explain that Ana had changed her mind, withdrawing her consent to the interview. As I drove off, I thought about what others had said about her, and I wondered if Ana was in her cell chanting, attempting to conjure up snakes in my path.

On second thought, however, I live in Texas, where, although I'd rarely seen one in more than three decades, I know that snakes are plentiful. And in retrospect, perhaps the song wasn't so odd either since I was listening to a seventies music station. Of course, it did take me back a bit when I realized that I'd unwitting walked into a case that involved the occult in what was to be my thirteenth book. But still, coincidences do happen, more often than we realize, I think.

One thing I became certain of working on the book was that, true or not, Ana Trujillo thought she had powers and communicated with spirits.

First, nearly everyone who crossed paths with her during those later years thought she was sincere when she described herself as a witch and carried her voodoo doll in her bra. In addition, there were those odd notes, including the one in which she appealed to a spirit to appear.

During long conversations with a Santeria priestess I contacted through the Voodoo Museum in New Orleans, I heard many theories about Ana's conversion. She described Ana as "a jumper," someone who cobbled together her beliefs by grabbing thoughts and practices from a variety of sources. The Santeria priestess suggested that Ana opened a door into the spirit world while living in the Rice Lofts, playing with her Ouija board and holding her rituals, and that she'd unwittingly released a demon into her life. When I showed the priestess a photo of that woven tower Annika found in Ana's things, it reminded her of a tool used by some practitioners to house conjured spirits. "People think they can control demons, but they can't. They grow stronger, especially the truly evil ones," the woman told me one night, in hushed tones. "Eventually, they take over, and they want violence and blood."

It wasn't Ana's descriptions of herself as a witch and claiming powers that convinced me she truly believed in her powers. Rather, it was something I heard on her 9-1-1 call, while talking with the police dispatcher. The woman was attempting to clarify what was taking place in the apartment, asking Ana what she meant when she said someone was about to die. After an undecipherable response, Ana's voice changed, and became clear.

"Be quiet!" she hissed.

"Hello?" the dispatcher responded, sounding confused.

Who was Ana talking to? Not the dispatcher. Stefan? This was more than an hour after the neighbor heard the last of the shouting in the apartment. It seems likely, based on the condition of his body when police arrived, that he was dead. If he was still technically alive, he certainly wasn't in any condition to be talking. Did she believe she could still communicate with him, that he was there with her?

At that moment, Ana was alone in the apartment, perhaps sitting near Stefan's body, rocking back and forth, at last aware of what she'd done. And she apparently believed someone or something was there with her, talking to her. Why else would she order, "Be quiet!"

Whatever the reality of her situation, the Ana Trujillo

who murdered Stefan Andersson had traveled a long and dangerous road from the days when she lived in a big white-brick house in a Houston suburb with her husband and daughters. Along the way, she threw away her own life, and she murdered a good man.

In the end, Ana Trujillo wasn't special at all, and there was only sadness.

"I love you, may you live forever in us within you," she wrote in one of her disjointed notes dated the day before Stefan died. Was she thinking of him? Envisioning what she already knew deep inside that she would ultimately do? "Til I see feel you, Ana."

Acknowledgments

There are always so many people who help with each book, it's difficult to decide where to start. But here goes.

Thank you to:

- All the folks who talked to me for this book, told me their stories, named and unnamed.
- Those who read the manuscript and gave me feedback: Terry Bachman and Sharlene Nelson.
- Edward Porter, always amenable to giving advice.
- Sue Behnke, for helping with research.
- All the folks at HarperCollins, especially my editors on this book—Emily Krump, Kelly O'Connor, and Erin Brown—along with Sara Schwager, the copyeditor, and Nadine Badalaty, who designed the cover.
- All the wonderful people who read my books, especially those who recommend them to others. I couldn't do this without you. I never forget that.
- My family and friends. You've all supported me over the years, especially when I'm elbow deep in a case or running late on a deadline. That means a bunch.

Finally, I'd like to say a few words about the woman this book is dedicated to, my friend and mentor, Ann Rule, who passed away in the summer of 2015 at the age of eighty-four.

Ann was the matriarch of true crime for a generation.

A wonderful writer, a determined researcher, she was also a great human being. Early on, she sought me out to tell me that she enjoyed one of my books. From that point forward, we talked and e-mailed. She offered encouragement, she talked me through some tough times when I hit snags, and she steered me in alternate directions when I confronted dead ends.

Over the years, Ann and I shared our stories, talking of family, writing, destiny, even the afterlife. I will always remember those conversations, and I'm sorry they've come to an end. I will think of her often, always with a smile.

Here's to Ann Rule and a life well lived. Thank you for the memories. Good-bye my friend, for now.